The History of the Origins of Christianity

Christianity

Book IV - The Antichrist

By Joseph Ernest Renan

Edited by Anthony Uyl

Devoted Publishing

Woodstock, Ontario, 2017

The History of the Origins of Christianity Book IV - The Antichrist
By Joseph Ernest Renan
Member of the French Academy.
Edited by Anthony Uyl

Originally Published by:
London: Mathieson & Company, 25, Paternoster Square E.C.

What kind of philosophies do you have? Let us know!

Contact us at: devotedpub@hotmail.com
Visit us on Facebook: @DevotedPublishing
Get more products via our website: www.devotedpublishing.com

Published in Woodstock, Ontario, Canada 2016

For bulk educational rates, please contact us at the email address above.

ISBN: 978-1-988297-72-9

Table of Contents

INTRODUCTION...4

CHAPTER I..14

CHAPTER II...19

CHAPTER III..22

CHAPTER IV 27

CHAPTER V...33

CHAPTER VI 36

CHAPTER VII...42

CHAPTER VIII..47

CHAPTER IX 50

CHAPTER X...55

CHAPTER XI 60

CHAPTER XII 63

CHAPTER XIII...70

CHAPTER XIV 74

CHAPTER XV...77

CHAPTER XVI 84

CHAPTER XVII...96

CHAPTER XVIII..101

CHAPTER XIX 105

CHAPTER XX...110

APPENDIX...115

INTRODUCTION

Review of the Principal Documents used in this Work.

After the three or four years of the public life of Jesus, the period which the present volume embraces wise the moat extraordinary the whole development of Christianity. We shall see by a strange play of that grand unconscious artist who seems to preside over the apparent caprices of history, Jesus and Nero, the Christ and the Antichrist, opposed and facing each other, if I dare say it, like Heaven and Hell. The Christian conscience is complete. Up till now it has scarcely known to do ought but love; the persecutions of the Jews, although bitter enough, have been unable to change the bond of affection and recognition which the budding church keeps within its heart for its mother the synagogue, from which she is scarcely separated. Now the Christian has somewhat to hate. In front of Jesus there appears a monster who is the ideal of evil even as Jesus is the ideal of good. Reserved like Enoch or like Elias to play a part in the final tragedy the universe, Nero completes the Christian mythology, inspires the first sacred book of the new canon, founds, by a hideous massacre, the primacy of of the Roman Church, and prepares the revolution which shall make Rome a Holy City, a second Jerusalem. At the same time, by one of those mysterious coincidences which are not rare in the moments of the great crises of humanity, Jerusalem is destroyed, the temple disappears, Christianity, disembarrassed from what has been irksome to it, emancipates itself more and more, and follows outside of conquered Judaism its own destinies.

The last epistles of St. Paul, the Epistle to the Hebrews, the epistles attributed to Peter and James, and the Apocalypse among the canonical writings the principal documents of this history. The first epistle of Clemens Romanus, Tacitus and Josephus furnish us also with valuable indications. On a large umber of points, notably on the death of the Apostles and the relations of John with Asia, our picture will remain in semi-obscurity; upon others we shall be able to concentrate real rays of light. The material facts of the Christian origins are almost all obscure; what is clear is the ardent enthusiasm, the superhuman boldness, the sublime contempt for reality which makes this movement the most powerful effort towards the ideal whose memory has been preserved to us.

In the introduction to our St. Paul we have discussed the authenticity of all the epistles which have been attributed to the Great Apostle. The four epistles which are connected with this volume, the epistles to the Philippians, Colossians, Philemon and the Ephesians are those which suggest certain doubts. The objections raised against the epistle to the Philippians are of such little value that we need scarcely dwell upon them. We have seen and we shall see in what follows that the epistle to the Colossians gives much more ground for reflection, and that the epistle to the Ephesians, although well authenticated, presents a separate aspect in the work of Paul. Nothwithstanding the great difficulties which can be raised, I hold the epistle to the Colossians as authentic. The interpolations which in these last times some skilful critics have proposed to see there are not clear. The system of M. Holtzmann on this point is worthy of its learned author; but what dangers are there in this method too much accredited in Germany, where they start from an a priori figure which must serve as a fixed criterion for the authorship of the works of a writer! That the interpolation and supposition of apostolic writings had been often practised during the first two centuries of Christianity cannot be denied. But to make in such a matter a strict discernment between the true and the false, the apocryphal and the authentic is a task impossible to carry out. We see with certainty that the Epistle to the Romans, the Corinthians, and the Galatians are authentic. We see with the same certainty that the Epistles to Timothy and Titus are apocryphal. In the interval, between these two poles of critical evidence we hesitate. The great school led by Christian Baur has as principal defect, its representing the Jews of the first century as complete characters, fed upon dialectics and obstinate in their arguments. Peter, Paul, Jesus even, in the writings of this school, resemble some Protestant theologians of a German University having all one doctrine, having but one, keeping always the same. Now, what is true is that the wonderful men who are the heroes of this history changed and contradicted themselves much. They accepted during their lives three or four theories; they made borrowings from those of their adversaries against whom at another time they had been most severe. These men, looked at from our point of view, were susceptible, personal, irritable, mobile; what makes fixity of opinion, science, and rationalism was foreign to them. They had among them, like the Jews, in all times, violent disagreements; but, nevertheless, they made up very solid body. To understand them we must place ourselves at a great distance from the pedantry inherent in every scholastic; we must study rather the little coteries of a pious society, the English and American congregations, and, principally, what has passed since the foundation of all the religious orders. Under this view the faculties of theology in the German Universities, which can alone supply the amount of work necessary to arrange the chaos of documents relative to these curious origins, are the places, in all the world, in which the true history of it could be written. Now, history is the analysis of a life which develops itself, of a germ which expands, and theology is the inverse of life. Only attentive to what confirms or weakens his dogmas, the theologian, even the most liberal, is always, without thinking it, an apologist; he seeks to defend or to refute. The historian only seeks to recount. Facts materially false, documents even apocryphal, have for him a value, for they paint the soul, and are often more true than the dry truth itself. The greatest error in his eyes is to transform into factors of abstract theory those good and artless missionaries whose dreams have been the consolation and the joy of so many centuries.

What we are about to say of the Epistle to the Colossians, and especially of the Epistle to the Ephesians, must be said with stronger reason of the first epistle attributed to St. Peter and the epistles attributed to James and Jude. The second epistle, attributed to Peter, is certainly apocryphal. We recognise at the first glance an artificial composition, an imitation composed of scraps of apostolic writings, especially from the Epistle of Jude. We do not dwell upon this point, for we do not believe that II. Peter has among true critics a single defender But the falseness of II. Peter, an epistle whose principal object is to encourage patience among the faithful who are wearied by the long delay of the reappearance of Christ, proves in a sense the authenticity of I. Peter. For, to be apocryphal, II. Peter is a writing old enough; now the author of II. Peter thoroughly believed that I. Peter was the work of Peter, since he refers to it, and represents his writing as a "second epistle," making a sequence to the first (iii., 1-2). I. Peter is one of the writings of the New Testament which are most anciently and most unanimously quoted as authentic. One grave objection only is drawn from the borrowings which may be remarked there from the Epistles of St. Paul, and in particular from that to the Ephesians. But the secretary whom Peter used to write the letter, if he really wrote it, might well be allowed to make such borrowings. At all times preachers and publicists have been unscrupulous in appropriating to themselves those phrases which have become public property, and which are in a sort of way "in the air." We see, likewise, Paul's secretary, who has the epistle called to the Ephesians copying largely from the Epistle to the Colossians. One of the features which characterizes the literature of the epistles is to present many borrowings from writings of the same kind composed previously.

The first four verses of Chapter v. of I. Peter excite, indeed, some suspicions. They recall the pious recommendations, a little insipid, impressed upon a hierarchical mind which fill the false epistles to Timothy and Titus. Besides, the affectation which the author shows in representing himself a "witness of the suffering of Christ," raises apprehensions analogous to those which the pseudo-Johannine writings cause by their persistence in representing themselves as the accounts of an actor and spectator. We do not require, however, to stop at that, Many features also are favourable to the hypothesis of authenticity. Thus the progress towards hierarchy is scarcely sensible in I. Peter. Not only is there no mention of Episcopos, each Church has not even a Presbyteros; it has some presbyteri or "elders," and the expressions which the author uses do not imply that these elders formed a distinct body. A circumstance which deserves to he noted is that the author, while seeking to exalt the abnegation of which Jesus gives proof in his passion, omits an essential feature recorded by Luke, and gives us also to believe that the legend of Jesus had not yet arrived, at the time he wrote, at its full development.

As to the eclectic and conciliatory tendencies which we observe in the Epistle of Peter, they only constitute an objection for those who, with Christian Baur and his pupils, represent the diversity between Peter and Paul as an absolute opposition. If the hatred between the two parties in primitive Christianity had been as deep as this school believes, the reconciliation would never have been made. Peter was not an obstinate Jew like James. It is not necessary in writing this history to consider only the pseudo-Clementine Homilies and the Epistle to the Galatians. It is necessary to take take account of the Acts of the Apostles. The art of the historian should consist in presenting things in a manner which should in nothing lessen the divisions of parties (these divisions were deeper than we can imagine), and which, nevertheless, permits of explaining how such divisions have been able to weld themselves into a fine unity.

The Epistle of James presents itself to criticism very nearly under the same conditions as the Epistle of Peter. The difficulties of detail which can be opposed to that have not much importance. What is serious is that general objection drawn from the facility of the suppositions of writings at a time when there existed no guarantee of authenticity, and which there would be no scruple as to pious frauds. As to writers like Paul, who have left us by universal admission certain writings, and whose biography is well enough known, there are two certain criteria for discerning false attributions; it is (1st) to compare the doubtful work with the universally admitted works, and (2nd) to see if the matter in dispute answers to the biographical data we possess. But if it concerns a writer of whom we have some disputed pages, and whose biography is little known, we have often to decide only on the grounds of sentiment which do not weigh with us. By showing one's self easy certainly risk taking as serious things that are false; by showing one's self rigorous we risk rejecting as false things that are true. The theologian who believes that he proceeds upon certainties is, I repeat, a bad judge of such questions. The critical historian has a conscience at rest when he sets himself to investigate thoroughly the different degrees of certain, probable, plausible, and possible. If he has skill he will know what so true as much by the general colour, while he is prodigal of particular allegations, the signs of doubt and the "may-bes."

A consideration which I have found favourable to these writings (the 1st Epistle of Peter, the Epistles of James and Jude), very rigorously excluded by a certain criticism, is the fashion in which they are adapted to an organically received recital. While the 2nd Epistle attributed to Peter; the pretended Epistles of Paul to Timothy and Titus, are excluded from the limits of a logical history, the three epistles which we have named enter these, so to speak, of themselves. The features of circumstances which one meets there seem anticipative of facts known through evidence from without, and are embraced in it. The Epistle of Peter answers well to what we know, especially through Tacitus, as to the situation of the Christians at Rome about the year 63 or 64. The Epistle of James, on the other hand, is the perfect picture of the state of the Ebionim, at Jerusalem in the years which preceded the revolt. Josephus gives us some statements of the some kind. The hypothesis which attributes the Epistle of James to a James different from the Lord's brother has no advantage. This epistle, it is true, was not admitted in the first centuries in a manner as unanimous as that of Peter; but the motives for these hesitations appear to have been rather dogmatic than critical; the small taste of the Greek fathers for the Judeo-Christian writings was the principal cause of it.

A remark that at least applies with clearness to the small apostolic writings of which we speak is that they had been composed before the fall of Jerusalem. That event introduced into the situation of Judaism and Christianity such changes that one can easily discern a writing subsequent to the catastrophe of the year 70, from a writing contemporaneous with the third temple. Pictures evidently relating to the anterior struggles among the different classes of Jerusalem society, like that which the Epistle of James presents to us (v., 1, & ff), could not be conceived after the revolt of the year 66, which put an end to the reign of the Sadducees. From what there is in the pseudo-apostolic epistles, such as the epistles to Timothy, Titus, II. Peter, the epistle of Barnabas, works where we have as a rule an imitation or expansion of the more ancient writings; it follows, then, that there were some writings really apostolic, surrounded by respect, and whose number it was desired to augment. Just as each Arabic poet of the classical period has had his kasida, the complete expression of his personality; in like manner each apostle has his epistle more or less authentic, in which it was believed that the fine flower of his thought was preserved. We have already spoken of the Epistle to the Hebrew. We have proved that this work is not by St. Paul, as has been believed in certain branches of Christian tradition, but we are shown that the date of its composition allows it to be fixed with considerable verisimilitude about the year 66. It remains for us to examine whether it can be known who was the true author, where it was written, and who are those "Hebrews" to whom, according to the title, it was addressed. The circumstantial features which the epistle present are the following:--The author speaks to the Church named as a master well-known to it. He takes as his point of view almost a tone of reproach. That Church has received the faith a long time back, but it has so sunk in the matter of doctrine that it has need of elementary instruction, and is not capable of comprehending a high theology. This Church, besides, has shown, and shows still, much courage and devotion, especially in serving the saints. It had suffered cruel persecutions about the time when it received the full light of the faith. At that time it had been as a spectacle. That was but for a short period, for those who at that time actually composed the Church had had part in the merits of that persecution by sympathising with the confessors, by visiting the prisoners, and especially by courageously enduring the loss of their goods. In the trials, moreover, there were found some renegades, and the question was mooted as to whether those who by weakness had apostatised could re-enter the Church. At the time when the apostle wrote, it appears that there were still some members of the Church in prison. The believers of the Church in question had some illustrious heads who had preached to them the word of God, and whose death had been specially edifying and glorious. The Church had, notwithstanding, still some leaders with whom the author of the letter was on intimate relations. The author of the letter, in fact, has known was on the Church in question, and has exercised there a distinguished ministry. He has the intention of returning to it, and he desires that his return shall be brought about as quickly as possible. The author and those whom he addresses knew Timothy. Timothy has been imprisoned in a different town from that where the author is residing at the time he writes. Timothy had just been set at liberty. The author hopes that Timothy will go to rejoin him, then both of them will set forth together to visit the Church addressed. The author finishes with these words-- ἀσπάζονται ὑμᾶς οἱ ἀπὸ τῆς Ἰταλίας, words which can scarcely describe any other than Italians residing for the time being outside of Italy.

As to the author himself, his ruling feature is a perpetual use of the Scriptures, a subtle and allegorical exegesis, a most copious Greek style, very classical, a little dry, but at least as natural as that of most of the apostolic writings. He has a medium acquaintance with the worship which is practised at Jerusalem, and yet this cult inspires him with much pre-possession. He only uses the Alexandrian version of the Bible, and he founds some arguments upon the errors of Greek copyists. He is not a

Jerusalem Jew; he is a Hellenist in sympathy with Paul's school. The author, in short, does not give himself out for an immediate hearer of Jesus, but for a hearer of those who had seen Jesus--for a spectator of the apostolic miracles, and the first manifestations of the Holy Spirit. He no less holds an elevated rank in the Church; he speaks with authority; he is much respected by the brethren to whom he writes. Timothy appears to be subordinate to him. The single fact of addressing an epistle to a great Church indicates an important man, one of those personages who figure in the apostolic history, and whose name is celebrated.

All this, nevertheless, is not sufficient for us to pronounce with certainty as to the author of our epistle. It has been attributed, with more or less likelihood, to Barnabas, Luke, Silas, Apollo, and to Clemens Romanus. The attribution to Barnabas is the most likely. It has for it the authority of Tertullian, who represents the fact as recognised by everyone. It has especially in its favour this circumstance, that not one of the special features which the epistle presents are opposed to such an hypothesis. Barnabas was a Cypriote Hellenist, at that time associated with Paul, and independent of Paul. Barnabas was known by all and esteemed by all; it may be conceived, in short, how in this hypothesis the epistle has been attributed to Paul; it was, in fact, the lot of Barnabas to be always lost in some sense in the rays of the glory of the Great Apostle, and if Barnabas has composed some writing, as appears very probable, it is among the works of Paul that it is natural to seek for the pages really from his pen.

The determination of the Church addressed may be made with as much likelihood. The circumstances which we have enumerated scarcely permit of any choice but between the Church of Rome and that of Jerusalem. The title Πρὸς Ἑβραίους makes us think at once of the Church at Jerusalem, but it is impossible to be stopped by each a thought. Some passages--such as v., 11-14, vi., 11-12, and even 6 and 10--are nonsense if we suppose them addressed by a pupil of the apostle's to that mother Church--the source of all instruction. What said of Timothy is not better conceived; people as much engaged as the author, and as Timothy in Paul's party, would not have been able to address to the Church at Jerusalem a communication, supposing intimate relation. How can we admit, for example, that the author, with that exegesis, only founded on the Alexandrian version, that incomplete Jewish knowledge, that imperfect acquaintance with the affairs of the temple, would have dared to give a lesson so lofty to the masters par excellence, to people speaking Hebrew, or nearly so, living every day about the temple, and who knew much better than he all that he could tell them? How can we admit especially that he could treat them as catacumens scarcely initiated and incapable of a strong theology? On the contrary, if we suppose that the persons to whom the epistle was addressed are the faithful at Rome, everything is wonderfully arranged. The passages, vi., 10, x., 32 verse and ff., 3-7, are allusions to the persecutions of the year 64; the passage xiii., 7, applies to the death of the Apostles Peter and Paul; in short, οἱ ἀπὸ τῆς Ἰταλίας are then perfectly justified; for it is natural that the author should bear to the Church of Rome the salutations of the colony of Italians who were around him. Let us add that the 1st Epistle of Clemens Romanus (a work certainly Roman) makes from the Epistle to the Hebrews some distinct borrowings, and follows its mode of exposition very distinctly.

A single difficulty remains to be solved: Why the title of the epistle Πρὸς Ἑβραίους? Let us recall the fact that these titles are not always of apostolic origin, that they have sometimes been inserted later and falsely, as we have seen in the epistle called Πρὸς Ἐφεσίους. The epistle called to the Hebrews was written under the blow of persecution to the Church which was the most persecuted. In many passages (for example, xiii., 23) we feel that the author expresses himself in covert words. Perhaps the vague title Πρὸς Ἑβραίους was a password to save the letter from becoming a compromising matter. Perhaps, also, this title comes from this, that, in the second century, they looked upon the writing in question as a refutation of the Ebionites whom they called Ἑβραῖοι. A fact remarkable enough is that the Church of Rome had always, as to this epistle, some quite special lights; it is from thence it emerges, it is from thence that the first use is made of it. While Alexandria allows it be be attributed to Paul, the Church of Rome maintained always that it is not by that apostle, and that it is wrong to add it to his writings.

From whet city was the Epistle to the Hebrews written? It is more difficult to say. The expression Οἱ ἀπὸ τῆς Ἰταλίας shows that the author was out of Italy. One thing again, certainly, is that the town from which the epistle was written was a great city where there was a colony of Christians from Italy closely allied with those of Rome. These Christians of Italy were probably believers who escaped in the persecution of the year 64. We shall see that the current of Christian emigration fleeing from these terrors of Nero was directed towards Ephesus. The Church of Ephesus, besides, had had for the nucleus of its primitive formation two Jews come from Rome, Aquila and Priscilla; it remained always in direct relation with Rome. We are, therefore, led to believe that the epistle in question was written from Ephesus. Verse 23 of chap. xiii., it must be confessed, in that case, is singular enough. In what town other than Ephesus or Rome, and yet in relation with Ephesus and Rome, could Timothy have been imprisoned? What hypothesis we should adopt is an enigma difficult to explain. The Apocalypse is the principal feature of this history. The persons who will read attentively our chapters xv., xvi., and xvii., will realise, I believe, that there is no single writing in the Biblical canon which can be fixed with so much precision. We may determine this date to nearly a few days. The place where the work was written we are also at liberty to fix with probability. The question of the author of the book is, however, subject to greater uncertainty. Upon this point we cannot in my view express ourselves as fully assured. The author names himself at the head of the book (i., v. 9): "I, John, your brother and your companion in persecution for the kingdom and patience in Christ." But two questions arise here. First, is the assertion sincere, or is it not one of those pious frauds of which all the authors of apocalypses, without exception, have been found guilty Is the book, in other terms, not by an unknown person, who would be taken for a man of the first order in the opinion of the Churches for John the Apostle--a vision agreeable to his own ideas? Second, having admitted that verse 9 of chapter i. of the Apocalypse is sincere, may this John not be a namesake of the Apostle?

Let us discuss first this second hypothesis, for it is the easier to dispose of. The John who speaks, or who is reputed to speak in the Apocalypse, expresses himself with such vigour, supposes so clearly that he will be known, and that people will have no difficulty in distinguishing him from any of his namesakes; he knows so well the secrets of the Churches, he enters into them with such a resolute air, that they can scarcely refuse to see in him an apostle or an ecclesiastical dignitary all along the line. Now, John the Apostle had not in the second half of the first century any namesake who approached him in rank. Although M. Hitzig speaks of John Mark, he has really no place here, and was never on relations so intimate with the Churches of Asia that he should dare to address them in this tone. There remains a doubtful personage, that Presbyteros Johannes, a sort of likeness of the Apostle, who troubles like a spectre all the history of the Church of Ephesus, and causes critics so much embarrassment. Although the existence of this personage has been denied, and although we cannot peremptorily refute the hypothesis of those who see in him a shade of the Apostle John taken for a reality, we incline to believe that Presbyteros Johannes had, in fact, a separate identity; but that he had written the Apocalypse in 68 or 69, as M. Ewald still maintains, we absolutely deny. Such a personage would be known otherwise than by an obscure passage of Papias and an apologetic thesis of Dionysius of Alexandria. We should find his name in the Gospels, in the Acts, or in some epistle. We should we him leaving Jerusalem. The author of the Apocalypse is the best versed in the Scriptures, the most attached to the Temple, the most Hebraizing of the New Testament writers; such a personage could not have been introduced in the provinces; he must be originally from Judea; he holds with the chords of his heart to the Church of Israel. If Presbyteros Johannes existed, he was a disciple of the Apostle John, in the extreme old age of the latter. Papias appears to have been near enough to him, or at least to have been his contemporary. We admit, even, that sometimes he takes the pen for his master, and we regard as plausible the opinion which attributes to him the editing of the fourth gospel and of the first epistle called of John. The second and third epistles called "of John," where the author designs himself by the the words ὁ πρεσβύτερος, appear to us to be his personal work, and avowed as such. But, certainly, supposing that Presbyteros Johannes may have some position in the second class of Johannine writings (which include the fourth gospel and the three epistles), he has none in the composition of the Apocalypse. If anything is clear, it is that the Apocalypse, on the one hand, and the gospel and the three epistles on the other hand, do not come from the same pen. The Apocalypse is the most Jewish, the fourth gospel is the least Jewish of the writings of the New Testament. While admitting that the Apostle John may he author of some one of the writings which tradition attributes to him, it is assuredly the Apocalypse and not the Gospel. The Apocalypse answers well to the decisive opinion he appears to have adopted in the contest between the Judeo-Christians and Paul; the Gospel does not answer to it. The efforts which, in the third century, a party of the fathers of the Greek Church made to attribute the Apocalypse to the Presbyteros, came from the repulsion which the book then inspired in the orthodox doctors. They could not endure the thought that a writing whose style they found barbarous, and which appeared to them deeply impressed by Jewish hatred, should be the work of an apostle. Their opinion was the result of an induction a priori without value, not the expression of a tradition or of a critical reasoning.

If the ἐγὼ Ἰωάννης of the first chapter of the Apocalypse is sincere, the Apocalypse is then most assuredly by the Apostle John. But the essence of apocalypses is to be pseudonymous. The authors of the Apocalypses of Daniel, Enoch, Baruch, and Esdras represent themselves as being Daniel, Enoch, Baruch, and Esdras in person. The Church of the second century admitted upon the same footing as the Apocalypse of John an Apocalypse of Peter, which was decidedly apocryphal. If, in the Apocalypse which has remained canonical, the author gives his true name, there is there a surprising exception to rules of the kind. Well, that exception we believe must be admitted. An essential difference, indeed, separates the canonical Apocalypse from the other analogous writings which have been preserved to us. The greater number of the apocalypses are attributed to authors who have flourished, or have been reputed to flourish five or six hundred years--sometimes thousands of years back. In the second century they attributed apocalypses to the men of the apostolic century. The Shepherd and the pseudo-Clementine writings are 50 or 60 years later than the personages to whom they are attributed. The Apocalypse of Peter was probably in the same position; at least, nothing proves that it had anything special, topical, or personal. The canonical Apocalypse, on the contrary, if it is pseudonymous, would have been attributed to the Apostle John, in his lifetime, or a very short time after his death. Were it not for first three chapters, that would be barely possible; but is it conceivable that the falsifier would have the boldness to address his apocryphal work to the seven Churches which had been in relation with the apostle? And if one were to deny those relations, with M. Scholten, they would fall into a still greater difficulty, for it would be necessary to admit, then, that the falsifier, by an inaptness which has never been equalled, writing to churches which had never know John, presents his pretended John as having been at Patmos, quite near Ephesus, and knowing their deepest secrets, and as having full authority over them. Those churches, which, in the hypothesis of M. Scholten, knew well that John had never been in Asia, nor near Asia--could they be deceived by such a gross artifice? One thing which appears from the Apocalypse, in all hypotheses, is that the Apostle John was for some time head of the Churches of Asia. That being established, it is very difficult not to conclude that the Apostle John was really the author of the Apocalypse, for, the date of the book being fixed with absolute precision, we do not find the space of time necessary for a false one. If the apostle, in January 69, lived in Asia, or only had been there, the first four chapters are incomprehensible on the part of a falsifier. In supposing, with M. Scholten, that the Apostle John died at the beginning of the year 69 (which does not appear to agree with the truth), we are not without embarrassment. The book is written, in fact, if the recorder was still living; it is intended to spread at once in the Churches of Asia; if the apostle had been dead the fraud would have been too evident. What would they have said at Ephesus, in February 69, on receiving a book reputed to proceed from an apostle whom they knew no longer to exist, and whom, according to M. Scholten, they had never seen?

The critical examination of the book, far from weakening this hypothesis, strongly maintains it. John the Apostle appears to have been after James the most ardent of the Judeo-Christians; the Apocalypse, on its side, breathes out a terrible hatred against Paul, and against those who were relaxed in their observance of the Jewish law. The book answers wonderfully to the violent fanatical character which seems to have been that of John. It is indeed the work of the "son of thunder" the terrible Boanerges, of him who wished that the name of his master might be used only by those who belonged to the circle of the most strict of the disciples; of him who, if he could, would have made fire and brimstone to rain on the inhospitable Samaritans. The description of the heavenly court, with its quite material pomp of thrones and crowns, is indeed that of him who, when young, had set his ambition on being seated, with his brother, on thrones to the right and left of the Messiah. The two grand prepossessions of the author of the Apocalypse are Rome (ch. xiii. and ff.) and Jerusalem (ch. xi. and xii.). It appears that he had seen Rome, its temples, its statues, and the grand imperial idolatry. Now, a journey to Rome the part of John, accompanying Peter, can be easily supposed. What regards Jerusalem is more striking still. The author always reverts to "the beloved city;" he thinks only of it; he is acquainted with all the adventures of the Jerusalemite Church during the revolution of Judea (which calls forth the fine symbol of the woman and her flight into the desert); we feel that he has been one of the pillars of that Church, a devoted enthusiast of the Jewish party. That agrees well with John. The tradition of Asia Minor appears likewise to have preserved his memory an that of a severe Judaizer. In the Passover controversy, which troubled the Churches so deeply during the latter half of the second century, the authority of John is the principal argument which makes the Asian Churches maintain the celebration of Easter, conformably to Jewish law, on the 14th Nisan. Polycarpus, in the year 160, and Polycrates in 190, made appeal to his authority to defend their ancient usage against the innovators who, resting upon the fourth Gospel, would not have it that Jesus, the true passover, should have eaten the Paschal Lamb the evening before his death, and who transferred the festival to the day of the resurrection.

The language of the Apocalypse is likewise a reason for attributing the book to a member of the Church of Jerusalem. That language is quite apart from the other writing. of the New Testament. There is no doubt that the work has been written in Greek; but it is a Greek thought out in Hebrew, and which could be only understood and appreciated by people who knew Hebrew. The author has fed upon prophecies and apocalypses prior to his own to a degree which is astonishing; he evidently knows them by heart. He is familiar with the Greek version of the Sacred Books; but it is in the Hebrew texts the Biblical passages present themselves to him. What a difference from the style of Paul, Luke, or the author of the Epistle to the Hebrews, or even the synoptical Gospels! A man having passed some years at Jerusalem in the schools which surrounded the Temple could alone be impregnated to that extent with the Bible, or participate thus in a lively manner in the passions of the revolutionary people, and in its hopes and its hatred against the Romans.

Lastly, a circumstance which must not be neglected is that the Apocalypse presents some features which are in sympathy with the fourth Gospel and with the epistles attributed to John. Thus the expression ho logos tou theou so characteristic of the fourth Gospel is found, for the first time, in the Apocalypse. The image of "living waters" is common to the two works. The expression Lamb of God in the fourth Gospel recalls the expression of the Lamb which is common in the Apocalypse as designating

9

Christ. The two books apply to the Messiah, the passage in Zechariah xii. v. x., and translate it in the same manner. Far from us be the thought to conclude from these facts that the same pen has written the fourth Gospel and the Apocalypse, but it is not immaterial that the forth Gospel, whose author could not but have some connexion with the Apostle John, presents in its style and its images some sympathy with a book attributed for various reasons to the Apostle John. Ecclesiastical tradition is hesitating upon the question which occupies us. Up to about the year 150 the Apocalypse appears not to have had in the Church the importance which, according to our ideas, ought to have attached to a writing if they had been assured that in this writing they possessed a solemn manifesto coming from the pen of an apostle. It is doubtful if Papias admitted it as having been written by the Apostle John. Papias was a millenarian in the same style as the Apocalypse, but it appears that he declares that he holds this doctrine "from unwritten tradition." If he had alleged the Apocalypse as his ground, Eusebius would have said so, he who receives with so much enthusiasm all the quotations which that ancient father makes from the apostolic writings. The author of the Shepherd of Hermas knew, it would seem, the Apocalypse and copies it, but It does not follow from that that he held it to be a work of John the Apostle. It is St. Justin who, about the middle of the second century, declares as the first, distinctly, that the Apocalypse really is a composition of the Apostle John. Now, St. Justin, who did not come from the bosom of any of the great churches, is a mediocre authority on the question of traditions. Melito, who comments upon certain parts of the work, Theophilus of Antioch, and Apollonius, who used it much in their polemics, appear, nevertheless, like Justin, to have attributed it to the Apostle. As much must be said as to the Canon of Muratori. At the beginning of the year 200 the opinion is widespread that John of the Apocalypse was indeed the apostle. Irenæus, Tertullian, Clement of Alexandria, and Origen, the author of the Philosophumena, have not on this point any hesitation. The contrary opinion was always firmly held. To those who shook themselves free from Judeo-Christianity and from primitive millenarianism, the Apocalypse was a dangerous book, impossible to defend, unworthy of an apostle since it contained some prophecies which were not fulfilled. Marcion, Serdo, and the Gnostics rejected it absolutely. The Apostolic Constitutions omitted it in their canon, the old Peshito does not contain it. The enemies of the Montanist reveries, such as Caïus the Priest, and the Alogi, pretended to see it work of Cerinth. Lastly, in the second half of the third century, the School of Alexandria, in hatred of the millenarianism arising afresh in consequence of the persecution of Valerian, criticised the book with a severity and an undisguisedly bad disposition; the Bishop Dionysius demonstrated thoroughly that the Apocalypse could not have been by the same author as the fourth Gospel, and put in fashion the hypothesis of the presbyteros. In the fourth century the Greek Church was quite divided. Eusebius, although hesitating, is in the main unfavourable to the theory which attributes the work to the son at Zebedee. Gregory of Nazianzus, and nearly all the educated Christians of the same period, refuse to see an apostolic writing in a book which contradicts so keenly their taste, their ideas of apologetics, and their prejudices of education. We may say that if this party had been successful it would have relegated the Apocalypse to the rank of the Shepherd and the ἀντιλεγόμενα, whose Greek text has nearly disappeared. Fortunately, it was too late for such exclusions to be successful. Thanks to a skilful opposition, a book which includes some cruel accusations against Paul has been preserved alongside of the very works of Paul, and forms with them a volume reputed to come from a single inspiration.

This persistent protestation, which constitutes a fact so important in ecclesiastical history, is it really of considerable weight in the eyes of independent critics! We cannot tell. Certainly Dionysius of Alexandria is right when he establishes that the same man could not have written the fourth Gospel and the Apocalypse. But, placed in this dilemma, modern criticism has replied quite otherwise than the criticism of the third century. The authenticity of the Apocalypse has appeared to it more admissible than that of the Gospel, and if in the Johannine work it were necessary to give a share to this problematical presbyteros, it is indeed less the Apocalypse than the Gospel and the epistles which might properly be attributed to him. What motive could these adversaries of Montanism in the third and fourth centuries, those Christians educated in the Hebrew schools of Alexandria, Cesarea, and Antioch, have to deny that the author of the Apocalypse was the Apostle John? A tradition, a souvenir preserved in the churches? In no degree. Their motives were motives of theology, a priori. At first the attribution of the Apocalypse to the Apostle made it nearly impossible for an educated and sensible man to admit the authenticity of the fourth gospel, and they would have believed that they were giving up Christianity if they doubted the authenticity of this latter document. Besides, the vision attributed to John would appear an unceasing source of renewed errors; it went forth in perpetual recrudensces of Judeo-Christianity, of intemperate prophecy, of audacious millenarianism? What reply could one make to the Montanists and mystics of the same kind, disciples quite consistent with the Apocalypse, and to those troops of enthusiasts who ran to martyrdom, intoxicated as they were by the strange poetry of the old book of the year 69? One only; to prove that the book which served as a text for their chimeras was not of apostolic origin. The reason which led Caius and Dionysius and so many others to deny that the Apocalypse was really by the Apostle John is therefore just that which leads us to the opposite conclusion. The book is Judeo-Christian and Ebionite; it is the work of an enthusiast drunk with hatred against the Roman Empire and the profane world; it excludes all reconciliation between Christianity on the one hand, the empire and the world on the other; Messianism to entirely material there; the reign of the martyrs during 1,000 years is affirmed in it; and the end of the world is declared to be very near. These principles, in which the national Christians, led by the direction of Paul, then by the School of Alexandria, saw insurmountable difficulties, are for us works of ancient date and apostolic authenticity. Ebionism and Montanism do not make us afraid any longer; as simple historians, we even affirm that the adherents of these sects, repulsed by orthodoxy, were the true successors of Jesus, of the Twelve, and the family of the Master. The reasonable direction which Christianity took through moderate Gnosticism, by the tardy triumph of Paul's School, and, above all, by the influence of men such as Clement of Alexandria and Origen, ought not to make us forget its true beginnings. The chimeras, the impossibilities, the materialistic conceptions, the paradoxes, the enormities which made Eusebius impatient when he read those ancient Ebionite and millenarian authors, such at Papias, were the true primitive Christianity. That the dreams of those sublime enlightened ones should become a religion capable of living, it was necessary that men of good sense and fine spirit, as were the Greeks who became Christians at the beginning of third century, should take up the work of the old visionaries, and by taking it up should have singularly modified, corrected, and lessened it. The most authentic monuments of the artlessness of the first age became then embarrassing evidence which they tried to place in the shadow. There happened what occurs usually in the origin of all religious creations, that which is particularly observable during the first centuries of the Franciscan order; the founders of the house were ousted by the new comers; the true successors of the first fathers soon became "suspects" and heretics. Hence arises what we have had often occasion to remark, namely, that the favourite books of Ebionite and millenarian Christianity are much better preserved in the Latin and Oriental translations than in the Greek text, the Greek orthodox Church having always shown itself very intolerant in regard to those books and having systematically suppressed them.

The reasons which led to the attribution of the Apocalypse to the Apostle John remain therefore very strong, and I believe that the person who shall read our statement will be struck with the manner in which everything, in this hypothesis, is explained and connected. But, in a world where the ideas of literary ownership were so different from those of our days, a work could belong to an author in many ways. Did the Apostle John himself write the manifesto of the year 69? We may certainly doubt that. It is sufficient for our argument that he had cognizance of it, and that having approved it, he had seen it, without displeasure, passing from hand to hand under his name. The first three verses of chapter i., which have the appearance of another hand than that of the seer, may then be explained. By this would be explained also passages such as xviii., 20, and xxi., 4, which lead us to believe that he who held the pen was not the Apostle. In Ephesians ii., 20, we find an analogous feature, and there we are sure that between Paul and us there was the intermediary of a secretary or an imitator. The abuse which has been made of the name of the apostles to give value to certain apocryphal writings might to make us very suspicious. Many features of the Apocalypse do not suggest an immediate disciple of Jesus. We are surprised to see one of the members of the little party where the Gospel was elaborated presenting his old friend as a Messiah in glory, seated on the Throne of God, governing the peoples, and so totally different from the Messiah of Galilee that the seer trembles at his appearance and falls half-dead. A man who had known the true Jesus could with difficulty, even at the end of thirty-six years, have undergone such a modification in his remembrances. Mary of Magdala, on seeing Jesus risen, cried out, "Ω my Master!" and John saw the heavens opened only to discover Him whom he had loved transformed into Christ terrible! . . . Let us add that we are not less astonished to see coming from the pen of one of the principal personages of the Evangelical idyl an artificial composition, a veritable copy, in which the cool imitation of the visions of the old prophets shows itself in every line. The picture of the fishermen of Galilee which is presented to us by the synoptical evangelists scarcely answers to that of scribes, assiduous readers of ancient books of the learned Rabbis. It remains to enquire if it is not the picture of the synoptists which is false, and if the surroundings of Jesus were not more pedantic, scholastic, more analogous to the scribes and Pharisees than the narrative of Matthew, Mark, and Luke might lead one to suppose.

If we admit the hypothesis of which we have spoken, and according to which John rather accepted the Apocalypse as his, than written it with his own hand, we obtain another advantage, that is, of explaining how the book was so little known during the three-quarters of a century which followed its composition. It is probable that the author, after the year 70, seeing Jerusalem taken, the Flavii solemnly established, the Roman Empire reconstituted, and the world determined to last, in spite of the term of three years and a-half he had assigned to it, himself arrested the publicity of his work. The Apocalypse, in fact, only attained its complete importance in the middle of the second century, when millenarianism became a subject of discord in the Churches, and especially when the persecution gave some meaning and reference to the invectives pronounced against the Beast. The future of the Apocalypse was then attached to the alternatives of peace and trials which passed over the Church. Every persecution gave it a fresh popularity; it was when the persecutions were over that the book ran through real dangers, and we see it on the point of being expelled from the canons as a lying and seditious pamphlet.

Two traditions whose plausibility I have admitted in this volume, viz., the coming of Peter to Rome and the residence of John at Ephesus, having given cause for great controversies, I have made them the subject of an appendix at the end of the volume. I have specially discussed the recent memoir of M. Scholten the sojourn of the apostles in Asia as carefully as all the writings of the eminent Dutch critic deserve. The conclusions at which I have arrived, and which I only hold, besides, as probable, will certainly call forth, as did the use I have made of the fourth Gospel in writing the Life of Jesus, the disdain of a young presumptuous school, in whose eyes every statement is proved if it is negative, and which treats peremptorily as ignorant those who do not admit its exaggerations at first sight. I beg the serious reader to believe that I respect him enough to neglect nothing which can serve to the discovery of the truth in the order of studies which I undertake. But I hold, as a principle, that history and dissertation should be distinct from each other. History ought not to be written until after scholarship has accumulated whole libraries of critical essays and memoirs; but, when history comes to act, it only owes to the reader the original source on which each assertion rests. The notes occupy the third of each in those volumes which I dedicate to the origins of Christianity. If I had been obliged to set down the bibliography there, the quotations from modern authors, the detailed discussion of opinions, the notes would have filled at least three quarters of the page. It is true that the method I have followed supposes readers versed in researches in the Old and New Testament, which is the case with few people in France. But how would serious books have the right to exist if, before writing them, the author was bound to be certain that he would have a public to understand him? I affirm, besides, that even a reader who does not know German, if he is acquainted with what has been written in our language on these matters, can quite easily follow my discussion. The excellent collection entitled Revue de Theologie, which was printed up to a few years ago in Strasbourg is an encyclopædia of modern exigesis which does not dispense certainly with a reference to German and Dutch books, but where all the discussions of learned theology for half a century back have their echo. The writings of MM. Reuss, Reville, Scherer, Kienlen, Coulin, and generally the theses of the faculty of Strasbourg, will likewise present to readers desirous of more ample instruction, a solid acquisition. It "goes without saying" that those who can read the writings of Christian Baur, the father of all these studies; of Zeller, of Schougler, of Voltemar, Hitgenfeld, de Lucke, Lipsius, Holtzman, Ewald, Kelm, Hansrath, and Scholten, are much more edified still. I have declared all my life that Germany has acquired an eternal glory in founding the critical science of the Bible and the studies which are connected with it. I have spoken plainly enough to prevent myself being accused of passing silently over obligations which I have recognised a hundred times. The German School of exegetes has its defects; there defects are those which a theologian, however liberal he may be, cannot avoid; but the patience, the tenacity of mind, and the good faith which have been displayed in this work of analysis are truly admirable. Among many very beautiful stories which Germany has placed in the edifice of the human mind, erected at the common expense by all peoples, Biblical science is perhaps the block which has been cut with the greatest care, and which bears in the highest degree the stamp of the workman.

In regard to this volume, as in regard to the preceding, I owe much to the ever-ready scholarship and to the inexhaustible kindness of my learned confreres and friends, MM. Egger, Léon Renier, Derenbourg, Waddington, Bossier, de Longpérier, de Witte, Le Blant, Dulaurier, who have been quite willing that I should consult them constantly upon points connected with their special studies. M. Neubauer has reviewed the Talmudic portion. In spite of his labours in the Chamber M. Noel Parfait has been desirous not to discontinue his labours as an accomplished corrector. Lastly, I ought to express my extreme gratitude to MM. Amari, Pietro Rosa, Fabio Gori, Fiorelli, Minervini, and de Luca, who, during a journey in Italy which I made last year, were the most invaluable of guides to me.

We shall see how this journey will connect itself on many sides with the subject of the present volume. Although I had already known Italy, I was longing to salute once more that land of great memories, the learned mother of all Renaissance. According to a Rabbinical legend, there was at Rome during that long mourning of beauty which is called the middle ages an antique statue preserved in a secret place, and so beautiful that the Romans came by night to kiss it by stealth. The fruit of these profane embraces was, it is said, the Anti-Christ. This son of the marble statue was certainly at least a son of Italy. All the great protests of the human conscience against the extremes of Christianity have come in former times from that land; and thence they will still come in the future.

I should not conceal that the taste for history, the incomparable delight which one feels in seeing the spectacle of humanity unrolled, has especially enthralled me in this volume. I have had too much pleasure preparing it to ask for any other reward than that of having done so. Often I have reproached myself with so much enjoyment of it in my study while poor country is consuming itself in a prostrated agony, but I have had a tranquil conscience. At the time of the elections of 1869, I offered myself to the suffrages of my fellow citizens; all my addresses bore in large letters: "No Revolution; no War; a war will be as fatal as a revolution." In the month of September, 1870, I implored the enlightened spirits of Germany and Europe to think of the frightful misfortunes which were threatening civilization. During the siege in Paris, in the month in November, 1870, I exposed myself to much unpopularity by counselling the calling together of an Assembly having powers to treat for peace. At the the elections of 1871 I replied to the overtures which were made to me: "Such a mandate can be neither sought for nor refused." After the re-establishment of order I applied as much attention as I could to the reforms which I considered the most urgent to save our country. I have therefore done what I could. We owe our country to be sincere with here; we are not obliged to apply charlatanism to make her accept our services or agree with our ideas. Yet perhaps this volume, although addressed above all to the curious and the artistic, will contain much instruction. We shalt see crime pushed to its height, and the protest of the saints raised in the most sublime accents--such a spectacle shall not be without religious fruit. I never believed so thoroughly that religion is not a subjective duping of our nature, that it responds to an exterior reality, and that he who shall have followed its inspirations will have been the best inspired. To simplify religion is not to shake, it is often to fortify it. The little Protestant sects of our own day, like budding Christianity, are there to prove it. The great error of Catholicism is to believe that it can struggle against the progress of materialism with a complicated dogmatism, encumbering itself every day with a fresh addition of the marvellous. People cannot longer bear a religion founded on miracles; but such a religion might be very living still if it took a part of the dose of positivism which has entered into the intellectual temperament of the working classes. The people who have charge of souls should reduce dogma as much as possible, and make out of worship a means of moral education, of beneficent association. Beyond the family and outside of the State man has need of the Church. The United States of America could not have made their wonderful democracy last but through their innumerable sects. If, as one might suppose, Ultramontane Catholicism cannot succeed longer in the great cities in drawing people to its temples, there needs only the individual initiative created by the little centres where the weak find lessons, moral succour, patronage, and sometimes material assistance. Civil society, whether it calls itself a commune, a canton or a province, a State or father land, has many duties towards the improvement of the individual; but what it does is necessarily limited. The family ought to do much more, but often it is insufficient; some tunes it is wanting altogether. The association created in the name of moral principle can alone give to every man coming into this world a bond which unites him with the past, duties as to the future, examples to follow a heritage of virtue to receive and to transmit, and a tradition of devotion to continue.

CHAPTER I

PAUL CAPTIVE AT ROME

The times were strange, and perhaps the human race had never passed through a more extraordinary crisis. Nero was in his twenty-fourth year. The head of this wretched young man, placed by a wicked mother at the age of seventeen at the head of the world, finished by losing itself. For a long time some indications had disquieted those who knew him. His was a terribly declamatory mind, a bad, hypocritical, light, and vain nature; an incredible compound of false intelligence, deep wickedness, atrocious and cunning egotism, with unheard of refinements of subtlety; to make of him that monster who has no equal in history, and whose analogue is only found in the pathological annals of the scaffold, special circumstances were necessary. The school of crime in which he had grown up, the execrable influence of his mother, the obligation by which that abominable woman made him nearly begin life as a parricide, caused him soon to look on the world as a horrible comedy in which he was the principal actor. At the time we have reached, he has completely withdrawn himself from the philosophers his masters; he has killed nearly all his relations, and set the most shameful follies in the fashion; a portion of Roman society, by his example, has gone down to the last degree of depravity. The ancient harshness had reached its height; the reaction of popular and just instincts began. At the time when Paul entered Rome, the story of the day was this:--

Pedanius Secundus, prefect of Rome, a consular personage, had been assassinated by one of his slaves, not without extenuating circumstances being alleged in favour of the culprit. According to the law, all the slaves who, at the moment of the crime, had dwelt under the same roof as the assassin, ought to be put to death. There were nearly four hundred unfortunates in this case. When it became known that the atrocious execution was about to take place the feeling of justice which sleeps under the conscience of the most debased people was revolted. There had been an emeute; but the senate and the emperor decided that the law must take its course.

Perhaps among these four hundred innocents, destroyed in virtue of an odious law, there had been more than one Christian. Men had touched the bottom of the abyss of evil; they could only re-ascend. Certain moral facts of a singular kind took place even in the most elevated ranks of society. Four years before this there had been much talk of an illustrious lady, Pomponia Græcina, wife of Aulius Plautius, the first conqueror of Britain. They accused her of "foreign superstition." She always dressed in black, and never ceased her austerity. They attributed this melancholy to some horrible recollections, especially to the death of Julia, daughter of Drusus, her intimate friend, whom Messalina had put to death; one of her sons appears also to have been the victim of one of Nero's most monstrous enormities. But it was evident that Pomponia Græcina bore in her heart a deeper sorrow, and perhaps some mysterious hopes. She was remitted according to the ancient custom to her husband's judgment. Plautius assembled the relatives, examined the affair in a family council, and declared his wife innocent. That noble lady lived a long time afterwards tranquil under the protection of her husband, always sad--much respected. She appears to have told her secret to no one. Who knows if the appearances which superficial observers took for gloomy disposition were not the great peace of soul, the calm composure, the resigned waiting for death, disdain of a foolish and wicked society, the ineffable joy of renouncing joy? Who knows if Pomponia Græcina may not have been the first saint of the great world, the elder sister of Melania, Eustochia, and of Paula?

This extraordinary situation, if it exposed the Church of Rome to the opposing influence of politics, gave it on the other hand an importance of the first order, although it was not numerous. Rome under Nero in no way resembled the provinces. Whoever aspired to a great action must go there. Paul had in this point of view a sort of deep instinct which guided him. His arrival at Rome was an event in his life nearly as decisive as his conversion. He believed that he had attained to the summit of his apostolic career, and doubtless recalled to mind the dream in which after one of his days of struggle Christ appeared to him and said, "Courage! as thou hast borne witness of me in Jerusalem, thou shall also bear witness of me at Rome."

From the time when he approached the walls of the eternal city, the Centurion Julius conducted his prisoners to the Castra prætoriana, built by Sejan, near the Nomentan way, and handed them over to the prefect of the prætorium. The appellants to the Emperor were, on entering Rome, regarded as prisoners of the Emperor, and as such were entrusted to the imperial guard. The prefects of the prætorium were ordinarily two in number, but at this moment there was only one. This high office had been since the year 51 A.D., in the hands of the noble Afranius Burrhus, who a year afterwards, by a most miserable death, expiated the crime of having wished to do good by reckoning with evil. Paul had doubtless no direct communication with him. Perhaps, however, the humane fashion in which the apostle would appear to have been treated was due to the influence which this just and virtuous man exercised around him. Paul was appointed to the condition of custodia millitaris, that is to say entrusted with a prætorian guard to whom he was chained, but not in an inconvenient or continuous fashion. He had permission to live in rooms hired at his own expense, perhaps in the enceinte of the castra prætoriana, where all came freely to see him. He awaited for two years in this condition the appeal of his case. Burrhus died in March 62 A.D., and was replaced by Fenius Rufus and the infamous Tigellinus, the companion of Nero's debauches--the instrument of his crimes. Seneca just at this moment retired from public life. Nero had no longer any council save the Furies.

The relations of Paul to the believers in Rome had begun, we have seen, during the last stay of the apostle at Corinth. Three days after his arrival he wished, as was his habit, to put himself in communication with the principal hakamim; it was not in the bosom of the synagogue that the Christianity of Rome was formed; it was believers disembarking at Ostia or Puzzoli who, grouping themselves together, had constituted the first church of the capital of the world; this church had scarcely any affinities with the different synagogues of the same city. The immense size of Rome, and the mass of strangers who met there, were the reasons why they knew little of each other there, and why some very contrary ideas could be produced side by side without actual contact. Paul was thus led to follow the rule, which he had adopted from his first and second mission in the towns to which he brought the germ of the faith. He begged some of the heads of the synagogue to come to see him. He represented his situation to them in the most favourable light and protested that he had done nothing, and wished to do nothing against his nation--that he was actuated by the hope of Israel's faith in the resurrection. The Jews replied to him that they had never heard him spoken of nor received any letter from Judea on the subject, and expressed a desire to hear him expound his opinions himself. "For," added they, "we have heard it said the sect of which you speak provokes everywhere the most lively disputations." They fixed the hour for the discussion, and a considerable number of Jews met in the little room occupied by the apostle in order to hear him. The conference lasted nearly a whole day; Paul quoted all the texts from Moses and the prophets which proved, according to him, that Jesus was the Messiah: some believed, the greater number remained incredulous. The Jews of Rome piqued themselves upon a very strict observance. It was not there that Paul could have a very large success. They separated in great confusion; Paul, displeased, quoted a passage from Isaiah, very common among the Christian preachers, as to the wilful blindness of hardened men who shut their eyes and ears that they might not see or hear the truth. He closed, it is said, with his ordinary menace that he would carry to the Gentiles, who would receive him better, the kingdom of God which the Jews would not have. His apostolate among the Pagans was in fact crowned with a very great success indeed. His prisoner's cell became a theatre of ardent preaching. During the two years which he passed there he was not interfered with; he was not annoyed a single time in this exercise of proselytism. He had about him certain of his disciples, at least Timothy and Aristarchus. It appears that each of his friends in turn remained with him and shared his chain. The progress of the gospel was surprising. The apostle did miracles, and was believed to order heavenly power and spirits. Paul's prison was thus more fertile than his free activity had been. His chain, dragged along the prætorium, and which he showed everywhere with a sort of ostentation, was to them alone like a discourse. From his example, and animated by the manner in which he bore his captivity, his disciples and the other Christians of Rome preached boldly.

They did not encounter at first any great obstacle. The Campagna and the towns at the foot of Vesuvius received, perhaps from the Church of Puzzoli, the germs of Christianity which found there the conditions in which it was accustomed to increase, I mean with a first Jewish soil to receive it. Some strange conquests were made. The chastity of the believers was a powerful attraction. It was through this virtue that many noble Roman ladies were drawn to Christianity; the good families preserved still as to women an unbroken tradition of modesty and honour. The new sect had some adherents in the household of Nero, perhaps among the Jews, who were numerous in the lower ranks of the service, among those slaves and freed men, banded in guilds, whose condition bordered upon what had been basest and most elevated, the most brilliant and most miserable. Some vague indications would lead us to believe that Paul had certain relations with members of the Annoea family. A thing beyond doubt in any case, is that from this time the most sharp distinction between Jews and Christians was made at Rome among well informed persons. Christianity appeared a distinct "superstition" arising from Judaism, an enemy of its mother, and hated by its mother. Nero especially was sufficiently acquainted with what was going on, and took account of it with a certain animosity. Perhaps already some of the Jewish intriguers who surrounded him had inflamed his imagination from the Oriental point of view, and he had had promised to him that kingdom of Jerusalem, which was the dream of his last hours, his latest hallucination. We do not know with any certainty the names of any of the members of this Church of Rome at the time of Nero. A document of doubtful value enumerates as friends of Paul and Timothy, Eubulus, Pudens, Claudia, and that Linus whom ecclesiastical tradition will represent later on as the successor of Peter in the bishopric of Rome. The elements are likewise wanting to us to estimate the number of the faithful even in an approximate manner.

Everything appeared to go on in the best manner; but the implacable school, which had assumed as its task opposition to the ends of the world to the apostleship of Paul was not dormant. We have seen the emissaries of those ardent conservatives follow in a manner upon his track, and the Apostle of the Gentiles leaving behind him in the seas through which he passed a long streak of hatred. Paul, pictured as a baneful man, who teaches to eat meat sacrificed to idols, to fornicate with Pagans, is announced before in advance and marked for the vengeance of all. We scarcely believe it, but we cannot wholly doubt it, since it is Paul himself who states it. Even at this solemn and decisive moment, he found still in front of him some mean passions. Certain adversaries, members of that Judæo-Christian school which ten years previous he found everywhere in his footsteps, undertook to raise against him a species of counter-preaching to the gospel. Envious and bitter disputers, they sought occasions to contradict him, to aggravate his position as a prisoner, to enflame the Jews against him, and to lower the merit of his chains. The goodwill, the love, the respect which others manifested towards him, their loudly proclaimed conviction, that the chains of the apostle were the glory and best defence of the gospel, comforted him in all these vexations. "What does it matter, besides," wrote he about this time--

Provided that Christ be preached, whether the preacher be sincere, or the preaching be a pretext for him, I rejoice. I will always rejoice. As for me, I have the firm hope that, even at this time things will turn to my great benefit, to the liberty of the Church, and that my body, whether I live, or whether I die, shall be used to the glory of Christ. On the one hand, Christ is my life, and to die for me is an advantage; on the other hand, if I live, I shall see my work bring forth fruit; thus I know not which to choose. I am pressed by two opposing desires; on the one hand, to quit this world and to go to re-join Christ; on the other to remain with you. The first would be better for me, but the second would be better for you.

This greatness of soul gave him a marvellous assurance, gaiety, and strength. "If my blood," wrote he in one of his gospels, "is the libation by which the sacrifice of your faith must be watered, so much the better--so much the better. And you also say so much the better' with me." He, nevertheless, believed very willingly in his acquittal, and even in a prompt acquittal: he saw in that the triumph of the gospel, and he dated from that new projects. It is true that we no more see any of his thoughts directed to the West. It is to the Philippians and Colossians that he dreams of withdrawing himself until the day of the coming of the Lord. Perhaps had he acquired a more accurate knowledge of the Latin world, and had he seen beyond Rome and the Campagna countries becoming by Syrian immigration very analogous to Greece and Asia Minor, he would have met, had it only been because of the language, with great difficulties. Perhaps he knew a little Latin; but not enough for a fruitful preaching. Jewish and Christian proselytism in the first century was little exercised in the really Latin towns; it was confined to such towns as Rome and Puzzoli, where, in consequence of constant arrivals of Orientals, Greek had become wide-spread. Paul's programme was sufficiently full; the Gospel had been preached in the two worlds, it had attained, according to the wide pictures of the prophetic language, to the extremity of the earth, to all the nations which are under heaven. What Paul now dreamed of doing was to preach freely in Rome and then to return to his churches of Macedonia and Asia, and to wait patiently with them in prayer and extasy the advent of Christ.

In short, few years in the life of the Apostle were more happy than these. Immense consolations came from time to time to him; he had nothing to fear from the malevolence of the Jews. The poor lodging of the prisoner was a centre of marvellous activity. The follies of profane Rome, its spectacles, its scandals, its crimes, the disgraceful acts of Tigellinus, the courage of Thraseas, the horrible fate of the virtuous Octavia, and the death of Pallas, little moved our enlightened pietists. "The fashion of this world passeth away," they said. The great picture of a divine future made them shut their eyes to the blood-soaked soil in which their feet were plunged. Certainly the prophecy of Jesus had been accomplished. In the midst of outer darkness where Satan reigns; in the midst of tears and gnashing of teeth the little paradise of the elect is founded.

They were there in their secluded world, clothed internally with light and a clear sky in the kingdom of God their father, but without them what a hell!!! Oh, God, how frightful it is to remain in this kingdom of the Beast, where the worm never dies and the fire is never extinguished!

One of the greatest joys which Paul experienced at this period of his life was the arrival of a message from his dear Church of the Philippians, the first which he had founded in Europe and in which he had left so many devoted admirers. The rich Lydia whom he calls "his true spouse," did not forget him. Epaphroditus sent by the church brings him a sum of money, of which the apostle must have had great need, considering the expenses of his new condition. Paul, who had always made an exception of the Philippian Church and received from her what he did not wish to owe to any other, accepted it again with happiness. The news as to the church was excellent. A few quarrels which had occurred between the two deaconesses Euodia and Syntyche had come to trouble the peace. Some scandals awakened by evil-disposed persons and from which resulted imprisonments, only served to show the patience of the faithful. The heresy of the Judæo-Christians, the pretended necessity for circumcision, hung around them without disrupting them. Some bad examples of worldly and sensual Christians, of whom the apostle speaks with tears, did not come as it would appear from their church. Epaphroditus remained some time beside Paul, and had a sickness, the result of his devotion, which nearly brought him to death's door. A lively desire to see the Philippians possessed this excellent man; he sought himself to calm the disquietudes of his friends. Paul on his part wishing to make cease as soon as possible the fears of those pious ladies, quickly dismissed him, sending by him to the Philippians a letter full of tenderness written by the hand of Timothy. Never had he found such sweet expressions to describe the love which he bore to these entirely good and pure churches, which he carried in his heart.

He felicitated them not only on having believed in Christ, but on having suffered for him. Those among them who were in prison ought to be proud of enduring the treatment which they had seen before inflicted upon their apostle, and which they knew he had actually endured. They are like a little chosen group of the children of God, in the midst of a corrupted and perverse race--light in the midst of a dark world. He warned them against the example of less perfect Christians, that is to say, of those who were not released from all Jewish prejudices. The apostles of the circumcision are treated with the greatest hardness.

Beware of dogs, evil workers, of all these circumcised! It is we who are the true circumcised, we who worship according to the Spirit of God, who place our glory and confidence in Christ Jesus, not in the flesh. If I wished to exalt myself by these carnal distinctions, I should have a better right than anyone; I, circumcised the eighth day, of the pure race of Israel, of the tribe of Benjamin, a Hebrew and son of the Hebrews, formerly a Pharisee, formerly a persecutor, formerly a jealous observer of legal righteousness. Ah, well; all these advantages, I hold them from the point of view of Christ as inferiorities, as dust, since I have apprehended what is transcendent in the knowledge of Christ Jesus. To gain Christ I have lost all the rest, I have exchanged my own righteousness, arising from the observation of the law, against the true righteousness according to God, which comes from the faith in Christ, in order that I may participate in his resurrection and to rise again, I also, among the dead, as I have participated in his sufferings, and as I have taken upon me the image of his death. I am far from having attained this goal, but I pursue it. Forgetting what is behind, always reaching forth to that which is before, I aspire, like the racer, for the prize of the victory, placed at the extremity of the course. Such is the feeling of the perfect.

And he adds:--

Our country is in heaven, from whence we look for the Saviour, the Lord Jesus Christ, who shall transform our wretched body and make it like his glorious body, by the extension of his power, and thanks to the divine decree, which has submitted every thing to him. Behold, brethren whom I love and regret to see no longer, you, my joy and crown, this is the doctrine which should be held, my dearly beloved.

He especially exhorts them to concord and obedience. The form of life which he has given them, the manner in which they ought to practice Christianity, is good; but, after all, each believer has his revelation, his personal inspiration, which also comes from God. He prays "his true spouse" (Lydia) to reconcile Euodia and Syntyche, to go to help them and second them in their duties as servants of the poor. He wished that they should rejoice; "The Lord is at hand." His thanks for the sending of money on the part of the rich ladies of the Philippians, is a model of good grace and lively piety:

I have experienced a great joy in the Lord in connection with this late flourishing of your friendship, which has at last made you think of me: you thought well in that: but you had not an occasion. I do not say this to dwell upon my poverty. I have taught myself to be content with what I have. I know what it is to be in penury, and to have abundance. I am accustomed to everything, to be full and to suffer hunger, to have an overplus, and to want even what is necessary. I can do all things in Him who strengthens me. But you--you have done well to contribute so as to relieve my distress. It is not to the gift I look, but to the profit which will result from it to you. I have everything which is needful: I even abound, since I have received by Epaphroditus your offering, a sacrifice of a good odour, an offering most welcome, agreeable to God!

He recommends humility which makes us look on others as our superiors, charity which makes us think of others more than ourselves, according to the example of Jesus. Jesus had in Him all divinity and power; He could have, during His terrestrial life, shown himself in His divine splendour, but the economy of redemption would then have been reversed. Thus does He strip Himself of His natural distinction, to take the appearance of a slave. The world has seen Him like a man; looked at from without He would have been taken for a man. "He humbled Himself, making Himself obedient even to death, and that the death of the cross. Wherefore God has exalted Him and given Him a name above every other, willing that at the name of Jesus every knee shall bend in heaven, on the earth and under the earth, and in hell, and that every tongue shall confess the Lord Jesus Christ, to the glory of God the Father."

Jesus, we see, grew hour by hour greater in the consciousness of Paul. If Paul does not admit yet his full equality with God the Father, he believes in his divinity, and represents all His earthly life as the execution of a divine plan. Prison produced on him the effect which it usually produces on strong minds. It elevated him, and incited in his ideas some lively and deep resolutions. A little after having sent the letter to the Philippians, he sends Timothy to inform him of their condition, and to bear some new instructions to them. Timothy would return promptly enough. Luke would appear also at this time to have made an absence of short duration.

CHAPTER II

PETER AT ROME

Paul's chain, his entrance into Rome, quite triumphal according to Christian ideas, the advantages which his residence in the capital of the world gave him, did not allow of any repose for the party at Jerusalem. Paul was for that party a sort of stimulant, an active rival, against whom they murmured, and whom, nevertheless, they sought to imitate. Peter, in a remarkable degree, always hesitated, towards his audacious brother, between a lively personal admiration and the position his surroundings imposed on him; Peter (I say) passed his life, full also of numerous trials, in copying Paul, in following him at a distance in his course, in finding after him those strong positions which could assure the success of the common work. It was probably from the example of Paul that he settled, about the year 54, at Antioch. The report spreading into Judea and Syria in the second half of the year 61, of the arrival of Paul at Rome, was of itself enough to inspire him with the idea of a journey to the West.

It appears that he came with quite an apostolic company. First, his interpreter, John Mark, whom he called "his son," followed him usually. The apostle John, we have more than once observed, appeared likewise generally to have accompanied Peter. Some indications even lead us to believe that Barnabas was of the party. Lastly, it is not improbable that Simon of Gitton on his part might be drawn to the capital of the world, attracted by the kind of charm which that city exercised over all leaders of sects, charlatans, magicians, and thaumaturgists. Nothing was more common among the Jews than a journey to Italy. The historian, Josephus, came to Rome in the year 62 or 63 to obtain the deliverance of the Jewish priests, very holy personages, who, so as to eat nothing impure, lived in foreign countries on nuts and figs, and whom Felix had sent to give account to the emperor for some offence which is not known. Who were these priests? Was their affair entirely disconnected with Peter and Paul? The want of historic proof leaves us in much doubt as to all these points. The very fact on which modern Catholics base the edifice of their faith is far from being certain. We, however, believe that the Acts of Peter, such as the Ebionites recount, are only fabulous in detail. The fundamental idea of these Acts, Peter journeying through the world after Simon, the magician, to refute him, bearing the true gospel, which should overturn the gospel of the impostor, "coming after him like the light after the darkness, like knowledge after ignorance, like healing after sickness"--this conception is true when we put Paul's name in place of Simon's, and when, instead of the ferocious hatred which the Ebionites always exhibited against the preacher of the Gentiles, we picture between the two apostles a simple opposition of principle, excluding neither sympathy nor agreement on the fundamental point--the love of Jesus. In the journey undertaken by the old Galilean disciple to follow the track of Paul, we even willingly admit that Peter, following Paul closely, touched at Corinth, where he had, before his coming, a considerable party, and that he there much strengthened the Judæo-Christians, so much so that later on the Church of Corinth could pretend to have been founded by the two apostles, and to maintain, by making a slight error as to date, that Peter and Paul had been there at the same time, and from thence went forth in company to find death at Rome.

What were the relations of the two apostles at Rome? Certain indications would lead us to believe that they were good enough. We shall soon see Mark, Peter's secretary, charged with a mission from his master, to go to Asia with a recommendation from Paul; besides, the epistle, attributed to Peter, a writing of a very tenable authenticity, presents numerous borrowings made from Paul's epistles. Two truths must be maintained in this whole history; the first is that deep divisions (deeper indeed than those which were in the after history of the Church the ground of any schism) existed between the founders of Christianity, and that the form of the polemics, according to the usages of such people, was singularly bitter; the second is that a higher thought united them, even during their life, those brother-enemies, while wanting the great reconciliation which the Church should, of its own accord, make between them after their death, that is often seen in religious movements. There must also, in appreciating these debates, be great account taken of the Jewish character, quick and susceptible, given to violent language. In these little pious coteries, people quarrel and are reconciled continually; they have bitter words and, notwithstanding, love each other. A party of Peter, a party of Paul--these divisions did not possess more importance than those which in our day separate the different fractions of the Puritan Church. Paul had an excellent motto on this matter: "Let each one remain in the type of instruction which he has received," an admirable rule which the Roman Church did not much follow later on. The adherence to Jesus was sufficient; the confessional divisions, if one may so describe them, were a simple question of origin independent of the personal merits of the believer.

One fact, however, which is important, and which would lead us to believe that good relations had not been re-established between the two apostles is that, in the memory of the next generation, Peter and Paul are the leaders of opposing parties in the bosom of the Church; it is that the author of the Apocalypse, from the day of the death of the apostles, or at least of Peter, is, of all the Judæo-Christians, the most bitter against Paul. Paul looked on himself as the leader of the converted heathen wherever he found them; there was in this his interpretation of the agreement of Antioch; the Judæo-Christians regarded him evidently in a different manner. It is probable that this last party, which had always been very strong at Rome, drew from Peter's arrival a grand ground of preponderance. Peter became its leader and leader of the Church of Rome. Now the unequalled prestige of Rome gave to such a title the greatest importance. We can see something providential in the part played by this extraordinary city. Following the reaction which was thus produced against Paul, Peter became more and more, in virtue of a sort of opposition, the leader of the apostles. Reconciliation is quickly made between minds easily impressed. The chief of the apostles in the capital of the world! What more could be said? The grand association of ideas which was to dominate the destinies of humanity during thousands of years was being made. Peter and Rome became inseparable; Rome is predestined to be the capital of Latin Christianity; the legend of Peter, first Pope, is written in advance; but it will require four or five centuries to unwind itself. Rome in any case could scarcely doubt the day on which Peter set foot in it, that that day ruled its future, and that the poor Syrian who had entered within its walls had taken possession of it for centuries.

The moral, social, and political situation became graver day by day. People spoke only of signs and misfortunes; the Christians were more affected by these than any; the idea that Satan is the god of this world rooted itself among them more and more. The spectacles appeared to them devilish. They never went to them; but they heard the people around them speaking of them. One Icarus, who, in the wooden amphitheatre in the Field of Mars, pretended to be able to fly in the air, and who fell in front of Nero's own stall, covering him with his blood, struck them greatly and became the principal element in one of their legends. The crime of Rome attained the last bounds of the infernal sublime; it was already a custom in the sect--it may have been a precaution against the police, or from a taste for mystery--to call this city only by the name of Babylon. The Jews had the habit thus of applying to modern things some symbolical proper names borrowed from their ancient sacred literature.

This little disguised antipathy for a world which they did not understand became the characteristic feature of the Christians. "Hatred of the human race" passed as the résumé of their doctrine. Their apparent melancholy was an injury to the "happiness of the age;" their belief in the end of the world went against the official optimism, according to which everything renewed its youth. The signs of repulsion which they made while passing before the temples gave the idea that they only thought of burning them. These old sanctuaries of the Roman religion were extremely dear to patriots; to insult them was to insult Evander, Numa, and the ancestors of the Roman people, and the trophies of its victories. They charged the Christians with all misdeeds; their worship passed for a gloomy superstition, fatal to the empire, a thousand atrocious or shameful stories circulated about them; the most enlightened men believed them, and looked on those who were thus pointed out to their hatred as capable of all crimes.

The new sectaries gained scarcely any adherents except among the lower classes; well educated people avoided pronouncing their name, or, when they were obliged to do so, always excused themselves; but among the people the progress was extraordinary: they were like an inundation dammed up for a while which made an irruption. The Church of Rome was already quite a people. The court and the city began seriously to speak about it; its progress was for some time the news of the day. Conversatives thought with a sort of terror of this cloaca of impurity which they pictured to themselves in the depths of Rome; they spoke with anger of those kinds of evil ineradicable plants which they always snatched at and which always resisted.

As to the malevolent populace, it dreamed of impossible crimes to attribute to the Christians. They were rendered responsible for all public evils. They accused them of preaching rebellion against the emperor, and seeking to excite the slaves to insurrection. The Christian came to be looked on like the Jew of the middle ages, the scapegoat of all calamities, the man who only thinks of evil, the poisoner of wells, the child-eater, the incendiary when a crime was committed; the slightest indication was sufficient for the arrest of a Christian, and for putting him to the torture. Often the simple name of a Christian was sufficient to lead to arrest. When they were seen keeping back from heathen sacrifices they were blamed. The era of persecutions was really opened; it will continue with short intervals until Constantine. In the thirty years which had rolled away since the first Christian preaching, the Jews alone had persecuted the work of Jesus: the Romans had protected the Christians against the Jews: now the Romans became persecutors in their turn. From the capital, these terrors and hatreds spread into the provinces, and provoked the most clamant injustices. Many atrocious pleasantries mingled with him; the walls of the places where the Christians met were covered with caricatures and hateful and obscene inscriptions against the brothers and sisters. The habit of representing Jesus under the form of a man with the head of an ass was perhaps already established.

No one doubts at this day that these accusations of crimes and infamy were calumnious; a thousand reasons lead us even to believe that the directors of the Christian Church did not give the least pretext for the ill-will which soon produced such cruel violence against them. All the heads of the parties which divided the Christian society were agreed as to the attitude that should be taken against the Roman functionaries. They might well at heart hold the magistrates as emissaries of Satan, since they protected idolatry, and were the supports of a world given up to Satan; but in public the brothers were full of respect for them. The Ebionite faction alone showed the enthusiastic feelings of the zealots and other fanatics of Judea. In politics, again, the apostles were essentially legitimist and conservative. Far from encouraging the slave to revolt, they desired the slave to be submissive to his master, even if he was most harsh and unjust, as if he personally were serving Jesus Christ, and that not of necessity, to escape punishment, but for conscience, and because God would have it so. Behind the master was God Himself. Slavery was so far from seeming to be against nature, that the Christians had slaves, and Christian slaves. We have seen Paul repressing the tendency to political revolutions which was manifested about the year 57, preaching to the faithful of Rome, and doubtless of other countries, submission to the powers that be, whatever their origin, establishing in principle that the police is a minister of God, and that it is only the wicked who resist him. Peter, on his side, was the most peaceable of men; we shall soon find the doctrine of submission to the powers taught under his name, nearly in the same terms as by St. Paul. The school which connected itself later with John shared the same feelings on the divine origin of sovereignty. One of the greatest fears of the leaders was to see the faithful compromised in evil matters, whose odium fell on the whole church. The language of the Apostles, at this supreme moment, was of an extreme prudence. Some unfortunates put to the torture, some scourged slaves, were allowed to endure insult, calling their masters idolaters, menacing them with the wrath of God. Others, by excess of zeal, declaimed loudly against the heathen and reproached them with their vices; the reasonable brethren wittily called them "bishops," or "overseers of those without." Cruel misfortunes came upon them; the wise directors of the community, far from praising them, told them plainly enough that they had received what they deserved.

All kinds of intrigues, which the insufficiency of documents do not permit us to disentangle, aggravated the position of the Christians. The Jews were very powerful about the emperor and Poppea. The "mathematicians," that is, the soothsayers, among others a certain Balbillus, of Ephesus, surrounded the emperor, and, under pretext of exercising that portion of their art which consisted in turning away plagues and evil omens, gave him atrocious advices. Has the legend which has mixed with all this world of sorcerers the name of Simon the magician any foundation? That doubtless may be so; but the reverse may be also the case. The author of the Apocalypse is much pre-occupied about a "false prophet," whom he represents as an agent of Nero, as a thaumaturgist making fire fall from heaven, giving life and speech to statues, marking men with the stamp of the Beast. It is perhaps of Balbillus he speaks: we must however observe that the prodigies attributed to the False Prophet by the Apocalypse resemble much the juggling peculiarities which the legend attributes to Simon. The emblem of a lamb-dragon, under which the False Prophet is pointed out in the same book, agrees better likewise with a false Messiah such as Simon of Gitton was than a simple sorcerer. On the other hand, the legend of Simon falling from the sky is not without an analogue in the accident which happened in the ampitheatre under Nero to an actor who played the part of Icarus. The plan taken by the author of the Apocalyse of expressing himself in enigmas throws all these events greatly into obscurity; but we should not be deceived if we searched behind every line of that strange book for some allusion to the most minute anecdotal circumstances of Nero's reign.

Never, besides, has the Christian conscience been more oppressed, more out of breath, than at that moment. They believed in a provisional condition very short in duration. Each day they expected the solemn appearance. "He comes! Yet an hour longer! He is at hand!" were the words they said every moment. The spirit of martyrdom which thought that the martyr glorifies Christ by his death and that this death is a victory, was universally spread. For the heathen, on the other hand, the Christian became a body naturally devoted to punishment. A drama which about this time had much success was that of Laureolus, where the principal actor, a sort of rascal Tartuffe, was crucified on the stage amid the applause of the audience, and eaten by bears. This drama was prior to the introduction of Christianity to Rome; we find it represented in the year 41; but it appears as if at least they made an application of it to the Christian martyrs, the diminutive of Laureolus answering to Stephanos might suggest these allusions.

CHAPTER III

STATE OF THE CHURCHES IN JUDEA.--DEATH OF JAMES

The ill-will of which the Christian Church was the object at Rome, perhaps even in Asia Minor and Greece, made itself felt even in Judea; but the persecution there had other causes. There were rich Sadducees, the aristocracy of the Temple, who showed themselves enraged against the honest poor and blasphemed the name of "Christian." About the time we have reached there was circulated a letter of James, "servant of God and of the Lord Jesus Christ," addressed to "the twelve tribes of the Dispersion." It is one of the finest pieces of early Christian literature, recalling sometimes the Gospel, and at other times the sweet and restful wisdom of Ecclesiastes. The authenticity of such writings, seeing the number of false apostolic letters which circulated, is always doubtful. Perhaps the Judeo-Christian party, accustomed to use to its own taste the authority of James, attributed to him this manifesto in which the desire to oppose the innovators made itself felt. Certainly, if James had some share in it, he was not its editor. It is doubtful if James knew Greek; his language was Syriac; now the epistle of James is much the best written work in the New Testament, its Greek is pure and almost classical. As to this, the writing agrees perfectly with the character of James. The author is a Jewish Rabbi, he holds strongly by the Law; to express the meeting of the faithful, he makes use of the word "synagogue"; he is Paul's adversary; the tone of his epistle resembles the synoptical gospel which we shall see later on came from the Christian family of which James was the head. Nevertheless, the name of Jesus is only mentioned there two or three times, with the simple qualification of Messiah, and without any of the ambitious hyperboles which the ardent imagination of Paul had accumulated.

James, or the Jewish moralist who desired to cover himself with his authority, introduces us all at once into a little conventicle of the persecuted. Trials are a good thing, for in putting faith through the crucible, they produce patience; now patience is the perfection of virtue; the man who is tempted receives the crown of life. But what preoccupies our doctor especially is the difference between the rich and the poor. He must have produced in the community some rivalry between the favoured brothers of fortune and those who were not. Those complain of the harshness of the rich and their pride, while they groaned under them:

Let the brother of low degree rejoice in that he is exalted; but the rich, in that he is made low, because as the flower of the grass he shall pass away. . . . My brethren, have not the faith of our Lord Jesus Christ, the Lord of Glory, with respect of persons. For if there come into your assembly a man with a gold ring, in goodly apparel, and there come in also a poor man in vile raiment, and ye have respect to him that weareth the gay clothing, and say unto him, Sit thou here in a good place, and say to the poor, Stand thou there, or sit here under my footstool. Are ye not then partial in yourselves, and are become judges of evil thoughts? Hearken, my beloved brethren, hath not God chosen the poor of this world rich in faith, and heirs of the Kingdom which He hath promised to them that love Him? But ye have despised the poor. Do not rich men oppress you, and draw you before the judgment seats? Do not they blaspheme that worthy name by the which ye are called?

Pride, corruption, brutality, and the luxury of the rich Sadducees had indeed arrived at their height. The women bought the high priesthood from Agrippa II. with gold. Martha, daughter of Boethus, one of those Simonists, who went to see her husband officiate, made them stretch carpets from the gate of her house to the Sanctuary. The high-priesthood was thus fearfully debased. These worldly priests blushed for the most holy part of their functions. The offering of sacrifice had become repulsive to refined people, whom their duty condemned to the trade of butcher and knacker! Many of them did this in silk gloves not to soil the skin of their hands by contact with the victim. The whole tradition, agreeing on this point with the Gospels and the Epistle of James, represents to us the priests of the last year before the destruction of the Temple as gourmands, given up to luxury, and hard to the poor people. The Talmud contains the fabulous list of what was needed for the table of a high priest; it surpasses all likelihood, but indicates the dominant opinion. "Four cries come from the vestibule of the Temple," says one tradition; the first, "Come forth, ye descendants of Eli, you stain the Temple of the Eternal"; the second, "Come forth, Issachar of Kaphar-Barkai, who only dost respect thyself, and who profanest the victims consecrated to Heaven"--(it was he who wrapped his hands in silk while doing his service); the third, "Open, ye gates, let in Ishmael, the son of Phabi, the disciple of Phinehas, that he may fulfil the functions of the high-priesthood"; the fourth, "Open, ye gates, and let John, son of Nebedeus, the disciple of gourmands, enter in, that he may gorge himself with victims." A sort of song, or rather malediction, against the sacerdotal families, which ran its course in the streets of Jerusalem at the same period, has been preserved to us.

> *" Plague take the house of Boëthus!*
> *Plague take them because of their cudgels!*
> *Plague take the house of Hanan!*
> *Plague take them because of their conspiracies!*
> *Plague take the house of Cantheras!*
> *Plague take them became of their Kalams!*
> *Plague take the family of Ishmael, son of Phabi!*
> *Plague take them because of their fists!*

They are high-priests, their sons are treasurers, their sons-in-law are customs officers, and their servants beat us with their cudgels."

There was open war between these opulent priests, friends of the Romans, taking these lucrative appointments to themselves and their families, and the poor priests maintained by the people. Every day there were bloody brawls. The impudence and audacity of the high-priestly families went so far as to send their servants to the threshing-floors to collect the tithes which belonged to the high clergy, and they beat those who refused; the poor priests were in a wretched state. Fancy the feelings of the pious man, the democratic Jew, rich in the promises of all the prophets, maltreated in the Temple (his own house) by the insolent lackeys of unbelieving and epicurean priests. The Christians grouped around James made common cause with those oppressed ones who probably were like themselves, holy people (hasidim) favourites with the public. Mendicity appears to have become a virtue and the mark of patriotism. The rich classes were friends of the Romans, and could scarcely become that except by a sort of apostacy and treason. To hate the rich was thus a mark of piety. Obliged, so as not to die of hunger, to work in those constructions of the Herodians, in which they saw nothing but an ostentatious vanity, the hasidim looked on themselves as victims of the unbelieving. "Poor" passed as the synonym of "Saint."

"Now weep, ye rich, howl for your miseries that shall come upon you. Your riches are corrupted and your garments are moth-eaten. Your gold and silver is cankered and the rust of them shall be a witness against you, and shall eat your flesh as if it were fire. Ye have heaped treasures together for the last days. Behold the hire of the labourers who have reaped down your fields, which is of you kept back by fraud crieth, and the cries of them which have reaped are entered into the ears of the Lord of Sabaoth. Ye have lived in pleasure on the earth and been wanton. Ye have nourished your hearts as in a day of slaughter. Ye have condemned and killed the just; and he doth not resist you."

We feel in these pages that there is already fermenting the spirit of those social revolutions which some years later filled Jerusalem with blood. Nothing expresses with so much force the sentiment of aversion to the world which was the soul of Primitive Christianity. "To keep oneself unspotted from the world" is the supreme command. "He who would be the friend of the world is constituted the enemy of God." All desire is vanity--illusion. The end is so near? why complain of one another? why engage in litigation? the true judge is coming: He is at the door!

"And now you others who say: To-day or to-morrow we will go into such a city, and continue there a year, and buy and sell and get gain. Whereas ye know not what shall be on the morrow. For what is your life. It is even a vapour, that appeareth for a little time, and then vanisheth away. For that ye ought to say, if the Lord will we shall live, and do this or that."

When he speaks of humility, patience, mercy, the exaltation of the humble, and of the joy which is below tears, James seems to have kept in memory the very words of Jesus. We feel, nevertheless, that he holds much by the law. Quite a paragraph of his Epistle is dedicated to warn the faithful against Paul's doctrine on the uselessness of works and salvation by faith. A phrase of James (ii., 24) is the direct denial of a phrase in the Epistle to the Romans (iii., 28). In opposition to the Apostle of the Gentiles (Rom. iv., 1 and ff.) the Apostle of Jerusalem maintains (ii., 21 and ff.) that Abraham was saved by works, and that faith without works is a dead faith. The devils have faith and apparently are not saved. Departing here from his usual moderation, James calls his opponent a "vain man." In one or two other passages, we can see an allusion to the debates which already divided the Church, and which shall fill up the history of Christian theology some centuries later.

A spirit of lofty piety and touching charity animated this Church of the Saints. "Pure religion and undefiled before God and the Father is this, to visit the fatherless and widows in their affliction," said James.

The power of curing diseases, especially by anointing with oil, was considered as of common right among believers: indeed the unbelievers saw in this healing a gift peculiar to the Christians. The elders were reputed to enjoy it in a high degree, and became thus a band of spiritual physicians. James attaches to those practices of supernatural medicine the greatest importance. The germ of nearly all the Catholic Sacraments was laid here. Confession of sins, for a long time practised by the Jews, was looked on as an excellent means of pardon and healing, two ideas inseparable in the beliefs of the age.

"Is any among you afflicted? Let him pray. Is any merry? Let him sing. Is any sick among you? Let him call for the elders of the Church, and let them pray over him, anointing him with oil in the name of the Lord. And the prayer of faith shall save the sick, and the Lord shall raise him up, and if he have committed sins they shall be forgiven him. Confess your faults one to another and pray one for another that ye may be healed. The prayer of a righteous man is strong when it is made with a fixed object."

The apocryphal apocalypses where the religious passions of the people expressed themselves with so much fire, were greedily collected in this little group of enthusiastic Jews, or rather were born alongside of it, almost in its bosom, so much so that the tissue of these singular writings and that of the writings of the New Testament are often hard to disentangle from each other. They really took these pamphlets, born of yesterday, for the words of Enoch, Baruch and Moses. The strangest beliefs as to hell, the rebel angels, the wicked giants who brought on the flood, were spread about, and had as their principal source the books of Enoch. There were in all these fables some lively allusions to contemporaneous events. That foreseeing Noah, that pious Enoch, who did not cease to predict the Deluge to those heedless ones who, during this whole period, ate, drank, married, and enriched themselves, who are they if they be not the seers of these last days, vainly warning a frivolous generation, which is unwilling to admit that the world is nearly at an end? An entire branch, a sort of period of subterranean life is added to the legend of Jesus. It was asked what he did during the three days he passed in the grave. They would have it that during this time he had gone down, by giving battle to death, into the infernal prisons where were confined the rebellious or unbelieving spirits; that there he had preached to the shades and devils and prepared for their deliverance. That conception was necessary that Jesus might be, in the strongest sense of the term, the universal Saviour; as St. Paul presents the idea also in his last writings. Yet the fictions we speak of did not find a place within the limits of the Synoptical Gospels, doubtless because these limits had been already fixed when they were created. They remained floating outside the Gospel and did not find body until later in the apocryphal writing called the "Gospel of Nicodemus."

The work par excellence of the Christian conscience was, nevertheless, accomplished in silence in Judea or the adjacent countries. The Synoptical Gospels were created part by part, as a living organism is completed little by little, and attained, under the action of a deep mysterious reason, to perfect unity. At the date we have reached, was there already some text written on the acts and words of Jesus? Has the Apostle Matthew, if it is he who is in question, written in Hebrew the discourses of the Lord? Has Mark, or he who takes his name, entrusted to paper his notes on the life of Jesus? We may doubt it. Paul, in particular had certainly in his hands no writing as to the words of Jesus. Did he at least possess an oral tradition, mnemonic in some degree, of these words? We observe such a tradition for the account of the Supper, perhaps for that of the Passion, and up to a certain point for that of the Resurrection, but not for the parables and discourses. Jesus is in his eyes as expiatory victim, a superhuman being, a risen one, not a moralist. His quotation of the words of Jesus are undecided and are not related to the discourses which the Synoptical Gospels put into Jesus' mouth. The apostolical epistles which we possess, other than those of Paul, do not lead us to suppose any production of this kind.

What seems to result from this is that certain accounts, such as that of the Supper, of the Passion, and the Resurrection, were known by heart, in terms which admitted of little variety. The plan of the Synoptical Gospels was already probably agreed on: but while the Apostles lived, books which would have pretended to fix the tradition of which they believed themselves the sole depositories would not have had any chance of being accepted. Why, besides, write the life of Jesus? He is coming back. A world on the eve of closing has no need of new books. It is when the witnesses shall be dead that it will be important to render durable by the Scripture a representation which is effacing itself every day. In this point of view the Churches of Judea and the neighbouring countries had a great superiority. The knowledge of the discourses of Jesus was much more exact and extended than elsewhere. We remark under this connection a certain difference between the Epistle of James and the Epistle of Paul. The little writing of James is quite impregnated by a sort of evangelical perfume. We hear these sometimes like an echo of the word of Jesus; the sentiment of the life of Galilee is found there still with vivid power.

We know nothing historical as to the missions sent directly by the Church of Jerusalem. That Church, according to its own principles, ought scarcely to be looked on as a propaganda. In general there were few Ebionite and Judeo-Christian Missions. The strict spirit of the Ebionim only admitted of circumcised missionaries. According to the picture which is traced to us by some writings of the second century, suspected of exaggeration, but faithful to the Jerusalem spirit, the Judeo-Christianity preacher was held in a sort of suspicion; they made sure about him, they imposed on him some proofs, a noviciate of six years; he must have regular papers, a sort of labelled confession of faith, conformable to that of the Apostles of Jerusalem. Such impediments were a decided obstacle to a fruitful Apostleship: under such conditions Christianity would never have been preached. Thus the messengers of James appeared much more occupied in overturning Paul's foundations than in building on their own account, The Churches of Bithynia, Pontus and Cappadocia which appeared about this time alongside of the Churches of Asia and Galatia, did not proceed it is true, from Paul, but it is not likely that they were the work of James or Peter: they owed their foundation no doubt to that anonymous preaching of the faithful which was the most efficacious of all. We suppose, on the contrary, that Batania, the Hauran, Decapolis, and in general all the region to the east of the Jordan which were soon to be the centre of the fortress of Judeo-Christianity, were evangelized by some adherents of the Church of Jerusalem. They found the Roman limit very near on that side. Now the Arabian countries inclined in no way to the new preaching, and the countries subject to the Arsacides were little open to efforts coming from Roman lands. In the geography of the Apostles the earth was very little. The first Christians never thought of the barbarian or Persian world; the Arabian world itself scarcely existed for them. The missions of St. Thomas among the Parthians, of St. Andrew among the Scythians, and of Bartholomew in India are only legendary. The Christian imagination of the first ages turned little towards the East: the goal of Apostolic Pilgrimages was the extremity of the West; as to the East, they spoke as if the missionaries regarded the boundary as already reached.

Had Edessa heard of the name of Jesus in the first century? Was there at that time beside Osrhoene a Syriac-speaking Christianity? The fables by which the Church has surrounded its cradle do not permit us to express ourselves with certainty on that point. Yet it is very probable that the strong relations which Judaism had on this side were used for the propagation of Christianity. Samosata and Comagena had at an early period educated persons forming part of the Church or at least very favourable to Jesus. It was from Antioch in any case that this region of the Euphrates received the seed of the faith.

The clouds which were gathering over the East disturbed these pacific preachings. The good administration of Festus could do nothing against the evils which Judea carried in her bosom. Brigands, zealots, assassins, and impostors of all kinds overran the country. A magician presented himself, among twenty others, promising the people salvation and the end of evil, if they would accompany him to the desert. Those who followed him were massacred by the Roman soldiers; but no one was undeceived as to the false prophets. Festus died in Judea about the beginning of the year 62. Nero appointed Albinus as his successor. About the same time, Herod Agrippa II. took the high priesthood from Joseph Cabi to give it to Hanan, son of the celebrated Hanan or Annas, who had contributed more than anyone to the death of Jesus. He was the fifth of Annas' eons who occupied that dignity.

Hanan the younger was a haughty, harsh and audacious man. He was the flower of Sadduceeism, the complete expression of that cruel and inhuman sect, always ready to render the exercise of authority odious and insupportable. James, the brother of the Lord, was known in all Jerusalem as a bitter defender of the poor, as a prophet in the old style, inveighing against the rich and powerful. Hanan resolved on his death, and taking advantage of the absence of Agrippa, and of the fact that Albinus had not yet arrived in Judea, he assembled the judicial Sanhedrin and caused James and several other saints to appear before him. They accused them of breaking the law; they were condemned to be stoned. The authority of Agrippa was necessary to assemble the Sanhedrim, and that of Albinus would have been needed to proceed to punishment; but the violent Hanan went beyond all rules. James was, in fact, stoned near the temple. As they had a difficulty in accomplishing it, a fuller broke his head with his cudgel which was used to measure stuffs. He was, it is said, forty-six years old.

The death of this saintly personage had the worst effect on the city. The Pharisee devotees and the strict observers of the law were very discontented. James was universally esteemed; he was considered one of those men whose prayers were most efficacious. It is asserted that a Rechabite (probably an Essene), or according to others, Simeon son of Clopas, nephew of Jesus, cried while they stoned him, "Stop, what are you doing? What! you kill the just who prays for you?" They applied to him the passage in Isaiah, iii., 10, which they had heard from him, "Let us suppress they say, the righteous, because he is vexatious to us: this is why the fruit of their works is devoured." Some Hebrew Elegies were written on his death, full of allusion to Biblical passages and to his name of Obliam. Nearly everybody at last was found in sympathy asking Herod Agrippa II. to set bounds to the audacity of the high-priest. Albinus was informed of the actions of Hanan, when he had left Alexandria for Judea. He wrote Hanan a threatening letter, then he unseated him. Hanan thus only occupied the high-priesthood three months. The misfortunes which soon fell on the nation were looked on by many people as the consequence of James' murder. As to the Christians, they saw in this death a sign of the times, a proof that the final catastrophes were approaching.

The enthusiasm, indeed, assumed at Jerusalem great proportions. Anarchy was at its height. The zealots although decimated by punishment, were masters of everything. Albinus in no way resembled Festus; he only thought of making money by connivance with the brigands. On all sides, one saw prognostications of some unheard-of event. It was at the end of the year 62 that one named Jesus, son of Hanan, a sort of risen Jeremiah, began to run night and day through the streets of Jerusalem, crying, "A voice from the East! a voice from the West! a voice from the four winds a voice against Jerusalem and the temple! a voice against the bridegrooms and the brides! a voice against all the people!" They scourged him; but he repeated the same cry. They beat him with rods till his bones were seen; at each blow he repeated in a lamentable voice, "Woe to Jerusalem! woe to Jerusalem!" He was never seen to speak to anyone. He went along repeating, "Woe! woe to Jerusalem!" without reproaching those who beat him, and thanking those who gave him alms. He went on thus until the siege, his voice never appearing to grow weaker.

If this Jesus, son of Hanan, was not a disciple of Jesus, his weird cry was at least the true expression of what was at the core of the Christian conscience. Jerusalem had filled up its measure. That city which slew the prophets and stoned those who were sent to it, beating some, crucifying others, was henceforth the city of anathemas. About the time at which we have arrived were formed those little apocalypses which some attributed to Enoch, others to Jesus, and which offered the greatest analogies to the exclamations of Jesus, son of Hanan. These writings extend later into the framework of the synoptical gospels; they were represented as discourses, which Jesus had given in his last days. Perhaps already the mot d'ordre was given to leave Judea and flee to the mountains. The synoptical gospels always bear deeply the mark of these sorrows; they keep it like a birth-mark--an indelible impression. With the peaceful axioms of Jesus mingled the colours of a gloomy apocalypse, the presentiments of a disgusted and troubled imagination. But the gentleness of the Christians put them in the shadow compared with the madnesses which agitated the other parties in the nation, possessed like them by Messianic ideas. To them the Messiah had come; he had been in the desert, he had ascended to heaven after thirty years; the impostors or enthusiasts who sought to carry the people away after them were false Christs and false prophets. The death of James and perhaps of some other brethren, led them, besides, to separate their cause more and more from Judaism. A butt to the hatred of all, they comforted themselves by thinking of the precepts of Jesus. According to many, Jesus had predicted that, in the midst of all these trials, not a hair of their heads should perish.

The situation was so precarious, and they felt so plainly that they were on the eve of a catastrophe that an immediate successor was given to James in the presiding of the Church of Jerusalem. The other "brethren of the Lord," such as Jude, Simon, son of Clopas, continued to be the principal authorities in the community. After the war, we shall see them serving as a rallying point to all the faithful of Judea. Jerusalem had no more than eight years to live, and indeed, even before the fatal hour, the eruption of the volcano, will thrust to a distance the little group of pious Jews who are bound to one another by the memory of Jesus.

CHAPTER IV

FINAL ACTIVITY OF PAUL

Paul, nevertheless, was subjected in prison to the gentleness of an administration half distracted by the extravagance of the sovereign and his evil surroundings. Timothy, Luke, Aristarchus, and according to certain traditions, Titus, were with him. A certain Jesus, surnamed Justus, who was circumcised, one Demetrius, or Demas, an uncircumcised proselyte, who was, it appears, from Thessalonica, a doubtful personage of the name of Crescens, still were seen around him and served him as coadjutors. Mark, who according to our hypothesis had come to Rome in company with Peter, was reconciled, it appears, with him with whom he had shared the first apostolical activity, and from whom he had rudely separated: he served probably as an intermediary between Peter and the apostle of the Gentiles. In any case Paul, about this time, was very discontented with the Christians of the circumcision: he considered them as not very favourable to him, and declared that he did not find good fellow-workers among them.

Some important modifications, introduced probably by the new relations which he had in the capital of the empire, the centre and confluence of all ideas, were carried out about the time we are speaking of now in Paul's mind, and made the writings of that period of his life sensibly different from those he composed during his second and third mission. The informal development of the Christian doctrine worked rapidly. In some months of these fertile years, theology marched much faster than it did afterwards in some centuries. The new dogma sought its equilibrium and created props on all sides to support its feeble portions. They might have called it an animal in its genetic crisis, putting forth a limb, transforming an organ, cutting off a tail, to arrive at the harmony of life, that is to say, at the condition where everything in the living being answers, supports, and holds itself together.

The fire of a devouring activity had never till now allowed Paul leisure to measure the time, nor to consider that Jesus delayed his reappearance very long: but these long months of prison forced him to consider. Old age, besides, began to tell upon him; a sort of gloomy maturity succeeded to the ardour of his passion; reflection brought light, and obliged him to fill up his ideas, to reduce them to theory. He became mystical, theological, speculative, from being practical as he was. The impetuosity of a blind conviction, absolutely incapable of going backward, could not prevent him from being sometimes astonished that heaven did not open more quickly, and that the final trumpet did not sound sooner. The faith of Paul was not shaken, but it sought other points of support. His idea of Christ became modified. His dream henceforth is less the Son of Man appearing in the clouds, and presiding at the general resurrection, as a Christ established as divinity, incorporated with it, acting in it and with it. The resurrection for him is not in the future: it seems to have already taken place--When we change once, we change always; we may be at the same time the most impassioned and yet mobile of men. That which is certain is that the grand pictures of the final apocalypse and of the resurrection which were formerly so familiar to Paul, which present themselves in some way at every page of the letters of the second and third mission, and even in the Epistle to the Philippians, have a secondary place in the last writings of his captivity. They are then replaced by a theory of Christ, conceived like a sort of divine person, a theory very analogous to that of the Logos which, later on, shall find its definitive form in the writings attributed to John.

The same change is remarkable in his style. The language of the epistles of the captivity has more fulness: but it has lost a little of its force. The thought is advanced with less vigour. The dictionary differs very much from the first vocabulary of Paul. The favourite terms of the Johannine school, "light," "darkness," "life," "love," &c., become dominant. The syncretic philosophy of Gnosticism made itself already felt. The question of justification by Jesus is no longer so lively; the war between faith and works seems appeased in the bosom of the unity of the Christian life, made up of knowledge and grace. Christ, become the central being of the universe, conciliates in his person (thus become divine) the antinomianism of the two Christianities. Certainly it is not without reason that the authenticity of such writings has been suspected: there are for them, however, such strong proofs that we like better to attribute the differences of style and thought of which we speak to a natural progress in Paul's method. The earlier and undoubtedly authentic writings of Paul contain the germ of this new language. "Christ" and "God" are interchanged almost like synonyms; Christ exercises there divine functions; they invoke him as God, he is the necessary mediator with God. The ardour with which these were connected with

Jesus made them connect with him all the theories which had been in vogue in some part or other of the Jewish world. Let us suppose that a man replying to aspirations so different from the democracy should arise in our days. His partisans would say to some, "You are for the organisation of work," it is he who is the organisation of the work; to others, "You are for independent morality," he is the independent morality; to others again, "You are for co-operation," it is he who is the co-operation; and yet others, "You are for solidarity," it is he who is the solidarity.

The new theory of Paul can be summed up nearly as follows:--

This kingdom is the reign of darkness, that is to say of Satan and his infernal hierarchy who fill the world. The reign of the Saints on the contrary shall be the reign of light. Now the saints are what they are not by their own merit (before Christ all are enemies of God), but by the application which God makes to them of the merits of Jesus Christ the son of his love. It is the blood of this son, shed upon the cross, which blots out sins and reconciles every creature to God, making peace to reign in Heaven and earth. The Son is the image of the invisible God, the first-born of creatures; all has been created in him, by him and for him, things celestial and terrestrial, visible, and invisible, thrones, powers, and dominions. He was before all things and by him all things consist. The church and he form only one body, of which he is the head. As in everything he has always held the first rank, he shall also hold it in the resurrection. His resurrection is the commencement of the universal resurrection. The fulness of the Godhead dwells in him bodily. Jesus is thus the God of man, a sort of prime minister of the creation, placed between God and man. Everything that monotheism says of the relations between man and God may according to the then present theory of Paul, be said of the relations between man and Jesus. The veneration for Jesus, which with James does not exceed the cult of doulia or hyperdoulia, attains with Paul to the proportions of a true worship a latria such as no Jew had over yet vowed to a son of woman.

This mystery which God prepared from all eternity, the fulness of the times being come, he has revealed to his saints in these last days. The moment has come when each must complete for his part the work of Christ. Now the work of Christ is completed by suffering; suffering is therefore a good thing in which we should rejoice and glory. The Christian, by participating with Jesus, is filled like him with the fulness of the Godhead. Jesus by rising again has quickened all with himself. The wall of separation which the law created between the people of God and the Gentiles Christ has broken down; the two portions of reconciled humanity he has made a new humanity; all the old enmities he has slain upon the cross. The text of the law was like a bill of debt which humanity could not wipe off: Jesus has destroyed the value of that bill, nailing it to his cross. The world created by Jesus is therefore an entirely new world. Jesus is the corner stone of the Temple which God has built. The Christian is dead to the world, buried with Christ in the tomb; his life is hid with Christ in God. While waiting till Christ appears and associates him with his glory he mortifies his body, extinguishing all his natural passions, taking up in everything the opposition to nature, putting off "the old man" and clothing himself with "the new," renovated according to the image of his creator. From this point of view there is no more Jew nor Greek, circumcised nor uncircumcised, barbarian, Scythian, slave nor free man. Christ is all, Christ is in all. The saints are those to whom God by gratuitous gift has made application of the merits of Christ, and whom he has predestinated to the divine adoption before even the world began. The Church is one as God himself is one; his work is the edification of the body of Christ; the final goal of all this is the realization of perfect man, the complete union of Christ with all his members, a state in which Christ shall truly be the head of a humanity regenerated according to his own model, a humanity receiving from him movement and life by a series of members bound to each other and subordinated the one to the other. The dark powers of the air fight to prevent this consummation; a terrible struggle shall take place between them and the saints. It shall be an evil day, but, armed by the gifts of Christ, the saints will triumph.

Such doctrines were not entirely original. They were in part those of the Jewish school in Egypt and notably those of Philo. This Christ became a divine hypostasis, is the Logos of the Jewish Alexandrian philosophy, the Memera of the Chaldean paraphrases, prototype of everything, by which everything has been created. These powers of the air to which the empire of the world has been given, these bizarre hierarchies, celestial and infernal, are those of the Jewish cabbala and of Gnosticism. This mysterious pleroma, the final goal of the work of Christ, much resembles the divine pleroma which the gnosis places at the summit of the universal ladder, the Gnostic and cabbalistic theosophy which may be regarded as the mythology of monotheism, and which we believe we have seen weighing with Simon of Gitton, is represented from the first century with its principal features. To reject systematically in the second century all the documents in which are found traces of such a spirit is very rash. That spirit was in germ, in Philo, and in primitive Christianity. The theosophic conception of Christ would arise necessarily from the Messianic conception of the Son of Man, when it would be distinctly proved after a long waiting that the Son of Man had not come. In the most incontestably authentic epistles of Paul there are certain features which remain a little in advance of the exaggerations which are presented by the epistles written in prison. The epistle to the Hebrews dating before the year 70, shows the same tendency to place Jesus in the world of metaphysical abstractions. All this will become in the highest degree plain when we speak of the Johannine writings. According to Paul, who had not known Jesus, this metamorphosis in the idea of Christ was in some sort inevitable. While the school which possessed the living tradition of the master created the Jesus of the synoptical gospels, the enthusiastic man, who had only seen Jesus in his dreams, transformed him more and more into a superhuman being, into a sort of metaphysical archon whom they would say had never lived.

This transformation besides did not operate only on the ideas of Paul. The Churches raised by him advanced in the same views. Those of Asia Minor especially were impelled by a sort of a secret work to the most exaggerated ideas as to the divinity of Jesus. This might be imagined. To the fraction of Christianity which had sprung from the familiar conversations by the lake of Tiberias Jesus must always remain the beloved Son of God, who had been seen moving among men with that charming manner and that gentle smile; but when they preached Jesus to the people of some province hidden away in Phrygia, when the preacher declared that he had never seen him, and affected to know scarcely anything of His earthly life, what could these good and artless hearers think of him who was preached to them? How would they picture him to themselves? As a sage? As a master full of charm? It is not thus that Paul presents the rôle of Jesus. Paul was ignorant of, or pretended to be ignorant of, the historic Jesus. As the Messiah, as the Son of Man coming to appear in the clouds in the great day of the Lord? These ideas were strange to the Gentiles and supposed a knowledge of the Jewish books. Evidently the picture which would most often he presented to these good country people would be that of an incarnation, of a God clothed with a human form and walking upon the earth. This idea was very familiar in Asia Minor; Apollonius of Tyana was soon to ventilate it for his own prophet. To reconcile such a style of view with worn theism only one thing remained, to conceive Jesus as a divine hypostasis become incarnate, as a sort of reduplication of the one God, having taken the human form for the accomplishment of a divine plan. It must be remembered that we are no longer in Syria. Christianity has passed from the Semitic world into the hands of races intoxicated with imagination and mythology. The prophet Mahomet, whose legend is so purely human among the Arabs, has become the same among the Schiites of Persia and India, a being completely supernatural, a sort of Vishnu or Buddha. Some relations which the apostle had with his Churches of Asia Minor exactly about this time furnished him with the occasion of expounding the new form which he was accustomed to give to his ideas. The pious Epaphroditus, or Epaphras, the teacher and founder of the Church of Colosse and leader of the Churches on the shores of the Lycus, came to him with a mission from the said Churches. Paul had never been in that valley, but they admitted his authority there; They recognised him even as the apostle of the country and each one regarded himself as like him before conversion. When his captivity took place the churches of the Colossians, Laodicea upon the Lycus, and Hierapolis deputed Epaphras to share his chain, to console him, to assure him of the friendship of the faithful and probably to offer him the aid of money, of which he had need. What Epaphras reported of the zeal of the new converts filled Paul with satisfaction; faith, charity and hospitality were admirable, but Christianity took in these Churches of Phrygia a singular direction. Away from contact with the great Apostles, free entirely from Jewish influence, composed nearly entirely of heathens, these churches inclined to a sort of mixture of Christianity, Greek philosophy and the local cults. In this quiet little town of Colosse, with the sound of waterfalls, in the midst of wreaths of foam, facing Hierapolis with its frowning mountain, there increased every day the belief in the full divinity of Jesus Christ. Let us remember that Phrygia was one of those countries which had the most religious originality. Its mysteries included or claimed to include an exalted symbolism. Many of the rights which were practised there were not without analogy to those of the new cult. For Christians without an earlier tradition, not having gone through the same apprenticeship of monotheism as the Jews, the temptation became very strong to associate the Christian dogma with the old symbols which presented themselves here as the legacy of the most respectable antiquity. These Christians had been devoted Pagans before adopting the ideas which had come from Syria. Perhaps in adopting them they had not believed that they were breaking formally with their past. And besides, where is the truly religious man who repudiates completely the traditional teaching in the shadow of which he felt first his ideal, who does not seek some reconciliations, often impossible, between his old faith and that to which he has come by the advancement of his thought?

In the second century this need of syncretism shall take an extreme importance and shall complete the full development of the Gnostic sects. We shall see at the end of the first century some analogous tendencies filling the Church of Ephesus with troubles and agitation. Corinth and the author of the fourth gospel shared at bottom this identical principle from the idea that the conscience of Jesus was a heavenly being distinct from his terrestrial appearance. In the year 60 Colosse was already touched by the same disease--a theosophy made up of indigenous beliefs, Ebionitism, Judaism, philosophy and material borrowed from the new preaching found there already some skilful interpreters. A worship of uncreated æons, a largely developed theory of angels and devils, Gnosticism in short with its arbitrary practices, its realized abstractions, commenced to be produced, and by its sweet deceit threatened the Christian faith in its most lively and essential parts. There mingled here some renunciations against nature, a false taste for humiliation, a pretended austerity refusing to the flesh its rights, in a word all the aberrations of moral sense which would produce the Phyrigian heresies of the second century (Montanists Pepuzians, and Cata-Phrygians) which connected themselves with the old mystical leaven of Galli and Corybantes, and whose latest survivals are the dervishes of our days. The difference between the Christians of Pagan origin and those of Jewish origin are thus marked from day to day. Christian mythology and metaphysics were born in Paul's Churches. Springing from Polytheistic races the converted Pagans found quite simple the idea of a God-made man, while the incarnation of the divinity was for the Jews a thing blasphemous and revolting.

Paul wishing to keep Epaphras near him (whose activity he thought of utilizing) resolved to reply from the deputation to the Colossians by sending to them Tychicus of Ephesus, whom he charged at the same time with commissions for the churches of Asia. Tychicus was to make a journey into the valley of the Meander to visit the communities, to give them some news of Paul, to transmit to them with a living voice a knowledge as to the condition of the Apostle in regard to the Roman authorities--some details which he did not think it prudent to entrust to paper, in short to convey to each of the churches separate letters which Paul had addressed to them. He also recommended those churches who were nearest each other to communicate their letters reciprocally and to read them in turn in their meetings. Tychicus might besides be the bearer of a kind of Encyclical, traced upon the plan of the epistle to the Colossians and reserved for the churches to which Paul had nothing special to say. The apostle appeared to have left to his disciples or secretaries the care of editing this circular upon the plan which he gave them or after the system which he showed them. The epistle addressed in these circumstances to the Colossians has not been preserved to us. Paul dictated it to Timothy, signed it, and added in his own writing, remember my chains. As to the circular epistle which Tychicus took on his way to the churches which were not named by letter, it would appear that we have it in the Epistle called 'to the Ephesians.' Certainly this epistle was not destined for the Ephesians, since the apostle addresses himself exclusively to converted Pagans, to a Church which he had never seen and to which he had no special counsel to give. The ancient manuscripts of the epistle called to the Ephesians bore in blank in the superscription the designation of the Church to which it was destined, the Vatican manuscript and the codex Sinaïticus present an analogous peculiarity. It is supposed that this pretended letter to the Ephesians is in reality the letter to the Laodiceans, which was written at the same time as that to the Colossians. We have elsewhere given the reasons which prevent us from admitting this opinion, and which lead us rather to see in this writing what concerns a doctrinal letter which St. Paul desired to have reproduced in many copies and circulated in Asia. Tychicus, in passing to Asia, his own country, was able to show one of these copies to the elders; they could keep it as an edifying morceau, and it is perfectly admissible that it might be this copy which had remained, when the letters of Paul were collected; thence would come the title which the epistle in question bears to-day. What is certain is that the epistle called "to the Ephesians" is scarcely anything but a paraphrased imitation of the epistle to the Colossians, with some additions drawn from other epistles of Paul and perhaps lost epistles.

This epistle called to the Ephesians,' forms, along with the epistle to the Colossians, the best statement of Paul's theories about the close of his career. The epistles to the Colossians and the Ephesians have, for the last period in the life of the apostle, the same value as the epistle to the Romans has to the period of his great apostleship. The idea of the founder of Christian theology here reached the highest degree of clearness. We feel this last work of spiritualization to which great souls about to depart subject their thought, and after which there is nothing but death.

Certainly Paul was right when fighting this dangerous disease of Gnosticism, which was soon to threaten human reason, this chimerical religion of angels, to which he opposes his Christ as superior to all that is not God. We know there is still to come the last assault which he delivers against circumcision, vain works and Jewish prejudices. The morality which he draws from his transcendent conception of Christ is admirable from many points of view. But how much excess, great God! How does this disdain of all reason, this brilliant eulogy of madness, this burst of paradox, prepare us on the other hand for the perfect wisdom which shuns all extremes! That "old man," whom Paul attacks so harshly, is again brought forward. He will show that it does not deserve so many anathemas. All that past, condemned by an unjust sentence, will rediscover a principle of "new birth" for the world, carried by Christianity to the most exhaustive point. Paul shall be in that sense one of the most dangerous enemies of civilization. The recrudescences of Paul's mind shall be so many defeats for the human mind. Paul will die when the human mind shall triumph. What shall be the triumph of Jesus will be the death of Paul.

The apostle closes his epistle to the Colossians by sending to them compliments and good wishes of their holy and devoted catechist Epaphras. He begs them at the same time to make an exchange of letters with the Church at Laodicea. To Tychicus, who carries the correspondence, he joins as messenger a certain Onesimus, whom he calls "a faithful dear brother." Nothing is more touching than the history of this Onesimus. He had been the slave of Philemon, one of the heads of the Colossian Church; he fled from his master and sought to hide himself at Rome. There he entered into relations, with Paul, perhaps through the medium of Epaphras his compatriot. Paul converted him and persuaded him to return to his master, making him leave for Asia in the company of Tychicus. Finally, to calm the apprehensions of poor Onesimus, Paul dictated to Timothy a letter for Philemon, a perfect little chef d'oeuvre of the epistolary art, and placed it in the hands of the delinquent.

"Paul, the prisoner of Jesus Christ, and brother Timothy, and Philemon, our well beloved and our fellow-worker, and sister Appia, our companion in works, and to the Church which is in thy house. Grace to you and peace from God our Father, and the Lord Jesus Christ, I thank my God, making mention of thee always in my prayers; hearing of thy love and faith which thou hast toward the Lord Jesus, and toward all saints. May the communication of thy own faith become effectual by the acknowledging of every good thing which is in you in Christ Jesus. For we have great joy and consolation in thy love because the bowels of the saints are refreshed by thee, brother. Wherefore, though I might be much bold in Christ to enjoin thee that which is convenient; yet for love's sake I rather beseech thee, being such an one as Paul the aged, and now also a prisoner of Jesus Christ--I beseech thee for my son Onesimus, whom I have begotten in my bonds, which in time past was to thee unprofitable, but now profitable to thee and to me, whom I have sent again, thou therefore receive him that is mine own bowels; whom I would have retained with me that in thy stead he might have ministered unto me in the bonds of the gospel. But without thy mind would I do nothing, that thy benefit should be as it were of necessity, but willingly. For perhaps he therefore departed for a season that thou shouldest receive him for ever. Not now as a servant, but above a servant, a brother beloved, specially to me, but how much more unto thee, both in the flesh and in the Lord. If thou count me therefore a partner receive him as myself. If he hath wronged thee, or oweth thee ought put that on mine account."

Paul then took his pen, and to give his letter the value of a true credibility he added these words:

"I Paul, I have written it with mine own hand, I will repay it, albeit I do not say to thee how thou owest unto me, even thine own self besides. Yea, brother, let me have joy of thee in the Lord, refresh my bowels in the Lord."

Then he resumed his dictation:

"Trusting in thy obedience, I have written to thee, knowing that thou wilt do more than I say, prepare thyself also to receive me for I hope that, because of your prayers I shall be given back to you. Epaphras, my prison companion in Jesus Christ, Marcus, Aristarchus, Demas, Luke, my fellow labourers, salute thee. The grace of our Lord Jesus Christ be with your spirit!"

We have seen that Paul had some singular illusions. He believed himself on the eve of deliverance, he formed new plans of travel, and saw himself in the centre of Asia Minor, in the midst of the Churches which revered him as their apostle without ever having met with him. John Mark likewise was preparing to visit Asia, no doubt in Peter's name. Already the Churches of Asia had been informed of the approaching arrival of this brother. In the letter to the Colossians Paul inserted a new recommendation to his subject. The tone of this recommendation is cold enough. Paul feared that the disagreement he had had with John Mark and more still the sympathy of Mark with the Jerusalem party would place his friends in Asia in embarrassment, and that they would hesitate to receive a man whom they had up till then only known to be opposed. Paul was beforehand with these Churches and enjoined them to communicate with Mark, when he should pass through their country. Mark was cousin to Barnabas, whose name, dear to the Galatians, would not be unknown to the people of Phrygia. We do not know the result of the incidents. A frightful earthquake shook the whole valley of the Lycus. Opulent Laodicea was rebuilt by its own resources: but Colosse could not recover itself it almost disappeared from the number of the Churches, the Apocalypse in 69 does not mention it. Laodicea and Hierapolis invented all its importance in the history of Christianity.

Paul was comforted by his apostolic activity for the sad news which came from all parts. He said that be suffered for his dear Churches; he pictured himself as the victim who was opening to the Gentiles the gates of the family of Israel. About the last months of his imprisonment, he yet knew discouragement and desertion. Already writing to the Philippians he says, when opposing the conduct of his dear and faithful Timothy to that of others:

"Every one seeks his own interest, not that of Jesus Christ." Timothy alone appears never to have excited any complaint in this matter, severe, gruff,--difficult to please. It is not admissible to say that Aristarchus, Epaphras, Jesus called Justus had deserted him, but many among them were found absent occasionally. Titus was on a mission; others who owed everything to him, among whom may be quoted Phygellus and Hermogenes, ceased to visit him. He, once so surrounded, saw himself isolated. The Christians of the circumcision shunned him. Luke, at certain periods, was alone with him. His character, which had always been a little morose, exasperated him; people could scarcely live in his company. Paul had from that time a cruel feeling of the ingratitude of men. Every word which one reads of his about this time is full of discontent and bitterness. The Church of Rome, closely affiliated to that of Jerusalem, was for the most part Judeo-Christian. Orthodox Judaism, very strong at Rome, had fought roughly with him. The old Apostle; with a broken heart, called for death.

If the matter had concerned one of another nature and another race we might try to picture Paul, in these last days, arriving at the conviction that he had used his life in a dream, repudiating all the sacred prophets for a writing which he had scarcely read till then Ecclesiastes (a charming book, the only loveable book ever composed by a Jew), and proclaiming that man happy who, after having let his life flow on in joy even to old age with the wife of his youth, dies without losing a son. A feature which characterises great European men is, at certain times, that they admit the wisdom of Epicurus, by being taken with disgust while working with ardour, and after having succeeded, by doubting if the cause they have served was worth so many sacrifices. Many dare to say, in the heat of action, that the day on which they begin to be wise is that on which, freed from all care, they contemplate nature and enjoy it. Very few at least escape tardy regrets. There is scarcely any devoted person, priest or religious' who, at fifty years of age, does not deplore his vow, and nevertheless perseveres. We do not understand the gallant man without a little scepticism; we love to hear the virtuous man sometimes say, "Virtue, thou art but a word!" for he who is too sure that virtue will be rewarded has not much merit; his good actions do not appear more than an advantageous investment. Jesus was no stranger to this exquisite sentiment; more than once his divine rôle appears to have weighed him down. Certainly it was not thus with St. Paul; he has not his Gethsemane of agony, and that is one of the reasons which make him less loveable. While Jesus possessed in the highest degree what we regard as the essential quality of a distinguished person, I mean by that the gift of smiling in his work, of being its superior, of not allowing it to master him, Paul was not free from the defect which shocks us in sectaries; he believed clumsily. We could wish that sometimes, like ourselves, he had been seated fatigued on the roadside, and had perceived the vanity of absolute opinions. Marcus Aurelius, representing the most glorious of our race, yields to no one in virtue, and yet he does not know what fanaticisim is. That is never seen in the East; our race alone is capable of realizing virtue without faith, of uniting doubt with hope. Freed from the terrible impetuosity of their temperament, exempted from the refined vices of Greek and Roman civilization, these strong Jewish minds were like powerful fountains which never run dry. Up to the end doubtless Paul saw before him the imperishable crown which was prepared for him, and like a runner redoubled his efforts the nearer he approached the goal. He had, moreover, moments of comfort. Onesiphorus of Ephesus, having come to Rome, sought him, and without being ashamed of his chains, served him and refreshed his heart. Demas, on the contrary, was disgusted by the absolute doctrines of the apostle and left him. Paul appears always to have treated him with a certain coldness.

Did Paul appear before Nero, or, to put it better, before the council to which his appeal would be laid? That is almost certain. Some indications, of doubtful value it is true, tell us of a "first defence," where no one assisted him, and in which, thanks to the grace which sustained him, he acquitted himself to his own advantage, so much so that he compares himself to a man who has been saved from the teeth of a lion. It is very probable that his affair terminated at the close of two years of prison at Rome (beginning of the year 63) by an acquittal. We do not see what interest the Roman authority would have had in condemning him for a sect-quarrel, which concerned it little. Some substantial indications, moreover, prove that Paul, before his death, carried out a series of apostolic travels and preachings, but not in the countries of Greece or Asia, which he had evangelized already.

Five years before, a month previous to his arrest, Paul writing from Corinth to the faithful at Rome, announced to them his intention to visit Spain. He did not wish, he said, to exercise his ministry among them; it was only in passing that he reckoned on seeing them and enjoying some time with them; then they would bring him forward and facilitate his journey to the countries situated beyond them. The sojourn of the apostle at Rome was thus subordinated to a distant apostleship, which appeared to be his principal goal. During his imprisonment at Rome Paul appears sometimes to have changed his intention relative to his Western travels. He expresses to the Philippians and to the Colossian Philemon the hope of going to see them; but he certainly did not carry out that plan. When he left prison, what did he do? It is natural to suppose that he followed his first plan, and journeyed about where he could. Some grave reasons lead us to be believe that he realized his project of visiting Spain. That journey had in his mind a lofty dogmatic meaning; he held to it much. It was important that he should be able to say that the good news had touched the extremity of the West, to prove that the gospel was accomplished since it had been heard at the end of the world. This fashion of exaggerating slightly the extent of his travels was familiar to Paul.

The general idea of the faithful was that before the appearing of Christ, the kingdom of God should have been preached everywhere. According to the apostles' manner of speech it was enough that it had been preached in a city for it to have been preached in a country; and it was sufficient that it had been preached to a dozen people, for everyone in the city to have heard it.

If Paul made this journey, he no doubt made it by sea. It is not absolutely impossible that some port in the south of France received the imprint of the apostle's foot. In any case, there remained of this problematical visit to the West no appreciable result.

CHAPTER V

THE APPROACH OF THE CRISIS

At the close of Paul's captivity, the Acts of the Apostles and the Epistles fail us. We fall into a profound night, which contrasts singularly with the historical clearness of the preceding ten years. No doubt not to be obliged to recount facts in which the Roman authority played an odious part, the author of the Acts, always respectful to that authority, and desirous of showing that it has been sometimes favourable to the Christians, stops all at once. That fatal silence casts a great uncertainty over the events which we should like so much to know. Fortunately Tacitus and the Apocalypse introduce a ray of living light into this deep night. The moment has come when Christianity, up till now held in secret by insignificant people to whom it was a joy, was about to break into history with a thunderclap, whose reverberation should be long.

We have seen that the Apostles did not neglect any effort to recall to moderation their brethren exasperated by the iniquities of which they were the victims. They did not always succeed in that. Different condemnations had been pronounced against some Christians, and people had been able to represent these sentences as the repression of crimes or evils. With an admirable correctness of meaning the Apostles drew out the code of martyrdom. Was one condemned for the name of "Christian," he must rejoice. We see it recalled that Jesus had said: "Ye shall be hated by all because of My name." But, to have the right to be proud of that hatred, one must be irreproachable. It was partly to calm some inopportune effervescences, to prevent acts of insubordination against the public authority, and also to establish his right to speak in all the Churches, that Peter, about this time, thought of imitating Paul and writing to the Churches of Asia Minor, without making any distinction between Jews and converted heathens, a circular letter or catechetic. Epistles were in fashion; from simple correspondence the Epistle had become a kind of literature, a fictional form serving as a framework for little treatises on religion. We have seen St. Paul at the end of his life adopting this custom. Each of the Apostles, following his example, wished to have his Epistle, as a specimen of his method of instruction, containing his favourite maxims, and when one of them had none, they made one for him. These new Epistles which were at a later date called "catholic," do not suggest that they have anything to order of some one; they are the personal work of the Apostle, his sermon, his dominant thought, his little theology in eight or ten pages. There was mixed up in it some scraps of phrases drawn from the common treasure of homiletics and which, by dint of being quoted, have lost all signature, and no longer belong to anyone.

Mark had returned from his journey in Asia Minor, which he had undertaken at Peter's order, and with recommendations from Paul, a journey which probably was the sign of the reconciliation of the two Apostles. This journey had put Peter in relations with the Churches of Asia and authorised him to address to them a doctrinal instruction. Mark, according to his habit, served as secretary and interpreter to Peter for the editing of the Epistle. It is doubtful if Peter could speak Greek or Latin: his language was Syriac. Mark was at the same time in relations with Peter and Paul, and perhaps it is that which explains a singular fact which the Epistle of Peter presents, I mean some borrowings which the author of that Epistle makes from the writings of St. Paul. It is certain that Peter or his secretary (or the forger who has usurped his name), had under his eyes the Epistle to the Romans and the Epistle called "to the Ephesians," really the two "Catholic" Epistles of Paul, those which have some true general features, and which were universally circulated. The Church of Rome could have a copy of the Epistle called to the Ephesians, recently written, a sort of general formula of the latter faith of Paul, addressed in the style of a circular to many Churches. With much stronger reason it would possess the Epistle to the Romans. Paul's other writings, which indeed have more the character of special letters, would not be found at Rome. Some less characteristic passages of the Epistle of Peter appear to have been borrowed from James. Did Peter, whom we have seen always holding a floating position in the apostolic controversies, while he made, if we can express it so, James and Paul speak by the same mouth, wish to show that the contradiction between these two Apostles were only apparent? As a pledge of agreement, did he wish to become the demonstrator of Pauline conceptions, softened, it is true, and deprived of their necessary crowning--justification by faith? It is more probable that Peter, little accustomed to write and not concealing his literary barrenness, did not hesitate to appropriate some pious phrases which were continually repeated around him, and which, although parts of different systems, did not contradict each other in a formal way. Peter appears, fortunately for him, to have remained all his life a very mediocre theologian; the rigour of a consequent system ought not to be sought for in his writing.

The difference of the points of view in which Peter and Paul habitually placed themselves betrays itself, besides, from the first line of that writing: "Peter, an apostle of Jesus Christ, to the elect banished by the dispersion through Pontus, Galatia, &c." Such expressions are thoroughly final. The family of Israel, according to Palestinian ideas, was composed of two fractions--on the one hand, those who inhabited the Holy Land; on the other hand, those who did not inhabit it, comprehended under the general name of "the dispersion." Now, for Peter and James, the Christians, even heathens by origin, are so much a portion of the people of Israel that the whole Christian Church, outside of Jerusalem, enters in their views into the category of the expatriated. Jerusalem is still the only point in the world where, according to them, the Christian is not exiled.

The Epistle of Peter, in spite of its bad style, although more analogous to that of Paul than to that of James or Jude, is an affecting morceau where the state of the Christian conscience about the end of Nero's reign is reflected. A sweet sadness, a resigned confidence, fills it. The last times were at hand. These must be preceded by trials, from which the elect would come forth purified as by fire. Jesus, whom the faithful love without having seen him, in whom they believe without seeing him, will soon reappear, to their joy. Foreseen by God from all eternity, the mystery of the redemption is accomplished by the death and resurrection of Jesus. The elect, called to be born again in the blood of Jesus, are a people of saints, a spiritual temple, a royal priesthood, offering spiritual sacrifices.

"My dearly beloved, I pray you to comfort yourselves among the Gentiles who seek to represent you as evil-doers, as strangers and expatriated, so that they may by your good works, which they shall behold, glorify God in the day of visitation. Submit yourselves to every ordinance of man for the Lord's sake, whether it be to the king as supreme, or unto governors, as unto them that are sent by him for the punishment of evil-doers and for the praise of them that do well. For so is the will of God, that with well doing ye may put to silence the ignorance of foolish men. As free and not using your liberty for a cloke of maliciousness, but as the servants of God. Honour all men. Love the brotherhood. Fear God. Honour the king. Servants, be subject to your masters with all fear, not only to the good and gentle, but also to the forward. For this is thankworthy, if a man for conscience towards God endure grief, suffering wrongfully. For what glory is it, if when ye be buffeted for your faults ye shall take it patiently, but if when ye do well and suffer for it ye take it patiently, this is acceptable with God. For even hereunto were ye called, because Christ also suffered for us, leaving us an example that ye should follow in his steps. Who did no sin, neither was guile found in his mouth. Who when he was reviled, reviled not again, when he suffered he threatened not, but committed himself to him that judgeth righteously."

The ideal of the Passion, that touching picture of Jesus suffering without a word, exercised already, we have seen, a decisive influence on the Christian conscience. We may doubt if the account of it was yet written; that account was increased every day by new circumstances; but the essential features, fixed in the memory of the faithful, were to them perpetual exhortations to patience. One of the principal Christian positions was that "the Messiah ought to suffer." Jesus and the true Christian are more and more represented to the imagination under the form of a silent lamb in the hands of the butcher. They embraced Him in Spirit, this gentle lamb slain young by sinners; they dwelt lovingly on the features of affectionate pity and amorous tenderness of a Magdalen at the tomb. This innocent victim, with the knife plunged in his side, drew tears from all those who had known him. The expression "Lamb of God," to describe Jesus, was already coined; there mingled with it the idea of the paschal lamb; one of the most essential symbols of Christian art was in germ in these figures. Such an imagination, which struck Francis d'Assisi so greatly and made him weep, came from that beautiful passage where the second Isaiah, describing the ideal of the prophet of Israel (the man of sorrows) shows Him as a sheep which is led to death, and which does not open its mouth before its shearer.

This model of submission and humility Peter made the law of all classes of Christian society. The elders ought to rule their flock with deference, avoiding the appearance of commanding--the young ought to submit to the elder; the women, especially, without being preachers, ought to be, by the discreet charm of their piety, the great missionaries of the faith.

"And you, wives, likewise be in subjection to your own husbands, that if any obey not the word, they also may without the word be won by the conversation of the wives, while they behold your chaste conversation coupled with fear. Whose adorning let it not be that outward adorning of plaiting the hair, and of wearing of gold, or of putting on of apparel. But let it be the hidden man of the heart in that which is not corruptible, even the ornament of a meek and quiet spirit, which is in the sight of God of great price. For after this manner in the old time the holy women also, who trusted in God, adorned themselves, being in subjection unto their own husbands. Even as Sarah obeyed Abraham, calling him lord. Likewise, ye husbands, dwell with them according to knowledge, giving honour unto the wife as unto the weaker vessel, and as being heirs together of the grace of life. Finally, be ye all of one mind, having compassion one of another. Love as brethren, be pitiful, be courteous, not rendering evil for evil or railing for railing, but contrariwise blessing. And who is he that will harm you if ye be followers of that which is good? And if ye suffer anything for righteousness, happy are ye! "

The hope of the kingdom of trod held by the Christians gave room for some misunderstandings. The heathens imagined they spoke of a political revolution on the point of being carried out.

"Have a reason always ready for those who ask explanations from you as to your hopes, but make that answer with gentleness and meekness, strong in your own good conscience, so that those who caluminate the honest life in Christ you lead may be ashamed of their injuries; for it is better to suffer for doing good (if such is the will of God) than for doing evil. You have long enough done the will of the heathen, living in lust, evil desires, drunkenness, revelries, feastings, and the most abominable idolatrous worship. They are astonished now at your keeping from throwing yourselves with them into this excess of crime, and they insult you. They shall give an answer to him who shall soon judge the living and the dead. The end of all things is at hand. My dearly beloved, be not astonished at the fire which is lit to prove you, as if it were some strange thing; but rejoice in having part in the sufferings of Christ, so that you may triumph at the revelation of his glory. If you are insulted for the name of Christ happy are ye. Let none of you be punished as a murderer, a thief, or malefactor, as a judge of the affairs of those who are without but if anyone suffers as a Christian' let him not be ashamed; on the contrary, let him glorify God in that name; for the time is come when judgment must begin at the house of God. If it begin with us, what shall the end be of those that obey not the Gospel of God? The righteous shall scarcely be saved. What then shall become of the impious and the sinner? Let those therefore who suffer according to the will of God: commit to the faithful Creator their souls in all purity. Humble yourself under the mighty hand of God that he may exalt you in due time. Be sober and watch your adversary the devil, like a roaring lion, prowleth seeking for prey. Resist him, firm in the faith, knowing that the same trials which prove you, your brethren spread over the whole world endure also. The God of all grace, after you have suffered awhile will heal you, confirm and strengthen you. To Him be all power through all the ages." Amen.

If this epistle, as we readily believe, is truly Peter's, it does much credit to his good sense, to his right feeling, and his simplicity. He does not arrogate any authority to himself. Speaking to the elders, ho represents himself as one among themselves; he does not boast because he has been a witness of the sufferings of Christ, and hopes to be a participator in the glory that is so soon to be revealed. The letter was conveyed to Asia by a certain Silvanus, who could not have been distinct from the Silvanus, or Silas, who was Paul's companion. Peter would thus have chosen him as known to the faithful of Asia Minor, through the visit he had made to them with Paul. Peter sends the salutations of Mark to these distant churches in a way which supposes, moreover, that he was, likewise, not unknown to them. The letter is closed by the usual greetings. The Church of Rome is there described in these words: "The elect which is at Babylon." The sect was closely watched; a letter too clear, intercepted, might have led to frightful evils Thus to dis. arm the suspicions of the police, Peter terms Rome by the name of the ancient capital of Asiatic impiety, a name whose symbolic signification would not escape anyone, and which would soon furnish the material for a complete poem.

CHAPTER VI

THE BURNING OF ROME

The furious madness of Nero had arrived at its paroxysm. It was the most horrible adventure the world had ever passed through. The absolute necessity of the times had delivered up everything to one alone, to the inheritor of the great legendary name of Cæsar: another Government was impossible and the provinces usually found it well enough; but it concealed a terrible danger. When the Cæsar lost his mind, when all the arteries of his poor head, disturbed by an unheard of power shivered at the same moment, then there were madnesses without name! People were delivered up to a monster with no means of ridding themselves of him; his guard, made up of Germans who had everything to lose if he fell, were desperate around his person; the beast driven to bay acted like a wild boar and defended itself with fury. As for Nero, there was at the same time something frightful and grotesque, grand and absurd, about him. As Cæsar was well educated, his madness was chiefly literary. The dreams of all the ages, all the poems, all the legends, Bacchus and Sardanapalus, Ninus and Priam, Troy and Babylon, Homer, and the insipid poetry of the time, shook about in the poor brain of a mediocre, but very satisfied, artist to whom chance had entrusted the power of realising all his chimeras. We figure to ourselves a man very nearly as rational as the heroes of M. Victor Hugo, a Shrove-Tuesday character, a mixture of fool, cotquean and actor, clothed in all power and charged with the government of the world He had not the dark wickedness of Domitian, the love of evil for the sake of evil; he was not an extravagant like Caligula; he was a conscientious romancer, an emperor of the opera, a music-madman trembling before the pit and making it tremble, just like a citizen of our days whose good sense might be perverted by the reading of modern poems and who believed himself obliged to imitate Han of Islande and the Burgraves in his conduct. Government being the practical thing par excellence, romanticism is altogether out of place. Romance is with him in the domain of art; but action is the inverse of art. In what concerns the education of a prince especially, romance is fatal. Seneca, on this point, certainly did more harm to his pupil, by his bad literary taste, than good by his fine philosophy. He had a great mind, a talent above the average, and was a man at bottom respectable, in spite of more than one blemish, but quite spoiled by declamation and literary vanity, incapable of feeling or reasoning without phrases. By dint of exercising his pupil to express things he did not think, by composing in advance sublime sentences, he made a jealous comedian of him, a mendacious rhetorician, saying some words of humaneness when he was sure people were listening to him. The old pedagogue saw deeply into the evil of his time, that of his pupil and his own when he wrote in his moments of sincerity: Literarum intemperantia laboramus.

These ridiculous things appeared at first very offensive to Nero; the ape sometimes was circumspect and watched the position that had been taken towards him. Cruelty did not show itself till after Agrippina's death; soon it took complete possession of him. Every year, henceforth, is marked by his crimes; Burrhus is no more, and everybody believes that Nero killed him; Octavia has left the world filled with shame; Seneca is in retirement, expecting his arrest every hour, dreaming of nothing but tortures, strengthening his thoughts by meditation on punishment, trying to prove to himself that death is deliverance. Tigellinus being master of everything the saturnalia was complete. Nero proclaims daily that art alone should be held as a serious matter, that all virtue is a lie, that the brave man is he who is frank and avows his complete immodesty, and that the great man is he who can abuse, lose, and waste everything. A virtuous man is to him a hypocrite, a seditious person, a dangerous personage, and, above all, a rival; when he discovers some horrible baseness which gives proof to his theories, he shows great delight. The political dangers of bombast and that false spirit of emulation, which was from the first the consuming worm of the Latin culture, unveiled themselves. The player had succeeded in obtaining the power of life and death over his auditory; the dilettante threatened the people with the torture if they did not admire his verses. A monomaniac drunk with literary glory, who, turning the fine maxims which they have taught him into pleasantries of a cannibal, a ferocious gamin looking for the applauses of the street roughs--that is the master to which the empire is subjected. Nothing equal in extravagance has ever been seen. The Eastern despots, terrible and grave, had nothing of these mad jests, these debauches of a perverted æsthetic. Caligula's madness had been short; it was a fit, and he was, above all, a buffoon, although he certainly possessed some wit; on the contrary, the folly of this man, commonly nasty, was sometimes shockingly tragical. It was one of the most horrible things to see him, by way of declamation, playing with his remorse, making this the material for his verse. With that melodramatic air which belonged to himself, he spoke of himself as being tormented by the furies, and quoted Greek verses on the parricides. A jocular God appeared to have created him to present him as the horrible charivari of a human nature, all whose springs grated on each other, the obscene spectacle of an epileptic world, such as might a Saraband of Congo apes, or a bloody orgy of a king of Dahomey.

By his example all the world seemed struck with vertigo. He had formed a company of odious fellows who were called "the chevaliers of Augustus," having as their occupation to applaud the follies of the Cæsar, and to invent for him some amusements as prowlers in the night. We shall soon see an emperor coming forth from that school. A flood of fancies, bad tastes, platitudes, expressions claiming to be comic, a nauseous slang, analogous to the wit of the smallest journals, entered Rome and became the fashion. Caligula had already created this sort of wretched imperial actorship. Nero took him for his perfect model. It was not enough for him to drive chariots in the circus, to wrestle in public, or to make singing excursions in the country; people saw him fishing with golden nets which he drew with purple cords, arranging his claqueurs himself, and obtaining false triumphs, decreeing to himself all the crowns of ancient Greece, organising unheard-of fêtes, and playing at the theatres in nameless parts.

The cause of these aberrations was the bad taste of the century, and the misplaced importance they yielded to a declamatory art, looking at the enormous, dreaming only of monstrosities. In fact, what ruled him was the want of sincerity, an insipid taste like that of the tragedies of Seneca, a skill in painting unfelt sentiments, the art of speaking like a virtuous man without being one. The gigantic passed for great; the æsthetic was nowhere seen; it was the day of colossal statues, of that material theatrical and falsely pathetic art whose chef d'oeuvre is the Laocoon, certainly an admirable statue, but the pose being that of a first tenor singing his canticum, and where all the emotion is drawn from the pain of the body. They did not content themselves longer with the entirely moral pain of the Niobes, shining forth in beauty; they wished the likeness of physical torture. They would have delighted as the seventeenth century did in a marble by Puget. The senses were served; some grosser resources which the Greeks scarcely permitted in their most popular representations, became the essential element of art. The people were, thus literally, fascinated by shows, not serious spectacles, instructive tragedies, but scenes for effect, phantasmagoria. An ignoble taste for "tableaux vivants" had widely spread. People were no longer content to enjoy in imagination the exquisite stories of the poets; they wished to see the myths represented in the flesh, in whatever was most cruel or obscene; they went into ecstacies before the groupings and the attitudes of the actors; they sought there the effects of statuary. The applauses of 50,000 people, gathered together in an immense building, exciting one another, were such an intoxicating thing, that the sovereign himself came to envy the charioteer, the singer and the actor; the glory of the theatre passed as the first of everything. Not one of the emperors whose head had a weak spot was able to resist the temptations to gather crowns from these wretched plays. Caligula had left there the little reason he had; he passed his days in the theatre amusing himself with the idlers; and later, Commodus and Caracalla disputed with Nero for the palm of madness.

It became necessary to pass laws to prevent senators and knights from descending into the arena, from fighting the gladiators, or pitting themselves against the beasts. The circus had become the centre of life; the rest of the world seemed only made for the pleasures of Rome. There were unceasingly new inventions, each stranger than the other, conceived and ordered by the choragic sovereign. The people went from fête to fête, speaking only of the last day, waiting for the one that was promised them, and ended by becoming much attached to the prince who made such an endless bacchanalia of his life. The popularity Nero obtained by these shameful means cannot be doubted; it is sufficient that after his death Otho could obtain the government by reviving his memory, by imitating him, and by recalling the fact that he had himself been one of the minions of his coterie.

One cannot exactly say that this wretched man was wanting in heart, or all sentiment of the good and beautiful. Far from being incapable of friendship, he often showed himself to be a good companion, and it was that very fact which made him cruel; he wished to be loved and admired for himself, and was irritated against all who had not those feelings towards him. His nature was jealous and susceptible, and petty treasons put him beside himself. Nearly all his revenges were exercised on persons whom he had admitted to his intimate circle (Lucain, Vestinus), but who abused the familiarity he encouraged to wound him with their jests; for he felt his weaknesses and feared their being detected. The chief cause of his hatred to Thraseas was that he despaired of obtaining his affection. The absurd quotation of the bad hemistitch, Sub terris tonuisse putes, destroyed Lucain. Without putting aside the services of a Galvia Crispinilla, he really loved some women; and these women, Poppea and Actea, loved him. After the death of Poppea, accomplished by his brutality, he had a sort of repentance of feeling, which was almost touching; he was for a long time possessed by a tender sentiment, sought out everyone who resembled her, and pursued after the most absurd substitutions; Poppea on her side had for him feelings which a woman so distinguished would not have confessed for a common man. A courtesan of the great world, clever in increasing, by the charms of pretended modesty, the attractions of a rare beauty of the highest elegance, Poppea preserved in her heart, in spite of her crimes, an instinctive religion which inclined to Judaism. Nero seems to have been very sensible of that charm in women, which results from a certain piety associated with coquetry. These alternations of abandon and boldness, this woman who never went out but with her face partly veiled, this admirable conversation, and above all this touching worship of her own beauty which acted so that, her mirror having shown her some blemishes in it, she had a fit of perfectly womanlike despair, and wished to die; all this seized in a lively manner the imagination of a young debauches, on whom the semblances of modesty exercised an all-powerful illusion. We shall soon see Nero, in his rôle as the Antichrist, creating in a sense the new æsthetic, and being the first to feast his eyes on the spectacle of unveiled Christian modesty.

The devout and voluptuous Poppea retained him by analogous feelings. The conjugal reconciliation which led to her death supposes that in her most intimate relations with Nero she had never abandoned that hauteur which she affected at the outset of their connection. As to Actea, if she was not a Christian, as it has been thought she was, she could not have so much of this. She was a slave originally from Asia, that is to say, from a country with which the Christians of Rome had daily correspondence. We have often remarked. that the beautiful freed women who had the most adorers were much given to the oriental religions. Actea always kept her simple tastes, and never completely separated herself from her little society of slaves. She belonged first to the family of Annæa, about whom we have seen the Christians moving and grouping themselves; it was asserted by Seneca that she played in the most monstrous and tragical circumstances, a part which, seeing her servile condition, cannot perhaps be described as honourable This poor girl, humble, gentle, and whom many occasions show surrounded by a family of people bearing names almost Christian, Claudia, Felicula, Stephanus, Crescens, Phoebe Onesimus, Thallus, Artemas, Helpis, was the first love of Nero as a youth. She was faithful to him even to death; we find her at the villa of Phaon, rendering the last offices to the corpse from which every one drew aside in horror.

And we must say that singular as this should appear, we can quite imagine that in spite of everything, women loved him. He was a monster, an absurd creature, badly formed, an incongruous product of nature; but he was not a common monster. It has been said that fate, by a strange caprice, wished to realize in him the hircocerf of logicians, a hybrid bizarre, and incoherent being, most frequently detestable, but whom yet at times people could not refrain from pitying. The feeling of women resting more upon sympathy and personal taste than the vigorous appreciation of ethics, a little beauty or moral kindness, even terribly warped, is sufficient for their indignation to melt into pity. They are especially indulgent to the artist, misguided by the intoxication of his art, for a Byron, the victim of his chimera, and pushing artlessness so far as to translate his inoffensive poetry into acts. The day on which Actea laid the bleeding corpse of Nero in the sepulchre of Domitius she no doubt wept over the profanation of natural gifts known to her alone; that same day, we can believe more than one Christian woman prayed for him

Although of mediocre talent, he had some parts of an artist's soul; he painted and sculptured well, his verses were good, notwithstanding a certain scholarly pomposity, and, in spite of all that can be said, he made them himself; Suetonius saw his autograph drafts covered with erasures. He was the first to appreciate the admirable landscape of Subiaco, and made a delicious summer residence there. His mind, in the observation of natural things, was just and curious: he had a taste for experiments, new inventions, and in curious things he wanted to know the causes, and separated charlatanism clearly from pretended magical sciences, as well as the nothingness of the religions of his age. The biography we are now quoting from preserves to us the account of the manner in which the vocation of singer awoke in him. He owed his initiation to the most renowned harpist of the century, Terpnos. We see him pass entire nights seated by the side of the musician, studying his play, lost in what he heard, in suspense, panting, intoxicated, breathing with avidity the air of another world which opened before him through contact with a great artist. There was there also the origin of his disgust for the Romans, generally weak connaisseurs, and his preference for the Greeks, according to him, alone capable of appreciating him, and for the Orientals, who applauded him to distraction. Thenceforth he admitted no other glory than that of art: a new life revealed itself to him; the emperor was forgotten; to deny his talent was the. State-crime par excellence; the enemies of Rome were those who did not admire him.

His desire in everything to be the head of fashion was certainly absurd. Yet it must be said that there was more policy in that than one would think. The first duty of the Cæsar (seeing the baseness of the times) was to occupy the people. The sovereign was above all a grand organizer of fêtes; the amuser-in-chief must be made to expose his own person to danger. Many of the enormities with which they reproached Nero had their gravity only from the point of view of Roman manners, and the severe attitude to which people had been accustomed till then. This manly society was revolted by seeing the emperor give an audience to the senate in an embroidered dressing gown, and conducting his reviews in an intolerable négligé, without a belt, with a sort of scarf round his neck to preserve his voice. The true Romans were rightly indignant at the introduction of those Eastern customs. But it was inevitable that the most ancient and most worn-out civilization should dominate the younger by its corruption. Already Cleopatra and Antony had dreamed of an oriental empire There was suggested to Nero a royalty of the same kind; reduced to despair, he will think of asking the prefecture of Egypt. From Augustus to Constantine every year represents progress in the conquest of the portion of the empire which speaks Greek over the portion which speaks Latin.

It must be recollected, moreover, that madness was in the air. If we except the excellent nucleus of aristocratic society which shall arrive at power with Nerva and Trajan, a general want of the serious made the most considerable men play in some sort with life. The personage who represented and summed up the time, "the honest man" of this reign of transcendent immorality, was, Petronius. He gave the day to sleep, the night to business and amusements. He was not one of those dissipated men who ruin themselves by grosser debaucheries, he was a voluptuary, profoundly versed in the science of pleasure. The natural ease and abandon of his speech and actions gave him an air of simplicity which charmed. While he was pro-consul in Bithynia and later on consul, he shewed himself capable of great management. Coming back to vice or the boasting of vice, he was admitted into the inner court of Nero, and become the judge of good taste in everything; nothing was gallant or delightful Petronius did not approve. The horrible Tigellinus, who ruled by his baseness and wickedness, feared a rival whom he saw surpassing him in the science of pleasures; he determined to destroy him. Petronius respected himself too much to fight with this miserable man. He did not wish however to quit life rudely. After having opened his veins he closed them again, then he opened them anew, conversing on trifles with his friends, hearing them talk, not upon the immortality of the soul and the opinions of philosophers, but of songs and light poems. He chose this moment to reward some of his slaves and to have others chastised. He set himself down to table and fell asleep. This sceptical Merimée, with a cold and exquisite tone, has left us a romance of an accomplished and verve polish, at the same time of refined corruption, which is the perfect mirror of the time of Nero. After all, it is not the king of fashion who orders things. The elegance of life has its freedom outside of science and morality. The joy of the universe would want something if the world was only peopled by iconoclastic fanatics and virtuous blockheads.

It cannot be denied that the taste for art was not lively and sincere among the men of that age. They could scarcely produce any beautiful things, but they sought greedily for the beautiful things of the past ages This same Petronius an hour before his death made them break his myrrh vase so that Nero should not have it. Objects of art rose to a fabulous price. Nero was passionately fond of them. Fascinated by the idea of the great, but joining to that as little good sense as was possible, he dreamed fantastical palaces, of towns like Babylon, Thebes, and Memphis. The imperial dwelling on the Palatine (the ancient house of Tiberius), had been modest enough and of a thoroughly private character until Caligula's reign. This emperor, whom we must consider in everything as the creator of the school of government, in which it can be readily believed that Nero was not the master, considerably enlarged the house of Tiberius. Nero affected to find himself straitened there, and had not jests enough for his predecessors, who were content with so little. He made the first draught in provisional materials of a residence which equalled the palaces of China and Assyria. This house which he called "transitory," and which he meditated soon making real, was quite a world. With its porticos three miles long, its parks where great flocks fed, its interior solitudes, its lakes surrounded by perspectives of fantastic towns, its vines, its forests, it covered a space larger than the Louvre, the Tuileries and the Champs-Elysees put together; it stretched from the Palatine to the gardens of Mecoenus, situated upon the heights of the Esquiline. It was a perfect fairy land; the engineers Severus and Celer were surpassed there. Nero wished to have it executed in such a way that it could be called the "Golden House." People charmed him by speaking of foolish enterprises, which might make his memory eternal. Rome especially preoccupied his mind. He wished to rebuild it from top to bottom, and to have it called Neropolis.

Rome for a century back had been the wonder of the world; she equalled in grandeur the ancient capitals of Asia. Her buildings were beautiful, strong, and solid, but the streets appeared mean to the people of fashion, who every day went more and more in the direction of vulgar and decorative constructions; they aspired to those effects of harmony which make the delight of cockneys; they sought for frivolities unknown to the ancient Greeks. Nero was the head of the movement. The Rome which he imagined would have been something like the Paris of our day, or one of those artificial cities built by superior order on the plan which one has especially seen win the admiration of country people and foreigners. The irrational youth was intoxicated by these unwholesome plans. He desired also to see something strange, some grandiose spectacle worthy of an artist; he wished for an event which should mark a date in his reign. "Until me," said he "people did not know the extent that was permitted to a prince." All these inner suggestions of a disordered fancy appeared to take shape in a bizarre event which had for the subject which occupies us the most important consequences.

The incendiary mania being contagious and often complicated by hallucination, it is very dangerous to awake it in weak heads where it sleeps. One of the features of Nero's character was his inability to resist the fixed idea of a crime. The burning of Troy which he had played since his infancy, took possession of him in a terrible manner. One of the pieces which he had represented in one of his fêtes was the Incendium of Afranius, where a conflagration was seen upon the stage. In one of his fits of egotistical rage against fate, he cried: "Happy Priam, who could see with his own eyes his empire and his country perish at the same time!" On another occasion, having quoted a Greek verse from the Bellerophon of Euripedes, which signifies:--

When I am dead, the earth and the fire can mingle together;

"Oh, no," said he, "But while I am living!" The tradition according to which Nero burned Rome, only to have a repetition of the burning of Troy, is certainly exaggerated, since, as we shall show, Nero was absent from the city when the fire shewed itself. Yet this story is not destitute of all truth. The demon of perverse dramas who had taken possession of him was, as among wicked people of another age, one of the essential actors in the horrible crime.

On the 19th of July, 64, Rome took fire with a fear-fill violence. The conflagration began near the Capena gate, in the portion of the Grand Circus contiguous to the Palatine hill and Mons Coelius. That quarter contained many shops, full of inflammable material, where the fire spread with a prodigious rapidity. From that point it made the tour of the Palatine, ravaged the Velabra, the Forum, the Cannes, and mounted the hills, greatly damaged the Palatine, went down again to the valleys, consuming during six days and nights some districts which were compact and full of tortuous streets. An enormous abatis of houses which had been built at the foot of the Esquiline arrested it for some time; then it flamed up again and lasted three days more. The number of deaths was considerable. Of fourteen districts of which the city was composed, three were entirely destroyed, while other seven were reduced to blackened walls. Rome was a prodigious city closely built, with a very dense population. The disaster was frightful and such as has never been seen equalled.

Nero was at Antium when the fire broke out. He only entered the city at the moment the flames approached his "transitory" house. It was impossible for anything to resist the flames. The imperial mansions of the Palatine, the "transitory" house itself, with its dependencies, and the whole surrounding quarter, were destroyed. Nero evidently did not care much whether his residence could be saved or not. The sublime horror of the spectacle fascinated him. It was afterwards said that, mounted on a tower, he had contemplated the fire, and that there, in a theatrical dress, with a lyre in his hand, he had sung, to the touching rhythm of the ancient elegy, the ruin of Troy.

There was here a legend, a fruit of the age and of successive exaggerations; but one point upon which universal opinion pronounced itself was this, that the fire was ordered by Nero, or at least revived by him when it was about to go out. It was believed that members of his household were recognized setting fire to it at different points. In certain directions, the fire was kindled, it was said, by men feigning drunkenness. The conflagration had the appearance of having been raised simultaneously at many points at the same time. It is said that, during the fire, there had been seen the soldiers and the watchmen charged with extinguishing it, stirring it up, and hindering the efforts which were made to circumscribe it, and that with an air of threatening and in the style of people who executed official orders. Some large constructions of stone, in the neighbourhood of the imperial residence, and whose site he coveted, were turned over as in a siege. When the fire began again, it commenced in some buildings which belonged to Tigellinus. What confirmed these suspicions is that after the fire Nero, under pretext of cleaning the ruins at his expense to leave a free place to the owners took charge of removing the ruins, so much that he did not permit any person to approach them. It was much worse, when they saw him collect a good part of the ruins of the country, when they saw the new palace of Nero, that "House of Gold" which for a long time had been the plaything of his delirious imagination, rising upon the site of the old temporary residence, increased by the space which the fire had cleared. It was thought he had wished to prepare the grounds of this new palace, to justify the reconstruction which he had projected for a long time, to procure himself money by appropriating to himself the debris of the fire, in short, to satisfy his mad vanity, which made him desire to have Rome rebuilt, that it might date from him and that he might give it his name.

Everything leads us to believe that there was no calumny in that. The truth, so far as it concerns Nero, can scarcely be probable. It may be said that with his power he had more simple means than fire to procure the lands he desired. The power of the emperor, without bounds in one sense, soon found on another side its limit in the customs and prejudices of a people conservative in the highest degree of its religious monuments. Rome was full of temples, of holy places, of areæ, of buildings which no law of expropriation could cause to disappear. Cæsar and many other emperors had seen their designs of public utility, especially in what concerns the rectification of the course of the Tiber, met by this obstacle. To execute his irrational plans, Nero had but really one means--fire. The situation resembled that of Constantinople and in the great Mussulman cities, whose renovation is prevented by the mosques and the ouakouf. In the East, fire is only a weak expedient; for, after the fire, the ground, considered as a sort of inalienable patrimony of the faithful, remains sacred. At Rome, where religion is attached more to the edifice than to the site, the measure was efficacious. A new Rome, with large and stretched out streets, was reconstructed quickly enough according to the plans of the emperor and on the premiums which he offered.

All honest men who were in the city were enraged. The most precious antiquities of Rome, the houses of the ancient leaders decorated yet with triumphal spoils, the most sacred objects, the trophies, the ex-voto antiques, the most esteemed temples--all the material of the old worship of the Romans had disappeared. It was like the funeral of the reminiscences and legends of the fatherland. Nero had in vain taken on himself the expense of assuaging the misery he had caused; it was stated in vain that everything was limited in the last analysis to an operation of clearing up and rendering wholesome; that the new city would be very superior to the old; no true Roman would believe it; all those for whom a city is anything more than a mass of stones were wounded to the heart; the conscience of the country was hurt. This temple built by Evander, that other erected by Servius Tullius, of the sacred enceinte of Jupiter Stator, the palace of Numa, those penates of the Roman people, those monuments of so many victories, those triumphs of Grecian art, how could the loss be repaired? What value compared with that was there is sumptuousness of parades, vast monumental perspective, and endless straight lines? They conducted expiatory ceremonies, they consulted the Sibyl's books, and the ladies especially celebrated divers piacula. But there remained the secret feeling of a crime, an infamy; Nero began to feel that he had gone a little too far.

CHAPTER VII

MASSACRE OF THE CHRISTIANS--THE ÆSTHETICS OF NERO

An infernal idea then came into his mind. He asked himself if there were not in the world some wretches still more detested than he by the Roman citizens, on whom he had brought down the odium of the fire. He thought of the Christians. The honor which those last showed for the temples and the buildings most venerated by the Romans rendered acceptable enough the idea that they were the authors of a fire, the effect of which had been to destroy those sanctuaries. Their gloomy air before the monuments appeared an insult to the country. Rome was a very religious city, and one person protesting against the national cults was very quickly observed. It must be remembered that certain rigorous Jews went even so far as not to touch a coin bearing an effigy, and saw as great a crime in the fact of looking at or carrying about an image, as in that of carving it. Others refused to pass through a gate of the city surmounted by a statue. All this provoked the jests and the bad will of the people. Perhaps the talk of the Christians upon the grand final conflagration, their sinister prophecies, their affectation in repeating that the world was soon to finish, and to finish by fire, contributed to make them be taken for incendiaries. It is not even inadmissable that many believers had committed imprudences and that men had had some pretexts to accuse them for having wished, by preluding the heavenly flames, to justify their oracles at any price. What piaculum, in any case, could be more efficacious than the punishment of those enemies of the gods. In seeing them atrociously tortured the people would say: "Ah! no doubt, these are the culprits!" It must be recollected that public opinion regarded as established facts the most odious crimes laid to the charge of the Christians.

Let us put far from us the idea that the pious disciples of Jesus had been culpable to any degree of the crime of which they were accused: let us only say that many indications might mislead opinion. This fire it may be they had not lit, but surely they rejoiced at it. The Christians desired the end of society and predicted it. In the Apocalypse, it is the secret prayers of the saints which burn the earth and make it tremble. During the disaster, the attitude of the faithful would appear equivocal: some no doubt were wanting in showing respect and regret before the consumed temples, or even did not conceal a certain satisfaction. One could imagine such a conventicle at the base of the Transtevere, where it might be said: "is this not what we foretold?" Often it is dangerous to show oneself too prophetic. "If we wished to revenge ourselves," said Tertullian, "a single night and some torches would be sufficient" The accusation of incendiarism was very common against the Jews, because of their separate life. This very crime was one of these flagitia cohærentia nomini which made up the definition of a Christian.

Without having at all contributed to the catastrophe of the 19th July, the Christians could therefore be held, if one could so express it, incendiaries at heart. In four years and a half the Apocalypse will present a song on the burning of Rome, to which the event of 64 probably furnished more than one feature. The destruction of Rome by flames was indeed a Jewish and Christian dream; but it was nothing but a dream the pious secretaries were certainly contented to see in spirit the saints and angels applauding from high heaven what they regarded as a just expiation.

One can scarcely believe that the idea of accusing the Christians of the fire of the month of July should come of itself to Nero. Certainly, if Cæsar had known the good brothers closely, he would have strangely hated them. The Christians naturally could not comprehend the merit which lay in posing as an actor on the stage of the society of his age: now what exasperated Nero was when people misunderstood his talent as an artist and head of entertainments. Yet Nero could not but hear them speak of the Christians; he never found himself in personal relations with them. By whom was the atrocious expedient on which he acted suggested? It is probable besides that on many sides in the city some suspicions were entertained. The sect, at that time, was well known in the official world. We have seen that Paul had certain relations with some person attached to the service of the imperial palace. One thing very extraordinary is that among the promises which certain people had made to Nero, in case he should come to be deprived of the empire, was that of the government of the east and particularly of the kingdom of Jerusalem. The Messianic ideas among the Jews at Rome often took the form of vague hopes of a Roman oriental empire; Vespasian profited at a later date by those fancies. From the accession of Caligula up till the death of Nero, the Jewish cabals at Rome did not cease. The Jews had contributed greatly to the accession and to the support of the family of Germanicus. Whether through the Herods or other intriguers, they besieged the palace, too often to have their enemies destroyed. Agrippa II. had been very powerful under Caligula and Claudius; when he resided at Rome he played the part of an influential person. Tiberius Alexander on the other hand, occupied the loftiest functions. Josephus indeed shows himself to be very favourable to Nero; he says they have calumniated him, and lays all his crimes upon his evil surroundings. As to Poppea, he makes her out to be a pious person because she was favourable to the Jews, because she seconded the solicitations of the zealots, and also perhaps because she adopted a portion of their rites. He knew her in the year 62 or 63, obtained through her pardon for the arrested Jewish priests, and cherished the most grateful remembrance of her. We have the touching epitaph of a Jewess named Esther born at Jerusalem and freed by Claudius or Nero, who charges her companion Arescusus to keep watch that they put nothing on her tomb contrary to the Law, as for example, the letters D.M. Rome possessed some actors and actresses of Jewish origin: under Nero, there was in that a natural way of finding access to the emperor. There is named in particular a certain Alityrus, a Jewish player, much liked by Nero and Poppea; it was by him that Josephus was introduced to the empress. Nero, full of hatred for everything that was Roman, loved to turn to the east, to surround himself with orientals, and to concoct some intrigues in the east.

Is all this enough on which to found a plausible hypothesis? Is it allowable to attribute to the hatred of the Jews against the Christians the cruel caprice which exposed the most inoffensive of men to the most monstrous punishments? It was surely a pity that the Jews had this secret interview with Nero and Poppea at the moment when the emperor conceived such a hateful thought against the disciples of Jesus. Tiberius Alexander especially was then in his full favour, and such a man would detest the saints. The Romans usually confounded the Jews and the Christians. Why was the distinction so clearly made on this occasion? Why were the Jews, against whom the Romans had the same moral antipathy and the same religious grievances as against the Christians, not meddled with at this time? The sufferings of some Jews would have been a piacalum quite as effectual. Clemens Romanus, or the author (certainly a Roman) of the epistle which is attributed to him, in the passage where he makes allusion to the massacres of the Christians ordered by Nero, explains them in a manner very obscure to us, but very characteristic. All these misfortunes are "the result of jealousy," and this word "jealousy" evidently signifies here some internal divisions, some animosities among the members of the same confraternity. From that was born a suspicion, corroborated by this incontestable fact that the Jews, before the destruction of Jerusalem, were the real persecutors of the Christians, and neglected nothing which would make them disappear. A widespread tradition of the fourth century asserts that the death of Paul and even that of Peter, which they did not separate from the persecution of the year 64, had as its cause the conversion of the mistresses and one of the favourites of Nero. Another tradition sees in this a result of the defeat of Simon the magician. With a personage so fanciful as Nero every conjecture is hazarded. Perhaps the choice of the Christians for the frightful massacre was only a whim of the emperor or Tigellinus. Nero had no need of anyone to conceive for him a design capable of baffling, by its monstrosity, all the ordinary rules of historical induction.

At first a certain number of persons suspected of forming part of the new sect were arrested, and they were put together in a prison, which was already a punishment in itself. They confessed their faith, which was considered an avowal of the crime which was judged inseparable from it. These first arrests led to a great number of others. The larger portion of the accused appear to have been proselytes, observing the precepts and the rules of the pact of Jerusalem. It is not to be admitted that any true Christians had denounced their brethren; but some papers might be seized; some neophytes scarcely initiated might yield to the torture. People were surprised at the multitudes of adherents who had accepted these gloomy doctrines; they did not speak of them without fear. All sensible men considered the accusation of having caused the fire extremely weak. "Their true crime," it was said, "is hatred to the human race." Although persuaded that the fire was Nero's crime, many of the thoughtful Romans saw in this cast of the police net a way of delivering the city from a most fatal plague. Tacitus, in spite of some pity, is of that opinion. As to Suetonius, he ranks among Nero's praiseworthy measures the punishments to which he subjected the partisans of the new and malevolent superstition

These punishments were something frightful. Such refinements of cruelty had never been seen. Nearly all the Christians arrested were of the humiliores, people of no position. The punishment of those unfortunates, when it was a matter of lese-majesty or sacrilege, consisted in being delivered to the beasts or burned alive in the amphitheatre, with accompaniments of cruel scourgings. One of the most hideous features of Roman manners was to have made of punishment a fête, and the witnessing of slaughter a public game. Persia, in its moments of fanaticism and terror had known frightful exhibitions of torture; more than once it has tasted there a sort of gloomy pleasure; but never before the Roman domination had there been this looking at these horrors as a public diversion, a subject for laughter and applause. The amphitheatres had become the places of execution; the tribunals furnished the arena. The condemned of the whole world were led to Rome for the supply of the circus and the amusement of the people. Let us join to that an atrocious exaggeration in the penalty which caused simple offences to be punished by death; let us add numerous judicial blunders, resulting from a defective criminal procedure, and we shall conceive that all the ideas were perverted. The punished were considered very soon to be as much unfortunate as criminal; as a whole, they were looked on as nearly innocent, innoxia corpora.

To the barbarity of the punishments, this time they added insult. The victims were kept for a fête, to which no doubt an expiratory character was given. Rome reckoned few days so extraordinary. The ludus matutinus, dedicated to the fights with animals, made an extraordinary exhibition. The condemned, covered with the skins of wild beasts, were thrust into the arena, where they were torn by the dogs; others were crucified, others again, clothed in tunics steeped in oil, pitch, or resin, were fastened to stakes and kept to light up the fête at night. As the dusk came on they lit those living flambeaux. Nero gave for the spectacle the magnificent gardens he possessed across the Tiber, and which occupied the present site of the Borgo and the piazza and church of St. Peter. He had found there a circus, commenced by Caligula, continued by Claudius, and of which an obelisk brought from Hierapolis (that which at the present day marks the centre of the piazza of St. Peter) was the boundary. This place had already seen massacres by torchlight. Caligula caused to be beheaded there by the light of flambeaux a certain number of consular personages, senators, and Roman ladies. The idea of replacing those lights by human bodies impregnated by inflammable substances may appear ingenious. This punishment, this fashion of burning alive was not new; it was the ordinary penalty for incendiaries, what was termed the tunica molesta; but a system of illumination had never been made out of it. By the light of these hideous torches Nero, who had put evening races in fashion, showed himself in the arena, sometimes mingling with the people in the dress of a jockey, sometimes driving his chariot and seeking for their applause. But yet there were some signs of compassion. Even those who believed the Christians culpable and who confessed that they had deserved the last punishment, were horrified by these cruel pleasures. Wise men wished that they would do only what public utility demanded, that the city should be cleared of dangerous men, but that there should not be the appearance of sacrificing criminals to the cruelty of a single person.

Some women, some maidens, were mixed up with these horrible games. A fête was made out of the nameless indignities they suffered. The custom was established under Nero of making the condemned in the amphitheatre play certain mythological parts, involving the death of the actor. Those hideous operas, where the science of machinery attained prodigious results, were a new thing; Greece would have been surprised if they had suggested to it a similar attempt to apply ferocity to æsthetics, to produce art by torture. The unfortunate was introduced into the arena richly dressed as a god or a hero doomed to death, then represented by his punishment some tragic scene of fables consecrated by sculptors and poets. Sometimes it was the furious Hercules, burned upon mount OEta, drawing over his skin the lit tunic of pitch; sometimes it was Orpheus torn in pieces by a bear; Dedalus thrown from the sky and devoured by beasts; Pasipháe submitting to the embrace of the bull, or Attys murdered; at other times, there were horrible masquerades, where the men were dressed as priests of Saturn, with a red mantle on their backs; the women as priestesses of Ceres, with fillets on their foreheads; and lastly some dramatic pieces, in the course of which the hero was really put to death, like Laureolus, or representations of tragical acts like that of Mucius Scævola. At the close, Mercury, with a rod of red hot iron, touched every corpse to see if it moved; some masked servants, representing Pluto or the Orcus, drew away the dead by the feet, killing with mallets all who still breathed.

The most respectable Christian ladies bore their part in these monstrosities. Some played the part of the Danaïdes, others those of Dircé. It is difficult to say why the fable of the Danaïdes could furnish a bloody tableau. The punishment which all mythological tradition attributes to these guilty women, and in which they are represented, was not cruel enough to minister to the pleasure of Nero and the habitués of his amphitheatre. Probably they marched bearing urns, and received the fatal blow from an actor representing Lynceus; or Anonyms, one of the Danaïds, was seen pursued by a Satyr and outraged by Neptune. Perhaps, in short, these unfortunates passed through the punishment of Tartarus one after the other, and died after hours of torment. Representations of hell were in fashion. Some years before (41) certain Egyptians and Nubians came to Rome, and had a great success by giving exhibitions at night, where they showed the horrors of the lower world, according to the paintings on the Syringe of Thebes, especially those on the tomb of Sethos I.

As to the sufferings of the Dircés there can be no doubt, We know the colossal group known by the name of the Farnese Bull, now in the museum at Naples. Amphion and Zethus fasten Dirce to the horns of an untamed bull which would draw her across the rocks and precipices of Cithero. This mediocre Rhodian marble, brought to Rome in the time of Augustus, was the object of universal admiration. What finer subject for this hideous art which the cruelty of the age had put in vogue and which consisted in making tableaux vivants of famous statues? A text and a fresco from Pompeii appear to prove that this temple scene was often represented in the arena, when the person to be punished was a woman. Bound naked by the hair to the horns of a furious bull, the unfortunates satiated the lustful glances of the cruel people. Some of the Christian women thus sacrificed were weak in body; their courage was superhuman: but the infamous crowd had no eyes save for their opened entrails and their torn bosoms.

Nero was doubtless present at these spectacles. As he was short-sighted he had the habit of wearing in his eye, when he followed the gladiatorial fights, a concave emerald which he used as a lorgnon. He loved to parade his knowledge of sculpture; it is asserted that he made odious remarks over the corpse of his mother, praising this and disparaging that. Flesh palpitating under the teeth of the beasts, a poor timid girl veiling her nudity by a modest gesture, then tossed by a bull, and torn in pieces on the pebbles of the arena, would present some plastic forms and colours worthy of a connaisseur like him. He was there in the first rank upon the podium, mingling with the vestals and the curule magistrates, with his bad figure, his mean face, his blue eyes, his chestnut hair twisted in rows of curls, his cruel lips, his wicked and beastly air; at once the figure of a big ugly baby, happy, puffed up with vanity, while a brassy music vibrated in the air, waving through a stream of blood. He doubtless dwelt like an artist upon the modest attitude of these new Dirces, and found, I imagine, that a certain air of resignation gave to these poor women about to be torn in pieces a charm which he had never known till then.

For a long time that hideous scene was remembered, and even under Domitian when an actor was put to death in his part, especially one Loreolius, who really died upon the cross, they thought of the piacula of the year 64 and imagined him to represent an incendiary of the city of Rome. The names of sarmentitii or sarmentarii (people preparing the fagots) semaxii (the stakes) the popular cry of "The Christians to the lions" appeared also to date from that time. Nero, with a sort of clever art, had struck budding Christianity with an indelible impress; the bloody noevus inscribed on the forehead of the martyr church shall never be effaced.

Those of the brethren who were not tortured had in some sort their part in the sufferings of the others by the sympathy which they shewed them and the care which they took to visit them in prison. They bought often this dangerous favour at the price of all their goods; the survivors of the crisis were utterly ruined. They scarcely thought of that, however, they saw nothing but the enduring reward of heaven and said continually: "Yet a little while, and he that shall come will come."

Thus opened this strange poem of martyrdom, this epopee of the amphitheatre, which was to last for 250 years, and from which would come forth the ennoblement of women, the rehabitation of the slaves by such episodes as these: Blandina on the cross turning her eyes upon her companions, who saw in the gentle and pale slave the image of Jesus crucified: Potanugina protected from outrage by the young officer who was leading her to punishment. The crowd was seized with horror when it perceived the humid breasts of Felicita; Perpetua in the arena pinning up her hair trampled by the beasts not to appear disconsolate. Legend tells that one of these saints proceeding to punishment met a young man who, touched by her beauty, gave her a look of pity. Wishing to leave him a souvenir she took the kerchief which covered her bosom and gave it to him; intoxicated by this gage of love the young man ran a moment later to martyrdom. Such was in fact the dangerous charm of those bloody dramas of Rome, Lyons, and Carthage. The joy of the sufferers in the amphitheatre became contagious as under the Terror the resignation of the "Victims." The Christians presented themselves above all to the imagination of the times as a race determined to suffer. The desire for death was henceforward their mark. To arrest the too deep desire for martyrdom the most terrible threatenings became necessary--the stamp of heresy, expulsion from the church.

The fault which the educated classes of the empire committed in provoking this feverish enthusiasm cannot be blamed enough. To suffer for his belief is a thing so sweet to man that this attraction is alone sufficient to make him believe. More than one unbeliever was converted without any other reason than that; in the east, one even sees impostors lying only for the sake of lying and being victims of their own lies. There was no sceptic who did not regard the martyr with a jealous eye, and did not envy him that supreme happiness of affirming something. A secret instinct leads us besides to favour those who are persecuted. Whoever imagines that a religious or social movement can be arrested by coercive measures gives therefore a proof of his complete ignorance of the human heart, and shews that he does not know the true means of political action.

What happened once may happen again. Tacitus would have turned away with indignation if he had been shewn the future of those Christians whom he treated as wretches. The honest people of Rome would have cried out if any observer endowed with a prophetic spirit had dared to say to them: "These incendiaries will be the salvation of the world." Hence an eternal objection against the dogmatism of conservative parties, an irremediable warping of conscience, and a secret perversion of judgment. Some wretches despised by all fashionable people have become saints. It would not be good if madnesses of this kind were frequent. The safety of society demands that its sentences shall not be too frequently reformed. Since the condemnation of Jesus, since the martyrs have been found to have had success for their cause in their revolt against the law, there had always been in the matter of social crimes as a secret appeal from the thing judged. Not one of the condemned but could say: "Jesus was smitten thus. The martyrs were held to be dangerous men of whom society must be purged, and yet the following centuries have shewn that this was right." A heavy blow this to those clumsy assertions by which a society seeks to represent to itself that its enemies are wanting in all reason and morality.

After the day when Jesus expired on Golgotha, the day of the festivals of the gardens of Nero (one can fix it about the 1st of August in the year 64) was the most solemn in the history of Christianity. The solidity of a construction is in proportion to the sum of virtues, sacrifices and devotion which are laid as its foundations. Fanatics alone found anything. Judaism endures still by reason of the intense frenzy of its prophets and zealots; Christianity, because of the courage of its first witnesses. The orgy of Nero was the grand baptism of blood, which marked out Rome as the city of the martyrs to play a part in the history of Christianity, and to be the second holy city. It was the taking possession of the Vatican hill by these conquerors of a kind unknown till then.

The odious madcap who governed the world did not perceive that he was the founder of a new order, and that he signed for the future a character written with cinnebar, whose effects would be reclaimed at the end of eighteen hundred years. Rome, made responsible for all the bloodshed, became, like Babylon, a sort of sacramental and symbolic city. Nero took in any case that day a place of the first order in the history of Christianity. This miracle of horror, this prodigy of perversity, was an evident sign to all. A hundred and fifty years after Tertullian writes: "Yes, we are proud that our position outside of the law has been inaugurated by such a man. When one has come to know him he understands that he who was condemned by Nero could not but be great and good." Already the idea had spread that the coining of the true Christ would be preceded by the coming of a sort of an infernal Christ who should be in everything the contrary of Jesus. That could not longer be doubted; the Antichrist, the Christ of evil, existed. The Antichrist was this monster with a human face made up of ferocity, hypocrisy, immodesty, pride, who paraded before the world as an absurd hero, celebrated his triumph as a chariot driver with torches of human flesh, intoxicated himself with the blood of the saints, and perhaps did worse than that. One is tempted to believe in fact that it is to the Christians that a passage in Suetonius refers as to a monstrous game which Nero had invented. Some youths, men, women and young girls were fastened to stakes in the arena. A beast came forth from the caves glutting itself upon these bodies. The freed man Doryphorus made as if he were fighting the beast. Now if the beast was Nero clothed in the skin of a wild beast, Doryphorus was a wretch to whom Nero had been married sending forth cries like a virgin when she is violated . . . The name of Nero has been discovered; it shall be THE BEAST. Caligula had been the Anti-God. Nero shall be the Anti-Christ, the Apocalypse. The Christian virgin who, attached to a stake, was subjected to the hideous embraces of the beast, will carry that fearful image with her into eternity!

That day was likewise the one upon which was created by a strange autithesis, the charming ambiguity on which humanity has lived for centuries and partly lives still. This was an hour reckoned in Heaven as that in which Christian chastity, until then so carefully concealed, should appear in the full light before fifty thousand spectators, and placed, as in the studio of a sculptor, in the attitude of a virgin about to die. Revelations of a secret which antiquity does not know! Brilliant proclamation of this principle that modesty is a joy and a beauty itself alone! Already we have seen the great magician who is called fancy, and who modifies from century to century the ideal of woman, working incessantly to place above the perfection of the form the attraction of modesty (Poppea only ruled by putting that on) and of a resigned humility (in that was the triumph of the good Actea). Accustomed to march always at the head of his age in the paths of the unknown, Nero was, it appears, the introducer of this sentiment, and discovered in his artistic debauches the philtre of love in the Christian female esthetic. His passion for Actea and Poppea proves that he was capable of delicate feelings, and as the monstrous mingled with everything he touched, he wished to realise for himself the spectacle of his dreams. The image of the grandmother of Cymodocea refracted itself like the heroine of an antique cameo in the focus of his emerald. By obtaining the applause of a connaisseur, so exquisite, a friend of Petronius, who perhaps saluted the Moritura by some of those quotations from the classical poets whom he loved, the timid nudity of the young martyr became the rival of the nudity, confident in itself, of a Greek Venus. When the brutal hand of this worn out world which sought its festival in the torments of a young girl had drawn aside the veil from Christian modesty, that might have said, "And I also am beautiful." It was the beginning of a new art. Hatched under the eyes of Nero, the aesthetic of the disciples of Jesus, which did not know itself till then, owes the revelation of its magic to the crime which tearing aside its robe despoiled it of its virginity.

CHAPTER VIII

DEATH OF ST. PETER AND ST. PAUL

We do not know with certainty the names of any of the Christians who perished at Rome, in the horrible events of August, 64. The arrested persons had been lately converted and their names were scarcely known. Those holy women who had astonished the church by their constancy were not known by names. They had been styled in Roman history as "The Danaïdes and the Dirces." Yet the images of the places remained lively and deep. The circus or naumachy, the two boundaries, the obelisk, and a turpentine tree which served as a rallying point for the reminiscences of the first Christian generations, became the fundamental elements of a whole ecclesiastical topography whose result was the consecration of the Vatican and the pointing out of that hill for a religious destiny of the first order. Although the affair had been special to the city of Rome and as it was necessary to appease the public opinion of the Romans, irritated by the fire, the atrocity ordered by Nero must have had some counterpart in the provinces and excited there a renewal of persecution. The churches of Asia Minor were heavily tried; the heathen population of these countries were prompt to fanaticism. There had been some imprisonments at Syrmna. Pergamos had a martyr who is known to us by the name of Antipas, who appears to have suffered near the temple of Esculapius, probably in a wooden theatre not far from the temple in connection with some festival. Pergamos was, with Cyzicus, the only town of Asia Minor which had a regular organization for gladiatorial shows. We know now that these plays were placed at Pergamos under the authority of the priests. Although there had been no formal edict forbidding the profession of Christianity, that profession was in reality against the law; hostis, hostis patriæ, hostis publicus, humani generis inimicus, hostis deorum atque hominum, such were the appellations written in the laws to designate those who put society in danger and against whom every man according to the expression of Tertullian became a soldier. The name alone of Christian was consequently a crime. As the most complete judgment was left to the judges for the estimation of such crimes, the life of every believer from that day was in the hands of magistrates of a horrible harshness and filled with cruel prejudices against them.

It is allowable without unlikelihood to connect with the event of which we have given an account the deaths of the apostles Peter and Paul. A fate truly strange has decreed that the disappearance of these two extraordinary men should be enveloped in mystery. A certain thing is, that Peter died a martyr. Now it can scarcely be conceived that he had been a martyr elsewhere than at Rome, and at Rome the only historical incident known by which one could explain his death is the episode recorded by Tacitus. As to Paul, some solid reasons lead us also to believe that he died a martyr and died at Rome. It is therefore natural to connect his death likewise with the episode of July-August, 64. Thus was cemented by suffering the reconciliation of those two souls, the one so strong, the other so good; thus was established by legendary authority (that is to say, divine) this touching brotherhood of two men whose parties opposed each other, but who, we may believe, were superior to parties and always loved each other. The great legend of Peter and Paul parallel to that of Romulus and Remus founding by a sort of collaboration the grandeur of Rome--a legend which in a sense has had in the history of humanity nearly as much importance as that of Jesus--dates from the day which, according to tradition, saw them die together. Nero, without knowing it, was again in this the most efficacious agent in the creation of Christianity, he who placed the corner stone in the city of the Saints.

As to the nature of the death of the two Apostles, we know with certainty that Peter was crucified. According to ancient texts his wife was executed with him, and he saw her led to punishment. A story, accepted since the third century, says that, too humble to suffer like Jesus, he asked to be crucified with his head downwards. The characteristic feature of the butchery of 64 having been the search for odious rarities in the way of tortures, it is possible that Peter in fact had been offered to the crowd in this hideous attitude. Seneca mentions some cases where tyrants have been known to cause the heads of the crucified to be turned to the earth. Their Christian piety would have seen a mystic refinement in what was only a bazarre caprice of the executioners. Perhaps the passage in the fourth gospel: Thou shalt stretch forth thine hands and another shall gird thee, and shall lead thee whither thou would'st not," includes some allusion to a speciality in Peter's suffering. Paul in his capacity as honestior had his head cut off. It is probable besides that there had been in regard to him a regular decision, and that he was not

47

included in the summary condemnation of the victims of Nero's fêtes. Timothy was, according to certain appearances, arrested with his master and kept in prison.

At the beginning of the 3rd century two monuments were already seen at Rome connected with the names of the Apostles Peter and Paul. One was situated at the foot of the Vatican hill: it was that of St. Peter; the other on the way to Ostia: it was that of St. Paul. They were called in oratorical style, "the trophies" of the Apostles. These were probably some cellæ or some memoriæ consecrated to the saints. Some such monuments existed before Constantine; we are entitled besides to suppose that these trophies were only known to the faithful; perhaps even they were nothing else than that Terebinth of the Vatican, with which the memory of Peter has been associated for ages, that Pine of the Salvian Waters, which was, according to certain traditions, the centre of the souvenirs relating to Paul. Much later these trophies became the tombs of the Apostles Peter and Paul. About the middle of the 3rd century, in fact, there appeared two bodies which universal veneration held to be those of the Apostles, and which appeared to have come from the the catacombs of the Appian Way, where there had really been many Jewish Cemeteries. In the fourth century these corpses reposed in the neighbourhood of the "two trophies." Above these "trophies" were then raised two basilicas of which one had become the present basilica of St. Peter and of which the other, St. Paul-beyond-the-Walls, have kept their essential forms until our day.

Did the "trophies" which the Christians venerated about the year 200 really mark the places where the two Apostles suffered? That may be. It is not unlikely that Paul at the end of his life resided in the outskirts which stretch beyond the Lavernal gate upon the way from Ostia. The shadow of Peter, upon the other hand always wanders in the Christian legend towards the foot of the Vatican, the gardens and the circus of Nero especially about the obelisk. This arises, it will be seen, from the fact that the circus spoken of preserved the souvenir of the martyrs of 64, with whom, failing precise indications, Christian tradition would connect Peter; we like better to believe, notwithstanding, that there was mixed with that some indication, and that the old place of the obelisk of the sacristy of St. Peter, marked at the present day by an inscription, points out somewhat nearly the spot where Peter on the cross satiated by his frightful agony the eyes of a populace greedy to behold him suffer. Were the bodies which since the third century had been surrounded by an uninterrupted tradition of respect, the very bodies of the two Apostles? We scarcely believe it. It is certain that attention in keeping up the memory of the tombs of the martyrs was very ancient in the church; but Rome was about 100 and 120 the theatre of an immense legendary work relating especially to the two Apostles, Peter and Paul; a work in which pious claims had a large part. It is scarcely believable that in the days which followed the horrible carnage in August, 64. they could have reclaimed the corpses of the sufferers. In the hideous mass of human flesh stoned, roasted, and trampled, which was that day drawn by hooks into the spoliarium, then thrown into the puticuli, it would have perhaps been difficult to recognize the identity of any of the martyrs. Often doubtless an authorization was obtained to withdraw from the hands of the executioners the remains of the condemned; but while supposing (which is very admissible) that some brethren had braved death to go and demand the precious relics, it is probable that instead of these being given to them they would have been themselves sent to add to the heap of corpses. During some days the mere name of Christian was a sentence of death. It is besides a secondary question. If the Vatican basilica does not really cover the tomb of the apostle Peter, it does not the less mark out for our remembrance one of the most really holy places of Christianity. The spot where the bad taste of the seventeenth century constructed a circus of theatrical architecture was a second Calvary, and even supposing that Peter had not been crucified there, there at least no doubt suffered the Danaïdes and the Dirces.

If, as we may be allowed to believe, John accompanied Peter to Rome, we can find a plausible foundation for the old tradition according to which John would have been plunged in the boiling oil, in the place where stood much later the Latin Gate. John appears to have suffered for the name of Jesus. We are led to believe that he was the witness, and up to a certain point the victim, of the bloody episode to which the Apocalypse owes its origin. The Apocalypse is to us the cry of horror from a witness who lived at Babylon, who had known the Beast, who had seen the bleeding bodies of his brother martyrs, who himself had felt the embrace of death. The unfortunate condemned who were used as living torches would be previously dipped in oil, or in an inflammable substance (not boiling, it is true). John was perhaps devoted to the same suffering as his brethren, and intended to illuminate the evening of the fête of the Faubourg of the Latin Way, a chance, a caprice had saved him. The Latin Way is indeed situated in the quarter in which the incidents of those terrible days passed. The southern part of Rome (the Capena gate, the Ostia road, the Appian Way, the Latin Way), forms the region around which appears to concentrate, in the time of Nero, the history of the budding church.

A jealous fate has willed that on so many points which greatly excite our curiosity, we should never escape from the penumbra where legend dwells. Let us repeat it once more: the questions relating to the death of the Apostles Peter and Paul present nothing but likely hypotheses. The death of Paul especially is wrapped in deep mystery. Certain expressions in the Apocalypse, composed at the end of 68 or the beginning of 69, would incline us to think that the author of this book believed Paul to be alive when he wrote. It is in no way impossible that the end of the great Apostle had been altogether unknown. In the career that certain texts attributed to him from the Western side, a shipwreck, a sickness, or some accident might carry him off. As he had not at that moment his brilliant crown of disciples around him the details of his death would remain unknown; later on, the legend would be filled up by taking account, on the one hand, the position of Roman citizenship which the Acts gives him, and on the other hand, the desire which the Christian conscience had to carry out a reconciliation between him and Peter. Certainly, an obscure death for the ardent Apostle has something in it which pleases us. We like to dream of Paul sceptical, shipwrecked, abandoned, betrayed by his friends, struck by the disenchantment of old age; it pleases us that the scales should fall a second time from his eyes, and our gentle incredulity would have its little revenge if the most dogmatic of men had died sad, despairing (let us rather say, tranquil) on some Spanish road or shore, saying thus to himself, Ego errovi! But this would be to give too much to conjecture. It is certain that the two apostles were dead in 70; they did not see the ruins of Jerusalem, which would have made such a deep impression on Paul. We admit, therefore, as probable in all that follows of this history, that the two champions of the Christian conception disappeared at Rome during the terrible storm of the year 64. James was dead a little more than two years before. Of "apostle-pillars" there remained, therefore, only John. Some other friends of Jesus, no doubt, lived still in Jerusalem, but forgotten, as if lost in the gloomy whirlwind in which Judea was to be plunged for many years.

We shall show in the following book how the church consummated a reconciliation between Peter and Paul which, perhaps, death had sketched. Success was the reward. Apparently inalienable, the Judeo-Christianity of Peter and the Hellenism of Paul were equally necessary to the success of the future work. Judeo-Christianity represented the conservative spirit, without which it possessed nothing substantial; Hellenism, advance and progress, without which nothing really exists. Life is the result of a conflict between opposing forces. People die as well from the absence of all revolutionary feeling as from excess of revolution.

CHAPTER IX

THE DAY AFTER THE CRISIS

The conscience of a society of men is like that of an individual. Every impression going beyond a certain degree of violence leaves in the sensorium of the patient a trace which is equivalent to a lesion, and puts it for a long time, if not for ever, under the power of hallucination, or a fixed idea. The bloody episode of August, 64, had equalled in horror the most hideous dreams which a sick brain could conceive. For many years to come the Christian consciousness shall be as if possessed. It is a prey to a sort of vertigo; monstrous thoughts torment. A cruel death appears to be the lot reserved for all believers in Jesus. But is not itself the most certain sign of the nearness of the Great day?

. . . The souls of the victims of the Beast were conceived if as waiting the sacred hour under the divine altar and crying for vengeance. The angel of God calms them, tells them to keep themselves in peace, and wait yet a little while; the moment is not far off when their brethren, destined for immolation, shall be killed in their turn. Nero shall charge himself with that. Nero is this infernal personage to whom God will abandon for a little his power on the eve of the catastrophe; it is this hellish monster who should appear like a frightful meteor in the horizon of the evening of the last days.

The air was everywhere as if impregnated with the spirit of martyrdom. The surroundings of Nero appeared animated against morality by a sort of disinterested hatred; there was from one end to the other of the Mediterranean, a struggle to the death between good and evil. That harsh Roman society had declared war against piety in all its forms; piety saw itself driven, forced to leave a world delivered up to perfidy, to cruelty, and to debauchery; there were no honest people who would run such dangers. The jealousy of Nero against virtue had risen to its height, philosophy was only occupied in preparing its disciples for the tortures: Seneca, Thraseas, Barea, Soranus, Musonius, and Cornutus had submitted, or were about to submit, to the consequences of their noble protest. Punishment appeared the natural lot of virtue. Even the sceptical Petronius, because he was of polished manners, could not live in a world where Tigellinus ruled. A touching echo from the martyrs of this Terror has come to us through the inscriptions of the island of religious banishments, where one would not have expected it. In a sepulchral grotto near Cagliari a family of exiles, perhaps devoted to the worship of Isis, has left us its touching complaint, almost Christian. When the unfortunates arrived in Sardinia, the husband fell ill in consequence of the frightful insalubrity of the island; his wife, Benedicta, made a vow beseeching the gods to take her in place of her husband; she was heard.

The uselessness of the massacres was seen, besides, clearly in this circumstance. An aristocratic movement, peculiar to a small number of people, is stopped by a few executions; but it is not the same with a popular movement, for such a movement has neither need of leaders nor of learned teachers. A garden where the flowers have no root can exist no longer: a park mowed becomes better than before. Thus Christianity, far from being arrested by the lugubrious caprice of Nero, multiplied more vigorously than ever; an increase of anger took possession of the survivors' hearts; it would become more than a dream, they would become masters of the heathen ruling them, as they deserved, with a rod of iron. An incendiary, although another than he whom they accused of having lit this fire, shall devour this impious city, become the temple of Satan. The doctrine of the final conflagration of the world takes each day deeper roots. Fire only shall be capable of purging the earth from the infamies which soil it; fire appears the only righteous and worthy end to such a mass of horrors.

The greater part of the Christians at Rome who escaped the ferocity of Nero, doubtless quitted the city. During six or twelve years, the Roman Church found itself in extreme disorder, a large door was opened to legend. Yet there was not a complete interruption in the existence of the community. The Seer of the Apocalypse in December, 68, or January, 69, gives orders to his people to quit Rome. Even by making that passage a prophetic fiction, it is difficult not to conclude that the Church of Rome quickly resumed its importance. The chiefs alone definitively abandoned a city where their Apostolate for the moment could not bear fruit. The point in the Roman world where life was most supportable for the Jews was at that time the province of Asia. There was between the Jewish community at Rome, and that at Ephesus, increasing communication. It was to that side that the fugitives directed themselves. Ephesus was the point where resentment for the events of the year 64 shall be most lively. All the hatreds of Rome were concentrated there; thence shall come forth in four years a furious invective, by which the Christian conscience shall reply to the atrocities of Nero.

There is no unlikelihood in placing among the Christian notables who came from Rome, the Apostle whom we have seen follow in everything Peter's fortunes. If the accounts relative to the incident, which was placed later on at the Latin Gate, have any truth, we may be permitted to suppose that the Apostle John, escaping punishment as by miracle, should have quitted the city without delay, and afterwards it was natural that he should take refuge in Asia. Like nearly all the data relating to the life of the Apostles, the traditions as to the residence of John at Ephesus are subject to doubt; they have yet also their plausible side, and we are inclined rather to admit them than reject them.

The Church at Ephesus was mixed; one party owned Paul's faith, another was Judeo-Christian. This latter fraction would preponderate through the arrival of the Roman colony, especially if that colony brought with it a companion of Jesus, a Jerusalem doctor, one of those illustrious masters before even whom Paul himself bowed. John was, after the death of Peter and James, the only apostle of the first order who still lived; he had become the chief of all the Judeo-Christian Churches; an extreme respect attached to him; we are led to believe (and no doubt the apostle himself says it), that Jesus had for him a special affection. A thousand stories were founded already upon these data. Ephesus became for a time the centre of Christianity, Rome and Jerusalem being, in consequence of the violence of the times, residences nearly forbidden to the new religion.

The struggle was soon lively between the Judeo-Christian community, headed by the intimate friend of Jesus and the families of the proselytes made by Paul. This struggle reached to all the churches of Asia. There were nothing but bitter declamations against this Balaam, who had sown scandal among the sons of Israel, who had taught them that they could without sin intermarry with heathens. John, on the contrary, was more and more considered like a Jewish high priest. Like James, he bore the πέταλον, that is to say, the plate of gold upon his forehead. He was the doctor par excellence; they were even accustomed, perhaps because of the incident of the boiling oil, to give him the title of martyr.

It appears that among the number of fugitives who came from Rome to Ephesus was Barnabas. Timothy was imprisoned about the same time; we do not know in what place, perhaps in Corinth. At the end of some months he was set free. Barnabas, when he heard this good news, seeing the situation quieter, formed the project of visiting Rome with Timothy, whom he had known and loved as the companion of Paul. The apostolic phalanx dispersed by the storm of 64, sought to reform itself. Paul's school was the least consistent; it sought, deprived of its head, to support itself by one of the more solid portions of the Church. Timothy, accustomed to be led, would be little if anything after Paul's death. Barnabas, on the contrary, who had always kept in a middle path between the two parties, and who had not once sinned against charity, became the bond of the scattered debris after the great shipwreck. That excellent man was thus once more the saviour of the work of Jesus, the good genius of concord and peace.

It is the circumstances concerning him that, according to our view, connect the work which bears the title difficult to understand of the epistle to the Hebrews. This writing would appear to have been composed at Ephesus by Barnabas, and addressed to the Church of Rome in the name of the little community of Italian Christians who had taken refuge in the capital of Asia. By his position, in some degree intermediate at the point of meeting of many ideas hitherto never associated, the epistle to the Hebrews comes by right to the conciliatory man, who so many times prevented the different tendencies in the bosom of the young community from reaching an open rupture. The opposition of the Jewish Churches to the Gentile Churches appears, when one reads this little treatise, a question settled, or rather lost in an overflowing flood of transcendental metaphysics and peaceful charity. As we have said, the taste for the midraschim or little treatises of religious exegesis under an epistolary form had made great progress. Paul was set forth quite fully as to his doctrine in his Epistle to the Romans; later on, the Epistle to the Ephesians had been his most advanced formula; the Epistle to the Hebrews would appear to be a manifesto of the same order. No Christian book so much resembles the work of the Alexandrian Schools, especially the tractates of Philo. Apollos had already entered on that path. Paul, the prisoner, was singularly pleased with him. An element foreign to Jesus, Alexandrianism, infused itself more and more into the heart of Christianity. In the Johannine writings we see this influence exercising itself in a sovereign manner. In the Epistle to the Hebrews, the Christian theology is shown to be strongly analagous to that which we have found in the Epistles in Paul's last style. The theory of the Word developed rapidly. Jesus became more and more "the second God," the metratone, the assessor of the divinity, the firstborn by right of God, inferior to God alone. As to the circumstances of the time in which it was written, the author explains these only by a few covert words; we feel that he fears to compromise the bearer of this letter, and those to whom it is addressed. A grievous weight appears to oppress him; his secret anguish escapes in brief but deep features.

God, after having formally communicated His will by the ministry of the prophets, has used in these last days the instrumentality of the Son by whom He had created the world, and who maintains everything by his power. This Son, the reflex of the Father's glory and the imprint of his essence, whom the Father has been pleased to appoint heir of the universe, has expiated sin by his appearance in this world; then he has gone to sit down in the celestial regions at the right hand of the majesty, with a title superior to that of the angels. The Mosaic law had been announced by the angels; it contains only the shadow of the good things to come; ours has been announced first by the Lord, then it has been transmitted to us in a sure manner by those who heard it from him, God bearing them witness by signs, prodigies, and all sorts of miracles, as well as by the gifts of the Holy Spirit; thanks to Jesus all men have been made sons of God, Moses has been a servant, Jesus has been the Son; Jesus has especially been par excellence the high priest after the order of Melchisedic.

This order is much superior to the Levitical priesthood, and has totally abrogated it; Jesus is priest throughout eternity.

"For such an high priest became us who is holy, harmless, and separate from sinners, and raised higher than the heavens, who does not need each day like the other priests to offer sacrifices, first for his own sins and then for those of the people. The old law made high priests of men who were liable to fall: the new law has constituted the Son to all eternity. We have such a high priest, who is seated on the right hand of the throne of the Majesty, as the minister of the true sanctuary and of the true tabernacle which the Lord hath built. Christ is the high priest of good things to come. For if the blood of bulls and goats and the ashes of an heifer sprinkle those who are unclean, gives carnal purity: how much more shall the blood of Christ, who has offered himself to God, a spotless victim, purify our conscience from dead works? It is thus He is the Mediator of the New Testament; for to have a testament it is necessary that the death of the testator should be proved, as a testament has no effect while the testator lives. The first covenant, also, was inaugurated with blood. It is by means of blood that everything is legally purged, and without shedding of blood there is no pardon."

We are, therefore, sanctified once for all by the sacrifice of the body of Jesus Christ, who shall appear a second time to those who wait for him. The old sacrifices never attained their end since they were renewed unceasingly. If the expiatory sacrifice recurred every year on a fixed day, is that not a proof that the blood of the victims was powerless? In place of those perpetual holocausts Jesus has offered his single sacrifice, which renders the other useless. Consequently there is no longer need of a sacrifice for sin.

The feeling of the dangers which surrounded the Church fills the author's mind. He has before his eyes only a perspective of sufferings. He thinks of the tortures which the prophets and the martyrs of Antiochus have endured; the faith of many succumbed. The author is very severe on these falls.

" For it is impossible for those who were once enlightened, and have tasted of the heavenly gift, and were made partakers of the Holy Ghost, and have tasted the good word of God and the powers of the world to come, if they shall fall away, to renew them again into repentance; seeing they crucify to themselves the Son of God afresh and put him to an open shame. For the earth, which drinketh in the rain that cometh oft upon it, and bringeth forth herbs meet for them by whom it is dressed, receiveth blessing from God. But that which beareth thorns and briers is rejected, and is nigh unto cursing, whose end is to be burned. But beloved, we are persuaded better things of you, and things that accompany salvation, though we thus speak. For God is not unrighteous to forget your work and labour of love, which ye have showed towards His name in that ye have ministered to the saints and do minister. And we desire that every one of you do show the same diligence to the full assurance of hope unto the end. That ye be not slothful, but followers of them who through faith and patience inherit the promises."

Some believers already had shown themselves neglectful of attendance upon the gatherings in the church. The apostle declares that these gatherings are the essence of Christianity, that it is there we exhort, animate, and watch each other, and that it is necessary to be all the more assiduous in that as the great day of final appearance approaches.

For if we sin wilfully after that we have received the knowledge of the truth, there remains no more sacrifice for sins, but a certain fearful looking for of judgment, and fiery indignation which shall devour the adversaries. . . . . It is a fearful thing to fall into the hands of the living God. But call to remembrance the former days, in which, after ye were illuminated, ye endured a great fight of afflictions. Partly while ye were made a gazing-stock, both by reproaches and afflictions; and partly whilst ye became companions of them that were so used. For ye had compassion of me in my bonds, and took joyfully spoiling of your goods, knowing in yourselves that ye have in Heaven a better and an enduring substance. Cast not away therefore your confidence, which hath great recompense of reward. For ye have need of patience that, after ye have done the will of God, ye might receive the promise. For yet a little while he that shall come will come.

Faith sums up the attitude of the Christian. Faith is the steady waiting for that which is promised, the certainty of what is not yet seen. It is faith which made the great men of the ancient law, who died without having obtained the things promised, having only seen them and hailed them from afar, confessing themselves strangers and pilgrims upon this earth, always searching for a better country which they have not found, the heavenly. The author quotes on this subject the examples of Abel, Enoch, Noah, Abraham, Sarah, Isaac, Jacob, Joseph, Moses, and Rahab the harlot.

What more shall I say, for the time would fail me to tell of Gideon, and of Barak, and of Samson, and of Jepthah, of David also, and Samuel and of the prophets. Who through faith subdued kingdoms, wrought righteousness, obtained promises, stopped the mouths of lions, quenched the violence of fire, escaped the edge of the sword, out of weakness were made strong, waxed valiant in fight, turned to flight the armies of the aliens. Women received their dead raised to life again, and others were tortured, not accepting deliverance, that they might obtain a better resurrection. And others had trials of cruel mockings and scourgings, yea, moreover, of bonds and imprisonment. They were stoned, they were sawn asunder, were tempted, were slain with the sword, they wandered about in sheep skins and goat skins, being destitute, afflicted, tormented. Of whom the world was not worthy. They wandered in deserts, and in mountains, and in dens, and in caves of the earth. And these, all having obtained a good report through faith, received not the promise. God having provided some better thing for us, that they without us should not be made perfect. Wherefore, seeing we also are compassed about with so great a cloud of witnesses, let us lay aside every weight, and the sin which doth so easily beset us, and let us run with patience the race that is set before us; looking unto Jesus, the author and finisher of our faith, who for the joy that was set before him endured the cross, despising the shame, and is set down at the right hand of the throne of God. For consider him that endured such contradiction of sinners against himself, lest ye be wearied and faint in your minds. Ye have not yet resisted unto blood striving against sin.

The author then explains to the confessors that the sufferings which they endure are no punishments, but that they ought to be taken as paternal corrections such as a father administers to his son, and which are a pledge of his tenderness. He invitee them to hold themselves in readiness against light minds which, after the manner of Esau, give their spiritual patrimony in exchange for a worldly and momentary advantage. For the third time the author turns back upon his favourite thought that after a fall which has put one outside of Christianity, there is no return. Esau also sought to regain the paternal benediction, but his tears and regrets were useless. We know that there had been, in the persecution of 64, some renegades through weakness, who, after their apostacy, desired to re-enter the Church. Our doctor demands that they should be repulsed. What blindness, indeed, equals that of the Christian who hesitates or denies "after having come to the holy mountain of Sion, and the city of the living God, the heavenly Jerusalem and myriads of angels in their choir, the Church of the firstborn written in heaven, and of God the universal Judge, of the spirits of the just made perfect, and Jesus the Mediator of the new covenant, after having been purified by the blood of propitiation which speaks better things than that of Abel . . .?"

The apostle closes by recalling to his readers the members of the Church who were still in the dungeons of the Roman authorities, and especially the memory of their spiritual leaders who were no more--those great initiators who had preached the word of God to them, and whose death had been a triumph for the faith. Let them consider the close of these holy lives and they will be strengthened. Let them beware of false doctrines, especially those which make holiness consist in useless ritual practices, such as distinction in meats. The disciple or friend of St. Paul is met here again. The fact is, the entire epistle is like the epistles of Paul, a long demonstration of the complete abrogation of the law of Moses by Jesus; to bear the shame of Jesus, to go forth from the world, "for we have no permanent city--we seek one which is to come; "to obey the chief ecclesiastics, to be very respectful to them, to render their task easy and agreeable, "since they watch over souls and must render an account of them," that is the duty before them. No writing shows, perhaps, better than this the mystic rôle of Jesus increasing and closing by filling up completely the Christian conscience. Not only is Jesus the Logos who has created the world, but his blood is the universal propitiation, the seal of a new alliance. The author is so preoccupied with Jesus that he makes some errors in reading that he may find him everywhere. In his Greek manuscript of the Psalms, the two letters TIof the word ΩTIA, in Ps. xl. (xxxix.) v. 6, were a little doubtful; he has seen a M, and as the preceding word ends with an Σ, he reads $\sigma\tilde{\omega}\mu\alpha$ which presents a fine Messianic meaning: "Thou hast desired sacrifice no longer, but thou hast given me a body: then I said, Lo I come!'"

A singular thing! the death of Jesus in Paul's school takes a larger importance than his life. The precepts of the Lake of Gennesareth little interested this school, and appear to have been scarcely known to them; what they saw as the first plan was the sacrifice of the Son of God giving himself up for the expiation of the sins of the world. Absurd ideas which, restated later on by Calvinism, caused the Christian theology to deviate widely from the primitive ideal. The synoptical Gospels which are the really divine part of Christianity, are not the work of Paul's school. We shall soon see them coming forth from little quiet family which still preserved in Judea the true traditions of the life and person of Jesus.

But what was wonderful in the beginnings of Christianity was that those who draw the car in the contrary way most obstinately were those who worked best to make it advance. The Epistles to the Hebrews, marked definitively in the history of the religious evolution of humanity, the disappearance of sacrifice, that is to say of what up till then had constituted the essence of religion. To primitive man God is an all-powerful Being who must be appeased or bribed. Sacrifice comes either from fear or interest. To gain God's favour we offer him a present capable of touching him, a fine piece of meat of the fattest kind, a cup of cocoa or wine. Plagues and diseases were considered as the blows of an offended God; and it was thought that by substituting another person for the persons threatened, the anger of the Supreme Being could be averted; perhaps indeed, it was said, God will be pleased with an animal, if the beast be good, useful, or innocent. God was thus judged after the pattern of men, and in fact in our day in certain parts of the East and of Africa, the aborigenes hope to gain a stranger's favour by killing at his feet a sheep, whose blood runs over his boots, and whose flesh will serve him for food; in the same way they imagine that the Supernatural Being will be sensible of the offering of an object, especially if by that offering he who presents the sacrifice deprives himself of something. Up till the great transformation of prophecy in the eighth century, B.C., the idea of sacrifice was not much more elevated among the Israelites than among other nations. A new era commences with Isaiah, crying in the name of Jehovah: "Your sacrifices disgust me, what are your goats or bullocks to me?" The day on which he wrote that wonderful page (about 740 B.C.) Isaiah was the real founder of Christianity. It was decided on that very day, that of two supernatural functions as to which the respect of the old tribes was divided, the hereditary sacrifices of the sorcerer, or inspired book which they believed to be the depository of the divine secrets, it was the second that should determine the future of religion. The sorcerer of the Semitic tribes, the nabi became "the prophet," or sacred tribune, consecrated to the progress of social equity, and while the sacrificer (the priest) continued to boast the efficacy of the slaughters by which he profited, the prophet dared to proclaim that the true God cares much more for justice and mercy than for all the bullocks in the world. Ordained, however, by ancient rituals from which it was not easy to escape, and maintained by the interests of the priests, the sacrifices remained a law of ancient Israel. About the time of which we write, and even before the destruction of the third temple, the importance of these rites grew less. The dispersion of the Jews led to something secondary being seen in the functions which could not be accomplished at Jerusalem. Philo proclaimed that worship consisted especially in pious hymns, which must be sung by the heart as well as the mouth; he ventured to say that such prayers were worth more than offerings. The Essenes professed the same doctrine. St. Paul, in the epistle to the Romans, declares that religion is a worship of pure reason. The epistle to the Hebrews, in developing this theory that Jesus is the true High Priest, and that his death was a sacrifice abrogating all the others, struck a last blow at the bloody immolations. The Christians, even those of Jewish origin, ceased more and more to believe in the legal sacrifice, which they only countenanced by sufferance. The generating idea of the mass, the belief that the sacrifice of Jesus is renewed by the eucharistic act, appeared already, but in the still obscure distance.

CHAPTER X

THE REVOLUTION IN JUDEA

The state of enthusiasm which held possession of the Christian imagination was soon complicated by the events which passed in Judea. These events appeared to give reason to the visions of the most frenzied brains. A fit of fever which cannot be compared with anything but that which seized France during the revolution, and Paris in 1871, took hold of the entire Jewish nation. Those "divine diseases" before which the ancient medical skill declared itself powerless, appeared to have become the ordinary temperament of the Jewish people. We should have that, determined in extremes it would have gone on to the end of humanity. For four years the strange race, which appears created alike to defy him who blesses it and him who curses it, was in a convulsion, before which the historian, divided between wonder and horror, must halt with respect, as before all that is mysterious.

The causes of this crisis were old, and the crisis itself was inevitable. The Mosaic law, the work of enthusiastic Utopians, possessed by a powerful Socialistic idea, the least political of men, was, like Islam, exclusive of a civil, parallel to the religious, society. That law which appears to have arrived at a condition of being re-edited when we read of it in the twelfth century B.C. would have even independently of the Assyrian conquest, made the little kingdom of the descendants of David fly to pieces. Since the preponderance created by the prophetic element the kingdom of Judah, at enmity with all its neighbours, moved by a continuous rage against Tyre, a hatred against Edom, Moab and Ammon, could not live. A nation which devotes itself to religious and social problems is lost as to politics. The day when Israel became a flock of God, a kingdom of priests, a holy nation, it was written that it should not be a people like any other. Men do not accumulate contradictory destinies; they always expiate an excellence by some humiliation.

The Achemenidian empire put Israel a little at rest. That grand feudality, tolerant to all provincial diversities, was analogous to the caliphate of Bagdad, and the Ottoman empire, was the condition in which the Jews found themselves most pleasantly situated. The Ptolemaic domination in the third century B.C., appears likewise to have been sympathetic enough with them. It was the same with the Seleucidæ. Antioch had became a centre of active Hellenistic propaganda; Antiochus Epiphanes believed himself obliged to install everywhere, as a mark of his power, the image of Jupiter Olimpus. Then burst forth the first great Jewish revolt against profane civilization. Israel had borne patiently the disappearance of its political existence since Nebuchadnezzar; it could not keep any longer within bounds when it realized a danger for its religious institutions. A race, in general little military, was seized with a fit of heroism; without a regular army, without generals, without tactics, it conquered the Seleucidæ, maintained its revealed right, and created for itself a second period of autonomy. The Asmonean royalty nevertheless was always pervaded by deep interior vices; it did not last more than a century. The destiny of the Jewish people was not to be constituted a separate nationality; this people dreamed always of something international, its ideal was not the city, it was the synagogues; it is the free congregation. It is the same with Islam, which has created an immense empire, but which has destroyed all nationality among the peoples it has subjected, and has left them no other fatherland than the mosque and the zaouia. There is often applied to such a social condition the name of theocracy, and that is correct, if it is intended to say by that that the profound idea of the Semitic religious empires which have gone forth from it is the kingdom of God, conceived of as the sole master of the world and universal suzerain; but theocracy among these peoples is not synonymous with the domination of priests. The priest, properly speaking, plays a weak part in the history of Judaism and Islamism. The power belongs to the representative of God, to him whom God inspires, to the prophet and the holy man, to him who has received a mission from Heaven, and who proves his mission by miracle or success. Failing a prophet, the power rests in the maker of Apocalypses or Apocryphal books attributed to ancient prophets, or rather to the doctor who interprets the divine law, to the chief of the synagogue and, later still, to the head of the family, who keeps the deposit of the law and transmits it to his children. A civil power, a royalty, has nothing much to do with such a social organization. This organization is never better carried out than in the case where the individuals who are the subjects of it are widely spread, in the condition of foreigners tolerated in a great empire where no uniformity reigns. It is the nature of Judaism to be subordinated, since it is incapable of drawing forth from its own bosom a principle of military power. The same fact is noticeable in the Greeks of our day; the Greek communities of Trieste, Syrmna and Constantinople are indeed much more flourishing than the little kingdom of Greece, because these communities are free from political agitation, in which a free race put prematurely in possession of liberty finds its certain ruin. The Roman domination established in Judea in the year 63 B.C., by the arms of Pompey, appeared at first to realize some of the conditions of Jewish life. Rome at that time did not as a rule assimilate the countries which she one after another annexed to her vast empire. She gave them the right of peace and war, and scarcely claimed anything but arbitration in great political questions. Under the degenerate remnants of the Asmonean dynasty and under the Herods, the Jewish nation preserved that semi-independence which sufficed for it since its religious condition was respected. But the internal crisis of the people was too strong. Beyond a certain degree of religious fanaticism man is ungovernable. It must be said also that Rome tended unceasingly to render her power in the East more effective. The little vassal kingdoms which she had at first conserved disappeared day by day, and the provinces returned to the empire pure and simple. After the year 6 after Christ, Judea was governed by procurators subordinated to the imperial legates of Syria and having beside them the parallel power of the Herods. The impossibility of such a régime revealed itself day by day. The Herods were little thought of in the East as either truly patriotic or religious men. The administrative customs of the Romans, even in their most reasonable aspects, were odious to the Jews. In general, the Romans shewed the greatest condescendence with respect to the fastidious scruples of the nation, but that was not sufficient; things had come to a point where nothing more could be done without affecting a canonical question. Those fixed religions, like Islamism and Judaism, endure no sharing of power. If they do not rule they call themselves persecuted. If they feel themselves protected they become exacting, and seek to render life impossible to all other religions except their own. That is well seen in Algiers, where the Israelites, knowing themselves to be maintained against the Mussulmans, have become insupportable to them, and occupy without ceasing the attention of the authorities by their recriminations.

Certainly we would not believe, in this experience of an age which made the Romans and Jews live together, and which resulted in such a terrible disruption, that the faults were reciprocal. Many procurators were dishonourable men, others could be rough, harsh, and allow themselves to be led into impatience against a religion which annoyed them, and whose features they could not understand. It would have required one to be a perfect being not to be irritated by that narrow end haughty spirit, an enemy to Greek and Roman civilization, malevolent towards the rest of the human race, which superficial observers held to constitute the essence of a Jew. How could an administrator think otherwise of those always occupied in accusing him before the emperor, and forming cabals against him even when he was perfectly right? In that great hatred which for more than two thousand years existed between the Jewish race and the rest of the world, who had the first blame? Such a question ought not to be put. In such a matter all is action and reaction, cause and effect. These exclusions, these padlocks of the Ghetto, these separate costumes, are unjust things, but who first wished for them? Those who believed themselves soiled by contact with the heathen, those who sought for separation from them, a society apart. Fanaticism has created the chains, and the chains have redoubled the fanaticism. Hatred begets hatred, and there is only one means of escaping from this fatal circle: it is to suppress the cause of the hatred, those injurious separations which, at first desired and sought for by the sects, became afterwards their shame. In regard to Judaism modern France has solved the problem. By casting down all the legal barriers which surrounded the Israelite, she has removed what was narrow and exclusive in Judaism, I mean to say its practices and its isolated life, so much so that a Jewish family brought to Paris ceases almost altogether to lead the Jewish life in the course of one or two generations.

It would be unjust to reproach the Romans in the first century, for not having acted in this manner. There was a fixed opposition between the Roman empire and orthodox Judaism. It was Jews who were often the most insolent, tormenting and aggressive. The idea of a common law which the Romans brought in germ with them was in antipathy to the strict observers of the Thora. These had moral needs in total contradiction to a purely human society, without any mixture of theocracy, as Roman society was. Rome founded the State, Judaism founded the church. Rome created profane and rational government; the Jews inaugurated the kingdom of God. Between this strict but fertile theocracy and the most absolute proclamation of the laic state which had ever existed, a struggle was inevitable. The Jews had their faith founded upon quite other bases than the Roman law, and at bottom quite irreconcilable with that law. Before having been cruelly harassed they could not content themselves, with a simple tolerance, those who believed that they had the words of eternity, the secret of the constitution of a righteous city. They were like the Mussulmans of Algeria. Our society, although infinitely superior, inspires in these only repugnance; their revealed law, at once civil and religious, fills them with pride and renders them incapable of giving themselves to a philosophical legislation, founded upon the simple idea of the relations of men to each other. Add to that a profound ignorance which hinders fanatic sects from taking account of the forces of the civilized world, and blinds them to the issue of the war in which they engage with light-heartedness.

One circumstance contributed much to maintain Judea in a condition of permanent hostility against the empire: it was that the Jews took no part in military service. Everywhere else the legions were formed from the people of the country, and it was thus with armies numerically feeble, the Romans held immense regions. The soldiers of the Romans and the inhabitants of the country were compatriots. It was not so in Judea. The legions which occupied the country were recruited for the most part at Cesarea and Sebaste, towns opposed to Judaism. Hence the impossibility of any cordial relation between the army and the people. The Roman force was in Jerusalem confined to its trenches as if in a condition of permanent siege.

It was certain, moreover, that the sentiments of the different fractions of the Jewish world should be the same in regard to the Romans. If we except some worldlings like Tiberias Alexander, become indifferent to their old faith and regarded by their co-religionists as renegades, everyone bore ill-will to the foreign rulers, but still were far from inciting to rebellion. We can distinguish four or five parties in Jerusalem:

1st. The Sadducean and Herodian party, the remainder of the house of Herod and his clientele, the great families of Hanan and of Boëthus in possession of the priesthood. A society of Epicureans and voluptuous unbelievers, hated by the people because of its pride, for its little devotion and for its riches; this party, essentially conservative, found a guarantee for its privileges in the Roman occupation, and, without loving the Romans, were strongly opposed to all revolution.

2nd. The party of Pharisean middle-class, an honest party composed of people sensible, settled, quiet, steady, loving their religion, observing it punctiliously, devoted, but without imagination; well educated, knowing the foreign world, and clearly seeing that a revolt could not end in anything but the destruction of the nation and the temple; Josephus is the type of that class of persons whose fate was that which appears always reserved to moderate parties in times of revolution, powerlessness, versatility, and the supreme disagreeableness of passing for traitors in the eyes of most people.

3rd. The enthusiasts of every kind, zealots, robbers, assassins, a strange mass of fanatical beggars reduced to the last wretchedness by the injustice and the violence of the Sadducees, who looked upon themselves as the sole inheritors of the promises of Israel, of that poor "beloved" of God, nourishing themselves upon prophetic books such as those of Enoch, violent Apocalypses, believing the kingdom of God about to be revealed, arrived at last at the most intense degree of enthusiasm of which history has kept records.

4th. Brigands, people without vagrants, adventurers, dangerous scoundrels, the result of the complete social disorganization of the country; these people for the most part of Idmuean or Nabatean were little concerned about the question of religion; but they were creators of disorder, and they had a quite natural alliance with the enthusiastic party.

5th. Pious dreamers, Essenes, Christians, Ebionim, waiting peacefully for the kingdom of God, devoted persons grouped around the temple praying and weeping. The disciples of Jesus were of that number; they were still so small a body in the eyes of the public that Josephus does not reckon them among the elements of the struggle. We see all at once that in the day of danger these holy people knew only how to escape.

The mind of Jesus, full of a divine efficacy for drawing man away from the world, and consoling him, could not inspire the strict patriotism which created assassins and heroes.

The arbiters of the situation would naturally be the enthusiasts. The democratic and revolutionary side of Judaism showed itself in them in a terrible manner. They were persuaded, with Judas the Gaulonite, that all power came from the evil one, that royalty is a work of Satan (a theory which some sovereigns, such as Caligula and Nero, true demons incarnate, only justified too much) and they suffered themselves to be cut in pieces sooner than give to another than God the name of master; imitators of Matthias, the first of the zealots who, seeing a Jew sacrificing to idols, killed him; they avenged God by blows of the dagger. The mere fact of nearing an "uncircumcised" speak of God or of the law was enough to make them seek to surprise him alone; then they gave him the choice of circumcision or death. Executioners of those mysterious sentences which were left to "the hand of heaven," and believing themselves charged with rendering effectual that fearful penalty of excommunication, which is equivalent to placing beyond the law and giving up to death, they formed an army of terrorists in full revolutionary ebullition. It could be foreseen that these troubled consciences, incapable of distinguishing their gross appetite from passions which their frenzy represented to them as holy, went to the most extreme excess and stopped before no degree of folly.

Minds were under the influence of a permanent hallucination; some terrifying reports came from all directions. People only dreamed of omens; the apocalyptic colour of the Jewish imagination tinged everything with an aureole of blood. Comets, swords in heaven, battles in the clouds, a spontaneous light shining at night at the foundation of the temple, victims giving birth to unnatural productions at the moment of sacrifice, were what were spoken of in terror. One day, it was the enormous brazen gates of the temple which opened of themselves and refused to allow themselves to be shut. At the Passover of 65, about three hours after midnight the temple was for half-an-hour perfectly light as in the full day; it was believed that it was consuming inside. Another time, on the day of Pentecost, the priests heard the sound of many people making preparations in the interior of the sanctuary as if for removal, and saying to one another, "Let us go out from here! let us go out from here!" All this came only too late; but the deep trouble of souls was the best sign that something extraordinary was preparing.

It was the Messianic prophecies especially which excited in the people an unconquerable need of agitation. People would not resign themselves to a mediocre destiny when they claimed the kingdom of the future. The Messianic theories were summed up for the crowd in an oracle which was said to be drawn from Scripture, and according to which "there was to go forth at this time a prince who should be master of the universe." It is useless to reason against obstinate hope; evidence has no power to fight the chimera which a people has embraced with all the power of its heart.

Gersius Florus, of Clazomenes, had succeeded Albinus as procurator of Judea about the end of 64, or the beginning of 65. He was, as it would appear, a very bad man; he owed the position he occupied to the influence of his wife, Cleopatra, who was the friend of Poppea. The hatred between him and the Jews now grew to the last degree of exasperation. The Jews had become unbearable by their susceptibility, their habit of complaining about trifles, and the little respect they showed to the civil and military authorities; but it would appear that, on his side, he took a pleasure in defying them and making a parade of it. On the 16th and 17th May, of the year 66, a collision took place between his troops and the Jerusalemites on some absurd grounds. Florus retired to Cesarea, only leaving a cohort in the Antonian tower. There was here a very blameable act. An armed power owes it to a city it occupies, when a popular revolt shows itself, not to abandon it to its own passions until it has exhausted all its means of resistance. If Florus had remained in the city, it is not probable that the Jerusalemites would have forced it, and all the misfortunes which followed would have been avoided. Florus once gone, it was written that the Roman army should not re-enter Jerusalem except through fire and death.

The retreat of Florus was, nevertheless, far from creating an open rupture between the city and the Roman authority. Agrippa II. and Berenice were at this moment in Jerusalem. Agrippa made some conscientious efforts to calm the peoples' minds; all moderate persons joined with him, they used even the popularity of Berenice, in whom the imagination of the people believed they saw living again her great-grandmother Mariamne, the Asmonean. While Agrippa harangued the crowd in the Xystos the princess showed herself upon the terrace of the palace of the Asmonean, which overlooked the Xystos. All was useless. Sensible men represented that war would be the certain ruin of the nation; they were treated as people of little faith. Agrippa, discouraged or frightened, quitted the city and retired to his estates in Batanea. One band of the most ardent kind departed at once and occupied by surprise the fortress of Massada, situated on the shores of the Dead Sea, two days' journey from Jerusalem, and nearly impregnable.

There was here an act of definite hostility. In Jerusalem the fight became daily more vigorous between the party of peace and that of war. The first of those two parties was composed of the rich, who had everything to lose in a revolution. The second, besides the sincere enthusiasts, comprehended that mass of the populace to whom a state of national crisis, fully putting to an end the ordinary conditions of life, derives most benefit. The moderate people depended upon the little Roman garrison lodged in the Antonian town. The high priest was an obscure man, Matthias, son of Theophilus. Since the deprivation of Hanan the Young, who caused the death of St. James, it seems there was a system of no longer taking the high priest from the powerful sacerdotal families, the Hanans, the Cantheras, and the Boëthuses. But the true head of the sacerdotal party was the old high priest Ananias, son of Nabedeus, a rich and energetic man, little popular because of the pitiless vigour with which he enforced his rights, hated especially for the impertinence and rapacity of his servants. By a peculiarity which is not rare in times of revolution, the chief of the party of action was at this time Eleazar, son of this some Ananias; he held the important position of Captain of the Temple. His religious enthusiasm appears to have been sincere. Pushing to the extreme the principle that the sacrifices could not be offered but by Jews and for Jews, he caused to be suppressed the prayers that were offered for the Emperor and the prosperity of Rome. All the younger portion of the people were full of ardour. It is one of the characteristics of the fanaticism which the Semetic religions inspire that it shows itself with the utmost vivacity among the young. The members of the ancient sacerdotal families, the Pharisees, the reasonable and settled men, saw the danger. They put forward some authorized doctors, they had consultations of the rabbis, memorials from canonical laws, although quite in vain; for it was plain that the town clergy made common cause with the enthusiasts and Eleazar. The higher clergy and the aristocracy, despairing of gaining anything over the popular crowd, delivered up to the most superficial suggestions, sent to beg Florus and Agrippa to come and quickly put down the revolt, making them note that soon it would not be time to do so. Florus, according to Josephus, wished a war of extermination, which should cause the entire Jewish race to disappear from the world, and he evaded a reply. Agrippa sent to the party of order a body of three thousand Arab horsemen. The party of order with these horsemen occupied the upper city (the present Armenian and Jewish quarters). The party of action occupied the lower city and the temple (the present Mussulman, Mogharibi and Haram quarters). A real war was waged between the two quarters. On the 14th of August the rebels, commanded by Eleazar, Menahem, son of that Judas the Gaulonite, who first, sixty years previously, had raised the Jews by preaching to them that the true adorer of God ought not to recognise any man as his superior, stormed the higher town and burned the house of Ananias, and the palaces of Agrippa and Berenice. The horsemen of Agrippa, Ananias his brother, and all the notables who could join them, took refuge in highest parts of the palace of the Asmoneans.

The morning after this success the insurgents attacked the Antonian tower; they took it in two days, and set it on fire. They beseiged then the upper palace and took it (6th September). Agrippa's horsemen were allowed to go out. As to the Romans, they shut themselves up in the three towers named after Hippicus, Phasaël, and Mariamne. Ananias and his brother were killed. According to the rule in popular movements discord soon broke out among the leaders of the popular party. Menahem made himself intolerable by his pride as a democratic parvenu. Eleazar, son of Ananias, irritated beyond doubt by the murder of his father, pursued him and killed him. The remnant of Menahem's party retired to Massada, which was to be until the end of the war the bulwark of the most enthusiastic party of the zealots.

The Romans defended themselves a long time in the towers: reduced to extremity, they only asked that their lives should be spared. This was promised them, but when they had surrendered their arms, Eleazar put them all to death, with the exception of Metilius, primipilus of the cohort, who promised that he would be circumcised. Thus Jerusalem was lost by the Romans about the end of September A.D. 66, a little more than a hundred years after its capture by Pompey. The Roman garrison of the castle of Machero, fearing to be seen retreating, surrendered. The castle of Kypros, which overlooks Jericho, fell also into the hands of the insurgents. It is probable that Herodium was occupied by the rebels about the same time. The weakness which the Romans shewed in all these mutinies is something singular, and gives a certain likelihood to the opinion of Josephus, according to which the plan of Floras would have been to push everything to the extremes. It is true that the first revolutionary outbursts have something fascinating which makes it very difficult to stop them and causes wise minds to resolve to allow them to wear themselves out by their own excesses.

In five months the insurrection had succeeded in establishing itself in a formidable manner. Not only was it mistress of the city of Jerusalem, but by the desert of Judea it obtained communication with the region of the Dead Sea, all of whose fortresses it held; from thence it came in contact with the Arabs, the Nabateans, more or less the enemies of Rome. Judea Ideamea, Perea, and Galilee were with rebels. At Rome during this time a hateful sovereign had handed over the functions of the empire to the most ignoble and incapable. If the Jews had been able to group around them all the malcontents of the East there would have been an end of Roman rule in these quarters. Unhappily for them, the effect was quite the opposite; the revolt inspired in the populations of Syria a redoubled fidelity to the empire. The hatred which they had inspired in their neighbours sufficed during the kind of torpor of the Roman power to excite against them some enemies not less dangerous than the legions.

CHAPTER XI

MASSACRES IN SYRIA AND EGYPT

A sort of general mot d'ordre in fact appeared at this time to have run through the East, inciting everywhere to great massacres of the Jews. The incompatibility of the Jewish life with the Greco-Roman life became more and more apparent. Each of the two races wishing to exterminate the other, it was evident that there would be no mercy between them. To conceive of these struggles it is necessary to understand to what extent Judaism had penetrated all the Oriental portion of the Roman empire. "They have spread over all the cities," says Strabo, "and it is not easy to mention a place in the world which has not received this people, or rather which has not been occupied by them. Egypt and Cyrenia have adopted their manners, observing scrupulously their precepts and deriving great profit from the adoption which they have made of their national laws. In Egypt they are admitted to dwell legally, and a great part of the city of Alexandria is assigned to them; they have their Ethnarc, who administers their affairs, exercises justice and watches over the execution of contracts and wills, as if he were the president of an independent state". This contact of two elements as opposed to one another as water and fire, could not fail to produce the most terrible outbursts. It is not necessary to suspect the Roman government of being implicated in this. The same massacres had taken place among the Parthians, whose situation and interest were quite otherwise than those of the West. It is one of the glories of Rome to have founded its empire upon peace; on the extinction of local wars, and by never having practised that detestable means of government, become one of the political secrets of the Turkish empire, which consists in exciting against each other the different populations of mixed countries; as to a massacre for religious motives, no idea was farther from the Roman mind. A stranger to all theology, the Roman did not understand the sect, and did not grant that persons ought to be divided for such a small matter as a speculative proposition. The antipathy against the Jews was moreover in the ancient world a sentiment so general that it had no need to be forced then. That antipathy marks one of the deep lines of separation which have over been found in the human race. It concerns something more than race, it is the hatred of the different functions of humanity, the hatred on the part of the man of peace content with his internal joys against the man of war, the man of the shop and counter against the peasant and the noble. It is probably not without reason that this poor Israel has passed its life as a people in being massacred. Since all nations and all ages have persecuted them, there must have been some motive. The Jew up to our time insinuates himself everywhere, claiming common rights but in reality the Jew was not within the common law. He kept his own special code; he wished to have guarantees from all, and once above the market, made his exceptions and his laws for himself. He wished the advantages of the nations without being a nation, without participating in the expenditure of nations. No people has ever been able to tolerate that. The nations are military creations founded and maintained by the sword. They are the work of peasants and soldiers; the Jews have not contributed in any degree to their establishment. That is the great misunderstanding involved in the Israelite pretensions. The stranger is tolerated because he is useful in a country, but on condition that the country does not allow itself to be taken possession of by him. It is unjust to claim the rights of a member of a family in a house which one has not built, as those birds do who install themselves in a nest which is not their own, or like those crustaceans who take the shell of another species.

The Jew has rendered to the world so many good and so many bad services, that people can never be just to him. We owe him too much, and at the same time we see too well his defects not to be impatient at the sight of him. That eternal Jeremiah, "that man of sorrows," is always complaining, presenting his back to blows with a patience which annoys us. This creature, foreign to all our instincts of religion and honour, boldness, glory and refinement of art; this person so little a soldier, so little chivalrous, who loves neither Greece nor Rome nor Germany, and to whom nevertheless we owe our religion, so much so that the Jew has a right to say to the Christian, "Thou art a Jew with a little alloy," this being has been set as the object of contradiction and antipathy; a fertile antipathy which has been one of the conditions of the progress of humanity!

In the first century of our era it appears that the world had a dim consciousness of what had passed, it saw its master in this strange, awkward, susceptible, timid stranger without any exterior nobility; but honest, moral, industrious; just in his business, endowed with modest virtues; not military, but a good trader a cheerful and steady worker. This Jewish family illumined by hope, this synagogue--the life commonly was full of charm--created envy. Too much humility, such a calm acceptance of persecution and insult and outrage; such a resigned manner of consoling himself for not being of the great world because he has a compensation in his family and his church, a gentle gaiety like that which in our days distinguishes the rayah in the east and makes him find his good fortune in his inferiority itself. In that little world where he has as much happiness as outside he suffers persecution and ignominy,--all this inspires with aristocratic antiquity his fits of deep bad temper, which sometimes lead him to the commission of odious brutalities.

The storm commenced to growl at Cesarea nearly at the same moment as when the revolution had succeeded in making itself mistress of Jerusalem. Cesarea was the city where the situation with the Jews and non-Jews (those were comprised under the general name of Syrians) presented the greatest difficulties. The Jews composed in the mixed villages of Syria the rich portion of the population; but this wealth, as we have said, came partly through injustice, and from exemption from military service. The Greeks and the Syrians, from among whom the legions were recruited, were hurt by seeing themselves oppressed by people exempt from the dues of the state, and who took advantage of the tolerance which they had for them. There were perpetual riots, and endless claims presented to the Roman magistrates. Orientals usually make religion a pretext for rascalities; Use less religious of men become singularly so when it becomes a question of annoying one's neighbour; in our days the Turkish functionaries are tormented by grievances of this kind. From about the year 60 the battle was without truce between the two halves of the population of Cesarea. Nero solved the questions pending against the Jews; hatred had only envenomed them; some miserable follies, or perhaps inadvertances on the part of the Syrians became crimes and injuries on the side of the Jews. The young people threatened and struck each other, grave men complained to the Roman authority, who usually caused the bastinado to be administered to both parties. Gessius Floras used more humanity. He began by making them pay on both sides, then mocked those who claimed. A synagogue, which had a partition wall, a pitcher and some slain poultry which were found at the door of the synagogue, and which the Jews wished to pass off as the remains of a heathen sacrifice, were the great matters at Cesarea, at the moment Florus re-entered it, furious at the insult which had been given him by the people of Jerusalem. When it was known some months after that these people had succeeded in driving the Romans completely from their walls, there was much excitement. There was open war between the Jews and the Romans; the Syrians concluded that they could massacre the Jews with impunity. In one hour there were 20,000 throats cut. There did not remain a single Jew in Cesarea; in fact Florus ordered to the galleys all those who had escaped by flight. This crime provoked frightful reprisals. The Jews formed themselves into bands and betook themselves on their side to massacre the Syrians in the cities of Philadelphia and Hesbon, Gerasa, Pela and Scythopolis; they ravaged the Decapolis and Gaulonitis; set fire to Sebaste and Askelon, ruined Anthedon and Gaza. They burned the villages, and killed anyone who was not a Jew. The Syrians on their side killed all the Jews they met. Southern Syria was a field of carnage; every town was divided into two armies, who waged a merciless war. The nights were passed in terror. There were some atrocious episodes. At Scythopolis the Jews fought with the heathen inhabitants against their co-religionist invaders, which did not hinder them from being massacred by the Scythopolitans. The butcheries of Jews recurred with increased violence at Askelon, Acre, Tyre, Hippos, and Gadara. They imprisoned those whom they did not kill. The scenes of fury which occurred at Jerusalem made people see in every Jew a sort of dangerous mad-man whose acts of fury it is necessary to prevent. The epidemic of massacres extended as far as Egypt. The hatred of the Jews and the Greeks was at its height. Alexandria was half a Jewish town, the Jews formed there a true autonomous republic. Egypt had only some months previously as prefect a Jew, Tiberius Alexander, but a Jewish apostate little disposed to be indulgent to the fanaticism of his co-religionists. Sedition broke out in connection with an assembly at the amphitheatre. The first insults came, it would appear, from the Greeks. The Jews replied to that in a cruel manner. Arming themselves with torches they threatened to burn within the amphitheatre the Greeks to the last man. Tiberius Alexander tried in vain to calm them. It was necessary to send for the legions, the Jews resisted; the carnage was frightful. The Jewish quarter of Alexandria called the Delta was literally crowded with corpses; the dead were computed as amounting to 50,000.

These horrors lasted for a month. In the north, they were stopped at Tyre; for beyond that the Jews were not considerable enough to give umbrage to the indigenous populations. The cause of the evil indeed was more social than religious. In every city where Judaism came to dominate, life became impossible for pagans. It is understood that the success obtained by the Jewish revolution during the summer of 66, had caused a moment of fear to all the mixed towns which bordered on Palestine and Galilee. We have insisted often on this singular character which makes the simple Jewish people include in their own bosom the extremes, and if we may say so, the fight between good and evil. Nothing in fact in wickedness equals Jewish wickedness; and yet we have drawn from her bosom the ideal of goodness, sacrifice, and love. The best of men have been Jews; the most malicious of men have also been Jews. A strange race--truly marked by the seal of God, who has produced in a parallel manner and like two buds on the same branch the nascent church and the fierce fanaticism of the Jerusalem revolutionaries, Jesus and John of Gischala, the apostles and the assassin zealots, the Gospel and the Talmud; ought one to be astonished if this mysterious birth was accompanied by mysteries, delirium, and a fever such as never had been seen before?

The Christians were no doubt implicated in more than one direction in the massacres of September, 66. It is nevertheless probable that the gentleness of these worthy sectaries and their inoffensive character often preserved them. The larger number of the Christians of the Syrian towns were what were called "Judaizers," that is to say, people of converted countries, not Jews by race. They were looked on with hatred; but people did not dare to kill them; they were considered a species of mongrels--strangers from their own country. As to them, while passing through that terrible month, they had their eyes on heaven, believing that they saw in every episode of the frightful storm the signs of the time fixed for the catastrophe: "Take the comparison of the fig-tree; when its branches become tender and its leaves bud, ye conclude that summer is nigh: likewise, when ye see those things come to pass, know that He is near, that He is even at the door?"

The Roman authority was prepared meanwhile to re-enter by force the city it had so imprudently abandoned. The imperial legate of Syria, Cestius Gallus, marched from Antioch towards the south with a considerable army. Agrippa joined him as guide to the expedition; the towns furnished him with auxiliary troops, in whom an inveterate hatred of the Jews supplied what was wanting in the matter of military education. Cestius reduced Galilee and the coast without much difficulty; and on the 24th of October he arrived at Gabaon, ten miles from Jerusalem. With astonishing boldness, the insurgents went out to attack him in that position, and caused him to suffer a check. Such a fact would be inconceivable if the Jerusalem army should be represented as a mass of devotees; fanatical beggars and brigands. It possessed certain elements more solid and really military, the two princes of the royal family of Adiabenes, Monobazus and Cenedeus; one Silas from Babylon, a lieutenant of Agrippa II., who was among the national party; Niger of Perea, a trained soldier; Simon, son of Gioras, who began thenceforth his career of violence and heroism. Agrippa believed the occasion favourable for making terms. Two of his emissaries came to offer the Jerusalemites a full pardon if they would submit. A large portion of the population wished that this should be agreed to; but the enthusiastics killed the envoys. Some people who showed anger at such a shameful act were maltreated. This division gave Cestius a moment's advantage. He left Gabaon and pitched his camp in the district named Sapha or Scopus, an important position situated to the north of Jerusalem, scarcely an hour's distance from it, and from which the city and the temple could be seen. He remained there three days, waiting for the result of having some spies in the place. On the fourth day (30th October), he marshalled his army and marched forward. The party of resistance abandoned all the new town, and retired into the inner town (high and low) and into the temple. Cestius entered without opposition, and occupied the new town, the quarter of Bezetha, the wood market, to which he set fire, and approached the high town, disposing his lines in front of the palace of the Asmoneans.

Josephus declares that if Cestius Gallus had been willing to make the assault at this moment, the war would have been ended. The Jewish historian explains the inaction of the Roman general by intrigues in which the principal material was the money of Florus. It appears that they had seen on the wall some members of the aristocratic party, led by one of the Hanans, who called to Cestius, offering to open the gates to him. No doubt the legate feared some ambush. For five days he vainly tried to break through the wall. On the sixth day (5th November) he at length attacked the enceinte of the temple from the north. The fight was fearful under the porticoes; discouragement took hold of the rebels; the party of peace were making ready to admit Cestius, when he suddenly caused the retreat to be sounded. If Josephus' story is true, the conduct of Cestius is inexplicable. Perhaps Josephus, to support his argument, exaggerates the advantages Cestius had at first over the Jews, and lessens the real force of the resistance. What is certain is that Cestius regained his camp at Scopus and left the next day for Gabaon, harassed by the Jews. Two days after (8th November) he raised his camp, but was pursued as far as the descent from Bethoron, leaving all his baggage, and retreated not without difficulty to Antipatris.

The incapacity which Cestius showed in this campaign is truly surprising. The bad government of Nero must have indeed debased all the services of the state for such events to have been possible. Cestius only survived his defeat a short time; many attributed his death to chagrin. It is not known what became of Florus.

CHAPTER XII

VESPASIAN IN GALILEE--THE TERROR AT JERUSALEM--FLIGHT OF THE CHRISTIANS

While the Roman empire in the East was suffering this most terrible insult, Nero, passing from crime to crime, from one madness to another, was completely taken up by his chimeras as a pretentious artist. Every-thing which could be called taste, tact or politeness, bad disappeared around hint with Petronius. A colossal self-love gave him an ardent thirst to absorb the glory of the whole world; his enmity was fierce against those who occupied public attention; for a man to succeed in anything was a state crime. It is said that he wished to stop the sale of Lucan's works. He aspired to unheard-of fame; he turned in his brain some magnificent projects, such as piercing the isthmus of Corinth, a canal from Baia to Ostia, and the discovery of the sources of the Nile. A voyage to Greece had been his dream for a long time, not for any desire he had to see the chefs-d'-oeuvre of an incomparable art, but through the grotesque ambition he had to present himself in the courses founded in the different towns, and take the prize. These courses were literally innumerable: the founding of such games had been one of the forms of Greek liberality. Every citizen at all rich considered these, as in the foundation of our academical prizes, a sure method of transmitting his name to the future. The noble exercises which contributed so powerfully to the strength and beauty of the ancient race, and was the school of Greek art, had become like the tourneys of a later age, profitable to people who made it a trade, who made it their profession to run in the agones, and to gain crowns there. Instead of good and worthy citizens, there were seen there none except hateful and useless rascals, or people who created a lucrative specialty out of it. These prizes, which the victors showed as a species of decoration, kept the vain Cæsar from sleep. He saw himself already entering Rome in triumph, with the extremely rare title of periodonice or victor in the complete cycle of the solemn games.

His mania as a singer reached its height of folly. One of the reasons of Thrasea's death was that he never sacrificed to the "heavenly voice" of the emperor. Before the King of the Parthians, his guest, he wished only to show his talent in the chariot races. There were some lyrical dramas put on the stage where he had the principal part, and where the gods and goddesses, the heroes and heroines were masqued and draped like him, or like the woman he loved. He thus played OEdipus, Thyeste, Hercules, Alcmeon, Orestes, and Canacé; he was seen on the stage chained (with chains of gold) led like one blind, imitating a madman, feigning the appearance of a woman who is being confined. One of his last projects was to appear in the theatre, naked, as Hercules, crushing a lion in his arms, or killing it with a blow of his club. The lion was, it was said, already chosen and prepared when the emperor died. To quit one's place while he sang was so great a crime that the most ridiculous precautions were taken to do so unseen. In the competitions he disparaged his rivals, and sought to discountenance them; so much so that the unfortunates sang false in order to escape the danger of being compared to him. The judges encouraged him, and praised his bashfulness. If this grotesque spectacle made shame mount to anyone's forehead or gloom to his face he said that the impartiality of some people was suspected by him. Besides, he obeyed the rules as to the reward, and trembled before the agonothetes and the mastigophores, and prayed that they should not chastise him when he had deceived himself. If he had committed some blunder which would have excluded him he would grow pale; it was necessary to say to him quite low that this had not been remarked in the midst of the applauses and enthusiasm of the people. They overthrew the statues of the former laureates not to excite him to a mad jealousy. In the races they rode to let him come in first, even when he fell from his chariot. Sometimes, however, he allowed himself to be beaten, so that it might be believed that he played a fair game. In Italy, as we have said already, he was humiliated by having to owe his success only to a bland of claquers, knowingly organised and dearly paid, who followed him everywhere. The Romans became insupportable to him; he treated them as rustics, and said that an artist who respected himself could only be so among the Greeks.

The much desired departure took place in November 66. Nero had been some days in Achaia when the news of the defeat of Cestius was brought to him. He felt that this war required a leader of experience and courage; but he wished above all some one whom he did not fear. These conditions seemed to meet in Titus Flavius Vespasianus, a solid military man, aged sixty, who had always had much good fortune and whose obscure birth had only inspired him with great designs. Vespasian was at this time in disgrace with Nero, because he did not show sufficient admiration for his fine voice, when messengers came to announce to him that he was to have the command of the expedition to Palestine, he believed they had come with his death warrant. His son Titus soon joined him. About the same time Mucianus succeeded Cestius in the office of imperial legate of Syria. The three men who, in two years, will be the masters of the empire's fate were thus found gathered together in the East.

The complete victory which the rebels had gained over a Roman army, commanded by an imperial legate, raised their audacity to the highest point. The most intelligent and educated people in Jerusalem were sad; they saw with clearness that the advantage in the end could only be with the Romans; the ruin of the temple and nation appeared to them inevitable; and emigration began. All the Herodians, all the people attached to Agrippa's service, retired to the Romans. A great number of Pharisees, on the other hand, entirely pre-occupied by the observance of the law and the peaceful future they predicted for Israel, were of opinion that they ought to submit to the Romans, as they had submitted to the kings of Persia and the Ptolemies. They cared little for national independence: Rabbi Johanan ben Zaka, the most celebrated Pharisee of the time, lived quite apart from politics. Many doctors retired probably from that time to Jamnia, and there founded those Talmudic schools which soon obtained a great celebrity.

The massacres, moreover, began again and extended to some parts of Syria which up till now had been safe from the bloody epidemic. At Damas all the Jews were killed. The greater number of the women in Damas professed the Jewish religion, and there would certainly be some Christians among the number; precautions were taken that the massacre should be a surprise and quite unknown to them.

The party of resistance showed a wonderful activity. Even the slow were carried away. A council was held in the temple to form a national government, composed of the elite of the nation. The moderate group at this period were far from having abdicated. Whether they hoped to direct the movement, or that they had some secret hope against all the suggestions of reason by which one is lulled asleep easily in hours of crisis, it was left to them to conduct nearly everything. Some very considerable personages, many members of the Sadducean or sacerdotal families, the principal of the Pharisees, that is to say, the higher middle class, having at its head the wise and honest Simeon, Ben Gamaliel (son of the Gamaliel of the Acts, and the great-grandson of Hillel) adhered to the revolution. They acted constitutionally; they recognised the sovereignty of the Sanhedrim. The town and the temple remained in the hands of the established authorities, Hanan (son of the Hanan [Annas] who condemned Jesus) the oldest of the high priests, Joshua, Ben Gamala, Simeon, Ben Gamaliel, Joseph, Ben Gorion. Joseph, Ben Gorion and Hanan were named commissaries of Jerusalem. Eleazar, son of Simeon a demagogue without conviction, whose personal ambition was rendered dangerous by the treasures he possessed, was kept out designedly. At the same time commissiaries were chosen for the provinces; all were moderate with the exception of one only, Eleazar, son of Ananias, who was sent to Idumea. Josephus, who has since created for himself such a brilliant renown as a historian, was prefect of Galilee. There were in this selection many grave men who were willing, to a large extent, to try to maintain order, with the hopes of ruling the anarchical elements which threatened to destroy everything.

The ardour at Jerusalem was extreme. The town was like a camp, a manufactory of arms; on all sides were heard the cries of the young people exercising. The Jews in places remote from the East, especially in the Parthian kingdom, hastened thither, persuaded that the Roman Empire had had its day. They felt that Nero was approaching his end, and were convinced that the empire would disappear with him. This last representative of the title of Cæsar, lowering himself in shame and disgrace, appeared to be a pius omen. By placing themselves at this point of view they would consider the insurrection much less mad than it seems to be to us--to us who know that the empire had still within it the force necessary for many future rennaissances. They could really believe that the work of Augustus was broken up; they imagined any moment to see the Parthians rush into the Roman territories; and this would indeed have happened if through different causes the Arsacide policy had not been very weak at the time. One of the finest images of Enoch is that where the prophet sees the sword given to the sheep, and the sheep thus armed pursuing in their turn the savage beasts, whom they cause to flee before them. Such were the feelings of the Jews. Their want of military education did not allow them to understand how deceptive was their success over Florus and Cestius. Coins were struck copied from the type of those of the Macabees, bearing the effigies of the temple or some Jewish emblem, with the legends in archaic Hebrew characters. Dated by the years "of deliverance" or "of the freedom of Sion" these pieces were at first anonymous or sent forth in the name of Jerusalem; later on, they bore the names of the party leaders who exercised supreme authority by the will of some portion probably, indeed, in the first months of the revolt, Eleazar, son of Simon, who was in possession of an enormous quantity of silver, had dared to coin money while giving himself the title of "high priest." The monetary issues lasted, in any case, for a considerable time; they were called "the money of Jerusalem" or "the money of danger."

Hanan became more and more the chief of the moderate party. He hoped still to lead the mass of the people to peace; he sought under hand to stay the manufacture of arms, to paralyse resistance by giving himself the appearance of organising it. This is the most formidable game in a time of revolution:

Hanan was called a traitor by the revolutionaries. He had in the eyes of the enthusiasts the fault of seeing clearly; in the eyes of the historian, he cannot be absolved from having taken the falsest of positions, that which consists in making war without believing in it, only because he was impelled by ignorant fanatics. The commotion in the provinces was frightful. The complete Arab regions to the East and South of the Dead Sea threw into Judea masses of bandits, living by pillage and massacres. Order in such circumstances was impossible, for to establish order, it is necessary to expel the two elements which make up a revolution's strength--fanaticism and brigandage. Terrible positions those which give no alternative but that between appeal to the foreigner and anarchy! In Acrabatena, a young and brave partisan Simon, son of Gioras, pillaged and tortured all the rich people. In Galilee, Josephus tried in vain to maintain some discipline: a certain John of Gischala, a knavish and audacious agitator combining an implacable personality with an ardent enthusiasm, succeeded in carrying all before him. Josephus was reduced, according to the eternal custom of the East, to enrol the brigands and pay them regular wages as the ransom of the country.

Vespasian prepared himself for the difficult campaign which had been entrusted to him. His plan was to attack the insurrection from the north, to crush it first in Galilee, then in Judea, to throw himself in some sort upon Jerusalem; and when he should have moved everything towards this central point, where fatigue, famine and factions, could not fail to produce fearful scenes; to wait, or if that were not enough, to strike a heavy blow. He went first to Antioch where Agrippa came to join him with all his forces. Antioch had not till now had its massacre of Jews, doubtless because it had in its midst a large number of Greeks who had embraced the Jewish religion (most frequently under the Christian form) which moderated their hatred. Even at this moment the storm broke; the absurd accusation of having fired the city led to butcheries, followed by a very severe persecution, in which doubtless many disciples of Jesus suffered, being confounded with the adherents of a religion which was only the half of theirs.

The expedition set off in March, 67, and. following the ordinary route along the sea-shore, established its head-quarters at Ptolemais (Acre). The first shock fell on Galilee. The population was heroic. The little town of Jondifat, or Jotapata, recently fortified, made a tremendous resistance; not one of its defenders would survive; shut up in a position without issue, they killed each other. "Gallilean" became from that time the synonym for fanatic sectaries, seeking death as their part, taking it with a sort of stubbornness. Tiberias, Taricheus, and Gamala were not taken until after perfect butcheries; there have been in history few examples of an entire race thus broken. The waves of the quiet lake where Jesus had dreamed of the kingdom of Heaven were actually tinged with blood. The river was covered with putrefied corpses, the air was pestiferous, crowds of Jews took refuge on the coasts. Vespasian caused them to be killed or drowned. The rest of the population was sold. Six thousand captives were sent to Nero, in Achaia, to execute the most difficult work of piercing the Isthmus of Corinth; the old men were slaughtered. There was nothing but desertion. Josephus, whose nature had little depth, and who, besides, was always in doubt of the issue of this war, surrendered to the Romans, and was soon in the good graces of Vespasian and Titus. All his cleverness in writing had not succeeded in washing such a conduct from a certain varnish of cowardice.

The main part of the year 67 was employed in this war of extermination. Galilee had never recovered; the Christians who were found there took refuge beyond the lake. Henceforth there shall be nothing spoken of the country of Jesus in the history of Christianity. Gischala, which was taken last, fell in November or December. John of Gischala, who had defended it with fury, retreated, and sought to gain Judea. Vespasian and Titus made their winter quarters at Ceserea, preparing in the following year to lay siege to Jerusalem.

The great weakness of provisional governments organised for national defence is not being able to support defeat. In all cases, undermined by advanced parties, they fall on the day when they do not give to the superficial crowd what they have proclaimed--victory. John of Gischala and the fugitives from Galilee arriving each day at Jerusalem with rage in their hearts, still raised the diapason of fury in which the revolutionary party lived. Their breathing was hot and quick--"We are not conquered," they said, "but we seek better posts; why exhaust oneself is Gischala and these hovels when we have the mother city to defend?" "I have seen," said John of Gischala, "the machines of the Romans flying in pieces against the walls of the Gallilean villages; and, as they have not wings, they cannot break the ramparts of Jerusalem."

All the young people were for open war. Some troops of volunteers turned readily to pillage; bands of fanatics, either religious or political, always resemble brigands. It is necessary to live, and freebooters cannot live without vexing the people. That is why brigand and hero in times of national crisis are merely synonymous. A war party is always tyrannical; moderation has never saved a country, for the first principle of moderation is to yield to circumstances, and heroism consists generally in not listening to reason. Josephus, the man of order par excellence, is probably in the right when he represents the resolution not to retire as having been the deed of a small number of energetic people, drawing by force after them some tranquil citizens who would have asked nothing better than to submit,

It is more often thus; people obtain a great sacrifice from a nation without a dynasty which terrorises it. The mass is essentially timid, but the timid count for nothing in times of revolution. The enthusiasts are always small in number, but they impose themselves upon others by cutting the road to reconciliation. The law of such situations is that power falls necessarily into the hands of the most ardent, and that politicians are fatally powerless.

Before this intense fever, increasing every day, the position of the moderate party was not tenable. The bands of pillagers, after having ravaged the country, fell back upon Jerusalem, those who fled from the Roman armies came in their turn to huddle up in the town and to starve. There was no effective authority; the zealots ruled; all those who were even suspected of "moderantism" were massacred without mercy. Up to the present the war and its excesses were arrested by the barriers at the temple. Now the zealots and brigands dwelt pell-mell in the holy house; all the rules of legal purity were forgotten, the precincts were soiled with blood, men walked with their feet wet with it. In the eyes of the priest this was no doubt a most horrible state of affairs; to many devotees the "abomination" foretold by Daniel as installing himself in the holy place just before the last days. The zealots, like all military fanatics, made little of rights and subordinated them to the sacred work par excellence--the fight. They committed a fault not less grave in changing the order of the high priesthood. Without having regard to the privilege of the families from whom it had been the custom to take the high priests, they chose a branch little considered in the sacerdotal race, and they had recourse to the entirely democratic plan of the lot. The lot naturally gave absurd results. It fell upon a rustic whom it was necessary to bring to Jerusalem and clothe in spite of himself with the sacred garments, the high priesthood saw itself profaned by scenes of carnival. All the staid people, Pharisees, Sadducees, the Simeons, Ben Gamaliels, the Josephs, Ben Gorions were wounded in what was dearest to them.

So much excess at last decided the aristocratic Sadducean party to attempt a reaction. With much skill and courage Hanan sought to reunite the honest middle-class and all those who were reasonable, to over-turn this monstrous alliance between fanaticism and impiety. The zealots were arranged near, and obliged to shut themselves in the temple, which had become an ambulance for the wounded. To save the revolution they had recourse to a supreme effort; it was to call into the city the Idumeans--that is to say, troops of bandits accustomed to all manner of violence which raged around Jerusalem. The entrance of the Idumeans was marked by a massacre. All the members of the sacerdotal caste whom they could find were killed. Hanan and Jesus, son of Gamala, suffered fearful insults. Their bodies were deprived of sepulture, an outrage unheard-of among the Jews.

Thus perished the son of the principal author of the death of Jesus. The Beni-Hanan remained faithful up to the end of their part, and, if I might say so, to their duty. Like the larger number of those who seek to put a stop to the extravagances of sects and fanaticism, they were hot-headed, but they perished nobly. The last Hanan appears to have been a man of great capacity; he struggled nearly two years against anarchy. He was a true aristocrat, hard sometimes, but grave, and penetrated by a real feeling on public subjects, highly respected, liberal in the sense that he wished the government of the nation to be by its nobility, and not by violent factions. Josephus did not doubt that if he had lived he would have succeeded in making an honourable arrangement between the Romans and the Jews, and he regarded the day of his death as the moment when the city of Jerusalem and the republic of the Jews were definitely lost. It was at least the end of the Sadducean party, a party often haughty, egotistical and cruel, but which represented according to him the opinion which alone was rational and capable of saving the country. By Hanan's death, people would be tempted to say, according to common language, that Jesus was revenged. It was the Beni-Hanan who, in presence of Jesus, had made this reflection: "The consequence of all this is that the Romans will come and destroy the temple and nation;" and who had added: "Better that one man should die than a whole people be lost!" Let us observe an expression so artlessly impious. There is no more vengeance in history than in nature; revolutions are no more just than the volcano which bursts or the avalanche that rolls. The year 1793 did not punish Richelieu, Louis XIV., nor the founders of French unity; but it proved that they were men of narrow views, if they did not feel the emptiness of what they had done, the frivolity of their Machiavellianism, the uselessness of their deep policy, the foolish cruelty of their reasons of State. Ecclesiastes alone was a sage, the day when he cried out, disabused: "All is vanity under the sun."

With Hanan (in the first days of 68) perished the old Jewish priesthood, entailed in the great Sadducean families who had made such a strong opposition to budding Christianity. Deep was the impression, people, those highly respected aristocrats, whom they had so lately seen clothed in superb priestly robes, presiding over pompous ceremonies, and regarded with veneration by the numerous pilgrims who came to Jerusalem from the whole world, thrown naked outside of the city, given up to the dogs and jackals, It was a world which disappeared. The democratic high-priesthood which was inaugurated by the revolution was ephemeral. The Christians at first believed to raise two or three personages by ornamenting their foreheads with the priestly πέταλον. All this had no result. The priesthood, no more than the temple on which it depended, was not destined to be the principal thing in Judaism. The principal thing was the enthusiast, the prophet, the zealot, the messenger from God. The prophet had killed royalty, the enthusiast, the ardent sectary, had killed the priesthood. The priesthood and the kingdom once killed, the fanatic remained, and he during two and a half years yet fought against fate. When the fanatic shall have been crushed in his turn, there will remain the doctor, the rabbi, the interpreter of the Thora. The priest and the king will never rise again.

Nor the temple neither. Those zealots who, to the great scandal of the priests who were friends of the Romans, made the holy place a fortress and a hospital, were not so far as would appear at first sight from the sentiment of Jesus. What mattered those stones? The mind is the only thing which is reckoned, and that which defends the mind of Israel, the revolution, has a right to defile the stones. Since the day when Isaiah said: "What are your sacrifices tome? they disgust me; it is the righteousness of the heart I wish," material worship was an old-fashioned routine which must disappear.

The opposition between the priesthood and the national party, at bottom democratic, which admitted no other nobility than piety and observance of the law, is felt from the time of Nehemiah, who was already a Pharisee. The true Aaron, in the mind of wise men, is the good man. The Asmoneans, at once priests and kings, only inspired aversion among pious men. Sadduceeism, each day more unpopular and ravenous, was only saved by the distinction which people made between religion and its ministers. No kings--no priests--such was at bottom the Pharisaic ideal. Incapable of forming a State of its own, Judaism must have arrived at the point at which we see it through eighteen centuries, that is to say, to live like a parasite in the republics of others. It was likewise destined to become a religion without a temple and without a priest. The priest rendered the temple necessary: its destruction shall be a kind of riddance. The zealots who, in the year 68, killed the high priest and polluted the temple to defend God's cause, were therefore not outside the real tradition of Israel.

But it was clear that, deprived of all conservative ballast, delivered to a frantic management, the vessel would go to frightful perdition. After the massacre of the Sadducees terror reigned in Jerusalem without any restraining counterpois. The oppression was so great that no one dared openly to weep nor inter their dead. Compassion became a crime. The number of suspects of distinguished condition who perished through the cruelty of these madmen was about 12,000. Doubtless it is necessary here to consider the statements of Josephus. The history of that historian as to the domination of the zealots has something absurd in it; some impious and wretched people would not have had to be killed as they were. As well might one one seek to explain the French Revolution by the going out from the prison of some thousands of galley slaves. Pure wickedness has never done anything in the world; the truth is that these popular movements being the work of an obscure conscience and not of reason, are compromised by their very victory. According to the rule of all movements of the same kind the revolution of Jerusalem was only occupied in decapitating itself. The best patriots, those who had most contributed to the success of the year 66, Guion, Niger, the Perea, were put to death. All the people in comfortable circumstances perished. We are specially struck by the death of a certain Zacharias, son of Barak, the most honest man of Jerusalem and greatly beloved by all good people. They introduced him before a traditional jury who acquitted him unanimously. The zealots murdered him in the middle of the temple. Thus Zacharias, the son of Barak, would be a friend of the Christians, for we believe that we can trace an allusion to him in the prophetic words which the evangelists attribute to Jeans as to the terrors of the last days.

The extraordinary events of which Jerusalem was the theatre struck indeed the Christians in the highest degree. The peaceable disciples of Jesus, deprived of their leader, James the brother of the Lord continued at first to lead in the holy city their ascetic life, and waited about the temple to see the great reappearance. They had with them the other survivors of the family of Jesus, the sons of Clopas, regarded with the greatest veneration even by the Jews. All that occurred would appear to them an evident confirmation of the words of Jesus. What could these convulsions be if not the beginning of what was called the sufferings of Messiah, the preludes of the Messianic Incarnation? They were persuaded that the triumphant arrival of Christ would be preceded by the entry upon the scene of a great number of false prophets. In the eyes of the presidents of the Christian community, these false prophets were the leaders of the zealots. People applied to the present time the terrible phrases which Jesus had often in his mouth to express the plagues which should announce judgments. Perhaps there were seen rising in the bosom of the Church some enlightened persons pretending to speak in the name of Jesus. The elders made a most lively opposition to them; they were assured that Jesus had announced the coming of such seducers and warned them concerning them. That was sufficient; the hierarchy, already strong in the Church, the spirit of docility, the inheritance of Jesus arrested all the impostures; Christianity benefited by the great skill with which it knew how to create an authority in the very heart of a popular movement The budding episcopacy (or to express it better, the presbytery) prevented those aberrations from which the conscience of crowds never escapes when it is not directed. We feel from this point that the spirit of the Church in human things shall be a sort of good average sense, a conservative and practical instinct, and practice a defiance of democratic chimeras contrasting strangely with the enthusiasm of its supernatural principles.

This political wisdom of the representatives of the Church of Jerusalem was not without merit.

The zealots and the Christians had the same enemies, namely, the Sadducees, the Beni-Hanan. The ardent faith of the zealots could not fail to exercise a great seduction on the soul, not less enthusiastic, of the Judeo Christians. Those enthusiasts who carried away the crowds to the deserts to reveal to them the Kingdom of God resembled much John the Baptist and Jesus a little. Some believers to whom Jesus appeared joined the party and allowed themselves to be carried away. Everywhere the peaceful spirit inherent in Christianity carried it with it. The heads of the Church fought with those dangerous tendencies by the discourses which they maintained they had received from Jesus. "Take heed that they do not seduce you," for many shall come in my name saying: "The Messiah is here, or he is there." Do not believe them. For there shall arise false Messiahs, and false prophets, and they shall do great miracles, so, as if it were possible, to seduce the very elect. Recollect what I have told you before. If then some come saying to you, "Come, see, he is in the desert" do not go forth; "Come, see, he is in a hiding-place" do not believe them. There were doubtless some apostacies and treasons of brethren by brethren. Political divisions led to a coldness of affection, but the majority, while feeling in the deepest manner the crisis of Israel, gave no countenance to anarchy even when coloured by a patriotic pretext. The Christian manifesto of that solemn hour was a discourse attributed to Jesus, a kind of apocalypse, connected perhaps with some words pronounced by the Master, and which explained the connection of the final catastrophe, thenceforth held to be very near, with the political situation through which they were passing, It was not much later after the siege that the niece was written entirely; but certain words they have placed in Jesus' mouth are connected with the moment we have arrived at. "When ye shall see the abomination of desolation of which the prophet Daniel speaks, set up in the holy place (let the reader here understand), then let those who are in Judea flee to the mountains; let him who is on the roof not come down to his house to remove anything; let him who is in the fields not return to seek his cloak! Unfortunate shall be they who either nurse children or bear them in these days. And pray that your flight should not take place in the winter or the Sabbath day; for there shall be a tribulation such as has never been since the beginning of the world and never shall be again."

Other apocalypses of the same kind, circulated it appears, under Enoch's name, and presented with the discourses, attributed to Jesus some singular conflicting thoughts. In one of them the Divine Wisdom, introduced as a prophetic personage, reproaches the people with their crimes, the murder of prophets, hardness of heart. Some fragments which may be supposed to be preserved appear to allude to the murder of Zacharias, the son of Barak. There was here also a matter as to the "height of offence," what would be the highest degree of honour to which human malice could rise, and which appears to be the profanation of the temple by the zealots. Such monstrosities prove that the coming of of the Well-Beloved was near, and that the revenge of the righteous would not tarry. The Judeo-Christian believers especially held still too much to the temple for such a sacrilege to fill them with fear. Nothing had been seen like this since Nebuchadnezzar.

All the family of Jesus considered it was time to flee. The murder of James had already much weakened the connections of the Jerusalem Christians with Jewish orthodoxy; the divorce between the Church and the Synagogue was ripening every day. The hatred of the Jews to the pious sectaries, being no longer supported by the Roman law, led without doubt to more than one act of violence. The life of the holy people who as a habit dwelt in the precincts and conducted their devotion then were very much distressed, since the zealots had transformed the temple into a place of arms and had polluted it by assassinations. Some allowed themselves to say that the name which suited the city thus profaned was no longer that of Sion, but that of Sodom, and that the position of the true Israelites resembled that of their captive ancestors in Egypt.

The departure seems to have been decided on in the early months of 68. To give more authority to that resolution a report was spread to the effect that the heads of the community had received a revelation on this matter; according to some this revelation was made by the ministry of an angel. It is probable that all responded to the appeal of the leaders, and that none of the brethren remained in the city, which a very correct instinct showed them was doomed to extermination.

Some indications lead us to believe that the flight of the peaceful company was not carried out without danger. The Jews, as it would appear, pursued them, the terrorists in fact exercised an active overlook on the roads, and killed as traitors all those who sought to escape, unless at least they could pay a good ransom. A circumstance which is only indicated to us in covert words saved the fleeing people. "The dragon vomited after the woman (the Church of Jerusalem) a river to overwhelm and drown her; but the earth helped the woman, opened its mouth and drank up the river which the dragon had vomited towards her, and the dragon was full of anger against the woman." Possibly the zealots were among those who wished to throw the whole body of the faithful into the Jordan, and that they succeeded in escaping by passing through a part where the water was low; perhaps the party sent to destroy them wandered and also lost the tracks of those whom they pursued. The place chosen by the heads of the community to serve as the primitive seat for the fugitive church was Pella, one of the towns of the Decapolis, situated near the left bank of the Jordan, in an admirable site commanding on one side the plan of the Ghor, on the other some precipices, below which rolled a torrent. They could not have made a better choice. Judea, Idumea, and Perea, were concerned in the insurrection; Samaria and the coast were profoundly troubled by war; Scythopolis and Pella were the two most neutral towns near Jerusalem. Pella, by its position beyond the Jordan, could afford more tranquility than Scythopolis, which had become one of the military stations of the Romans. Pella was a free city like all the places in the Decapolis, but it appears that it was given to Agrippa II. To take refuge there was to express strongly their horror of the revolt. The importance of the town dated from the Macedonian conquest; a colony of veterans from Alexandria was established there and changed the Semitic name to another which recalled their native country to the old soldiers. Pella was taken by Alexander Janneus; the Greeks who lived there refused to be circumcised and suffered much from Jewish fanaticism. Doubtless the heathen population had become rooted again there, for in the massacre of 66 Pella figures as a town of the Syrians and found itself again sacked by the Jews. It was in this Anti-Jewish town that the church of Jerusalem had its retreat during the horrors of the siege. It was well placed, and the church looked upon this locality as a safe abode, as a desert which God had prepared for it in which to wait in quietness, far from the torments of mankind, the home of the reappearance of Jesus. The community lived upon its savings, and they believed that God himself would take care to nourish it, and many saw in such a fate, so different from that of the Jews, a miracle which the prophets had foretold. Doubtless the Christians of Galilee on their side had passed to the East of the Jordan and the lake into Batanea and the Gaulonites. In this manner the lands of Agrippa II, were a country of adoption for Judeo-Christians of Palestine. What gave a special importance to this Christian body in retirement is that it carried with it the remainder of the family of Jesus, surrounded by the most profound respect, and designated in Greek by the name of Deposyni, the relations of the Master. We shall soon see indeed the Trans-Jordanic Christianity continued in Ebionism, that is to say the very tradition of the word If Jesus. The synoptical gospels were the product of it.

CHAPTER XIII

THE DEATH OF NERO

Since the first appearance of the spring of the year 68, when Vespasian undertook the campaign, his plan, we have already said, was to crush Judaism step by step, proceeding from the north and west towards the south and east, to force the fugitives to shut themselves up in Jerusalem, and there to slay without mercy that seditious multitude. He advanced as far as Emmaus, seven leagues from Jerusalem, at the foot of the great acclivity which stretches from the plain of Lydda to the Holy City. He did not consider that the time had yet come for this latter plan. He ravaged Idumea and Samaria, and on the 3rd of June he established his general quarters at Jericho, when he sent to massacre the Jews of Perea. Jerusalem was besieged on all sides, a circle of extermination surrounded it. Vespasian returned to Cesarea to assemble his entire forces, where he received news which made him stop short, and whose effect was to prolong by two years the resistance and the revolution at Jerusalem.

Nero died on the 8th of June. During the great struggles in Judea which we are relating, he had carried on in Greece the life of an artist; he only returned to Rome at the end of 67. He had never enjoyed himself so much; for his sake they had made all the games coincide in one year, all the towns sent him the prizes of their games, at every moment deputations came to seek him, to beg him to sing to them. The great child ninny, or perhaps jester, was entranced with joy. The Greeks alone know how to hear, said he, the Greeks alone are worthy of me and of my efforts. He extended to them great privileges, he proclaimed the liberty of Greece to the two isthmuses, paid liberally the oracles who prophecied to his taste, suppressed those who did not please him, and it is said caused to be strangled a singer who did not use his voice so that it did not appear better than his own. Hellius, one of the wretches to whom at his departure he had left full powers over Rome and the Senate, pressed him to return. The gravest political symptoms began to show themselves. Nero replied that his reputation was the first thing to be considered, and it obliged him to harbour his resources for a time when he should have no empire. His constant prepossession was indeed that if fortune should ever reduce him to a private condition he would be able quite well to make his art sufficient for him; and when they made the remark to him that he was fatiguing himself too much, he said that the exercise which for him was only the pastime of a prince, would perhaps be his bread winner. One of those things which most flatters the vanity of people of the world who occupy themselves a little in art or literature, is to imagine that if they should become poor they could live by their talents. As to that he had a voice which was weak and hollow, although he observed, in order to preserve it, medical prescriptions; his phonasque did not quit him and ordered him at every moment the most puerile precautions. We blush to think that Greece stained itself by this ignoble masquerade. Some towns indeed received him very well. The wretch did not dare to enter Athens; he was not asked. The most alarming news was brought to him; it was nearly a year since he had quitted Rome; he gave the order for return. In every town they gave him triumphal honours; they levelled the walls to let him enter. At Rome there was an extraordinary carnival. He mounted the car on which Augustus had his triumph; beside him was seated the musician Diodorus; upon his head he had the Olympic crown; in his right hand the Pythic crown, before him they bore the other crowns, and upon some placards the roll of his victories; the names of those he had conquered, the titles of the pieces in which he had played, the claquers, trained in three kinds of claque, and the knights of Augustus followed. They pulled down the arch of the grand circus to allow him to enter, and cries were heard: "Long live the Olympian! the Pythi hero Augustus! Augustus! Nero-Hercules! Nero-Apollo! only Periodonicist! The only one who has ever been Augustus! Augustus! So sacred voice! Happy those who could hear it!" The thousand eight hundred and eight crowns, which he had brought back from Greece, were placed in the grand circus and attached to the Egyptian obelisk, which Augustus had placed there to serve as a meta. At last the conscience of the noble portions of human nature awoke. The East, with the exception of Judea, bore without a blush this shameful tyranny and contented themselves with it; but the feeling of honour still lived in the West. It is one of the glories of France that the overthrow of such a tyranny was its work. While the German soldiers, full of hatred against the republicans and slaves for their principle of fidelity, played in regard to Nero as to all the emperors, the part of good Swiss and gardes du corps; the cry of revolt was raised by an Aquitanian, a descendant of the ancient kings of the country. The movement was truly French. Without calculating the consequences the Gallican regions threw themselves into the revolution with enthusiasm. The signal was given by Vindex about the 15th of March, 68. The news came quickly to Rome. The walls were soon chalked over with scandalous inscriptions, "By the dint of singing, say vile scoffers, he has awakened the cocks (Gallos)." Nero at first laughed. He felt quite glad, that he had been furnished with an occasion of enriching himself by pillaging the Gauls. He continued to sing to amuse himself until the moment when Vindex began to post proclamations in which he was treated as a wretched artist. The actor wrote then from Naples, where he was, to the Senate to demand justice, and took the route for Rome. He affected only however to interest himself in some musical instruments newly invented, and especially in a kind of hydraulic organ, upon which he solemnly consulted the Senate and the Knights.

The news of the defection of Galba (3rd April) and the alliance of Spain with Gaul, which he received while he was at dinner, came upon him like a thunder-clap. He overturned the table where he ate, tore up the letter and smashed two engraved vases of great value, out of which he was accustomed to drink.. In the ridiculous preparations which he began, his principal care was for his instruments, the theatrical baggage for his women, whom he had dressed as Amazons, with targets and hatchets, and having their hair cut short. There were strange alternations of depression and buffoonery, which we hesitate sometimes whether to take as serious, or rather to treat as absurd; all the acts of Nero floating between the black wickedness of a cruel booby and the irony of a roué. He had not an idea which was not childish. The pretended world of art in which he lived had rendered him completely silly. Sometimes he thought less of fighting than going to weep without arms before his enemies. Thinking to touch their hearts, he composed already the epinicium which he should sing with them on the morning of the reconciliation; at other times he wished to have all the senate massacred, to bum Rome a second time, and to let loose the beasts of the amphitheatre upon the city. The French especially were the objects of his rage; he spoke of causing those who were in Rome to be killed, as being implicated with their compatriots and wishing to join them. At intervals he had the thought of changing the seat of his empire and retiring to Alexandria. He remembered that some prophets had promised him the empire of the east and especially the throne of Jerusalem, and he dreamed that his musical talent would give him a means of livelihood, and this possibility, which would be the better proof of his talents, afforded him a secret joy. Then he consoled himself with literature; he made the remark that his position had something particular about it, all that had happened to him was quite unheard of; never had any prince lost alive such a great empire. Never in the days of his most bitter anguish did he change any of his habits. He spoke more of literature than of the affairs of the French; he sang, he made jests, he went to the theatre incognito, wrote with his own hand to an actor who pleased him: "Keep a man so busy, it is bad."

The little agreement in the armies of Gaul, the death of Vindex, and the weakness of Galba would perhaps have adjourned the deliverance of the world, if the Roman army in its turn had not made itself heard. The praetorians revolted and proclaimed Galba; on the evening on the 8th of June Nero saw that all was lost. His ridiculous mind suggested to him nothing but grotesque ideas. Clothing himself in mourning habits he went to harangue the people in this dress, employing all his scenic power to obtain thus a pardon of the past, or, for want of better, prefecture of Egypt. He wrote his speech. He was told before he arrived at the forum he would be torn in pieces. He lay down; awaking in the middle of the night he found himself without guards. They already had pillaged his room. He rose and struck at different doors and no one replied. He came back, wished to die, and asked for the myrmillon Spicullus, a brilliant slayer, one of the celebrities of the amphitheatre. Everyone deserted him. He went out wandering alone in the streets, thought of throwing himself into the Tiber, and then retraced his steps. The world appeared to make a void about him. Phaon, his freed man, offered him then his villa residence, situated between the Salarian and Nomentan ways, about a league and a half off. The unfortunate man, slightly clothed, covered with a poor mantle, mounted on a wretched horse, his face covered so as not to be recognised, went forth, accompanied by three or four of his freed men, among whom were Phaon, Sporus, Epaphroditus, his secretary. It was not yet quite light; in going through Colline gate he heard in the camp of the Prætorians, near which he passed, the cries of the soldiers who cursed him and proclaimed Galba. A start of his horse caused by the stench of a corpse thrown in the way, caused him to be recognised. He was able to reach Phaon's villa by gliding flat on his belly under the bushwood, and concealing himself behind the rose trees.

His comical mind and vulgar slang did not abandon him. They wished him to squat in a hole like a pouzzalana, as is often seen in some places. This was for him the occasion of a joke. "What a fate, to go to live under the earth." His reflections were like a running fire intermixed with dull pleasantries and wooden-headed remarks. He had upon each circumstance a literary reminiscence, a cool antithesis; "he who once was proud of his numerous suite, has now no more than three freed men." Sometimes the memory of his victims would come back to him, but only struck him as figures of rhetoric, never led to a moral act of repentance. The comedian survived through all. His situation was for him nothing but a drama--a drama which he had recited. Recalling the parts in which he had figured as a patricide or princes reduced to the condition of beggars, he remarked that now he played all that on his own account and would sing this verse, which a tragedian had placed in the mouth of OEdipus:

71

"My wife, my mother, my father

Pronounce my death warrant."

Incapable of a serious thought, he wished them to dig his grave the size of his body, and made them beat pieces of marble, some water and wood at his funeral procession, weeping and saying. "What an artist this is who has died!"

The courier of Phaon meanwhile brought a despatch. Nero tore it from him; he read that the senate had declared him the public enemy and had condemned him to be punished according to the ancient custom. "What is that custom?" asked he. They told him that the head of the culprit, quite bare, was stuck into a fork while they beat it with rods until death followed. Then the body was drawn by a hook and thrown into the Tiber. He trembled, took two poignards which he had on him, tried their points, sheathed them again, saying the fatal hour had not yet come. He engaged Sporus to begin his funeral dirge, tried hard to kill himself and could not. His awkwardness, this kind of talent which he had for making all the fibres of the soul vibrate falsely, that laugh at once brutal and infernal, that pretentious stupidity which made his whole life resemble the memory of Agrippa's Sabbat, attained to the sublime of absurdity. He could not succeed in killing himself. "Is there no one here to set an example to me?" he said. He redoubled his quotations, spoke in Greek, and made some bits of verse. All at once they heard the noise of a detachment of cavalry which came to take him alive.

The steps of the heavy horses fall upon my ears,

said he. Epaphroditus then took his poignard and plunged it into his neck. The centurion came in nearly at the same moment. He wished to stop the blood, and sought to make him believe he had come to save him. "Too late!" said the dying man, whose eyes rolled in his head and glazed with horror, "Behold where fidelity is found!" added he, expiring. It was his last comic feature. Nero giving vent to a melancholy complaint upon the wickedness of his century, upon the disappearance of good faith and virtue! Let us applaud, the drama is complete! Once more, Nature, with the thousand faces, thou hast known how to find an actor worthy of such a part!

He had held much to this, that they should not deliver his head to insults, and that they should not burn him entirely. His two nurses and Actea, who loved him still, bound him secretly in a rich white shroud, embroidered with gold and with all the luxury they knew he loved. They laid his ashes in the tomb of Domitius, a great mausoleum which commanded the gardens (The Pincio) and made a fine effect from the Campus Martius. From thence his ghost haunted the Middle Ages like a vampire; to conquer the apparitions which haunted the district, they built the Church of Santa Maria del Popolo.

Thus perished, at thirty-one years of age, after having reigned thirteen years and eight months, the sovereign --not the most foolish or the most wicked, but the vainest and the most ridiculous, whom the chance of events had brought into the first ranks of history. Nero is beyond everything a literary perversion; he was far from being destitute of all talent or of all honesty; this poor young man, intoxicated with bad literature, drunk with acclamations, who forgot his empire for Terpnos, who, receiving the news of the revolt of the Gauls did not withdraw from the spectacle at which he assisted, shewed his favour to the athlete, and did not think during many days of anything but his lyre and his voice. The most culpable in all of this were the people most greedy of pleasure, who exacted above all that their sovereign should amuse them, and also the false taste of the time, which had inverted the order of greatness, and gave too large a value to the man of renown in letters and the artist. The danger of literary education is that it inspires an inordinate love of glory without ever affording a serious moral, which fixes the meaning of true glory. It was destined that a natural and subtle vanity, longing for the immense and the infinite, but without any judgment, should make a deplorable shipwreck. But his qualities, such as aversion to war, became fatal, by leaving him with no taste but for ways of shining which should not have been his. At least, as he was not a Marcus Aurelius, it was not good to be so far removed from the prejudices of his caste and his condition. A prince is a soldier, a great prince can and should protect letters. He ought not to be a literateur. Augustus, Louis XIV., presiding over a brilliant development of mind, are, after the cities of genius like Athens and Florence, the finest spectacle of history. Nero, Chilperic, King Louis of Bavaria, are caricatures. In the case of Nero the enormous nature of the imperial power, and the harshness of Roman manners, caused that caricature to appear outlined in blood.

It is often asserted, to shew the irremediable nature of the masses, that Nero was popular in some points of view. The fact is that he had upon his own account two currents of opposite opinion. All those who were serious and honest detested him, the lower people loved him, some artlessly and by the vague sentiment which makes the poor plebeian love his prince if he has a brilliant exterior, the others because he intoxicated them with feasts. During those fêtes they saw him mixing with the crowd, dining, eating in the theatre in the midst of the mob. Did he not besides hate the Senate, the Roman nobility, whose character was so harsh and so little popular? The companions who surrounded him were at least amiable and polite. The soldiers of the guard always preserved their affection for him. For a long time his tomb was found always ornamented with fresh flowers, and portraits of him were placed in the rostra by unknown hands. The origin of the good fortune of Otho was that he had been his confidant and that he imitated his manners. Vitellius, to make himself acceptable at Rome, affected openly to take Nero as his model, and to follow his methods of government. Thirty or forty years after, all the world wished he were still living, and longed for his return.

This popularity, in reward to which there is no need to be too much surprised, had in fact a singular result. The report was spread abroad that the object of so many regrets was not really dead. During the life of Nero, there had been seen to dawn in the staff of the emperor, the idea that he would be dethroned at Rome, but that there would commence for him a new reign, Oriental and almost Messianic. People have always had a difficulty in believing that men who have a long time occupied the attention of the world disappear for ever. The death of Nero at Phaon's villa in the presence of a small number of witnesses had not had a very public character. All that concerned his burial had passed among three women, who were devoted to him. Icellus almost alone had seen the corpse; nothing recognisable remained of his person. They might believe in a substitution; some affirmed that the body had never been found, others declared that the gash he had made in his neck had been bandaged and healed. Nearly all maintained that at the instigation of the Parthian ambassador at Rome, he had taken refuge among the Arsacides, his allies, eternal enemies of the Romans, or that he had gone to the king of Armenia, Tiridatus, whose journey to Rome in 66, had been accompanied by magnificent fêtes, which had struck the people. There he was planning the ruin of the empire. Soon they would see him return at the head of the cavaliers of the East to torture those who had betrayed him. His partisans lived in that hope. Already they raised statues to him, and made edicts even to be current in his signature. The Christians, on the contrary, considered him as a monster, and, when they heard such reports, in which they believed as much as the other people, were smitten with terror. The imaginations which he kindled lasted for a very long time, and, according to what occurs nearly always in similar circumstances, there were many false Neros. We shall see soon the counterpart of that opinion in the Christian church, and the place which it holds in the prophetic literature of the time.

The strangeness of the spectacles in which they has taken part left few winds in their sober senses. Human nature had been pushed to the limits of the possible, there remained the vacuum which follows fits of fever;--everywhere spectres and visions of blood. It was said that at the moment when Nero came out through the Colline gate to take refuge in Phaon's villa, a flash struck his eyes, and that at the same moment the earth trembled as if it were opening, and that the souls of all those whom he had killed threw themselves upon him. There was in the air as it were a thirst for vengeance. Soon we shall assist at one of the interludes of the grand heavenly drama, where the souls of the slain, lying under God's altar, cry with a loud voice "Oh Lord, how long till thou shalt demand our blood from those who inhabit the earth," and there shall be given to them a white robe because they have to wait a little longer!

CHAPTER XIV

PLAGUES AND PROGNOSTICS

The first impression on the Jews and Christians at the news of the revolt of Vindex had been that of extreme joy. They believed that the empire would end with Cæsar's house, and that the revolted generals, full of hatred to Rome, would not think of anything except rendering themselves independent in their respective provinces. The movement of the Gauls was accepted in Judea as having a significance analogous to that of the Jews themselves. There war was a deep error. No part of the empire, Judea excepted, wished to see broken up that great association which gave to the world peace and material prosperity. All the countries on the borders of the Mediterranean, once at enmity, were delighted to live together. Gaul itself, although less peaceful than the rest, limited its revolutionary desires to the overthrow of the bad emperors, to demanding reform, and to seeking for a liberal government. But we can imagine that people, accustomed to the ephemeral kingdoms of the East, should have regarded as finished an empire whose dynasty was about to be extinguished, and should have believed that the different nations subjugated one or two centuries before would form separate States under the generals who held the command. For eighteen months, in fact, none of the leaders of the revolted legions succeeded in putting down his rivals in a permanent way. Never had the world been seized with such a trembling; at Rome the nightmare of Nero scarcely dispelled; at Jerusalem a whole nation in a state of madness; the Christians under the stroke of the fearful massacre of the year 64; the earth itself a prey to the most violent convulsions; the whole world was as in a vertigo. This planet appeared to be shaken and unable to endure. The horrible degree of wickedness which heathen society had reached, the extravagances of Nero, his golden house, his absurd art, his colossi, his portraits more than a hundred feet in height, had literally made the world mad. Some natural plagues broke out in all directions, and held men's minds in a kind of terror.

When we read the Apocalypse without knowing the date or having its key, such a book appears the work of the most capricious and individual fancy; but when we replace the strange vision in this interregnum from Nero to Vespasian, in which the empire passed through the gravest crisis it had known, the work appears in the most extraordinary sympathy with the state of men's minds; we may add with the state of the globe, for we shall soon see that the physical history of the world at the same period furnishes its elements. The world really dotted on miracles; never had it been so impressed by omens. The God-Father appeared to have veiled his face; certain unclean larvæ, monsters coming forth from a mysterious slime, appeared to be wandering through the air. Everyone believed that the world was on the eve of some unheard-of event, Belief in the signs of the times and prodigies was universal; scarcely more than a few hundreds of educated men saw their absurdity. Some charlatans, more or less authentic depositaries of the old chimeras of Babylon, played on the ignorance of the people and pretended to explain omens. These wretches became personages; the time was passed in expelling and then recalling them; Otho and Vitellius especially were entirely given up to them. The highest politics did not disdain to take note of these puerile dreams.

One of the most important branches of Babylonian divination was the interpretation of monstrous births, considered as implying certain indications of coming events. This idea more than any other had overrun the Roman world; the many-headed foetus especially was considered as an evident omen, each head, according to a symbolism we shall see adapted by the author of the Apocalypse, representing an emperor. There were some real or pretended hybrid forms In that matter also the unwholesome visions and incoherent images of the Apocalypse are the reflection of the popular tales with which peoples' minds were filled. A pig with a hawk's talons was held to be the very picture of Nero. Nero himself was very curious in regard to these monstrosities.

Men were also preoccupied with meteors and signs in the sky. The bolides made the greatest impression. It is known that the frequency of the bolides is a periodic phenomenon, which occurs nearly every thirty years. On these occasions there are some nights when, literally, the stars have the appearance of falling from heaven. Comets, eclipses, parhelia, and aurora borealis, in which were seen crowns, swords, and stripes of blood; burning clouds of plastic forms, in which were designed battles and fantastic animals; were greedily remarked and never appear to have been observed with such intensity as during these tragic years. People spoke only of showers of blood, astonishing effects of lightning, streams flowing upwards to their course, and rivers of blood. A thousand things to which people had paid no attention obtained through the feverish emotion of the public an exaggerated importance. The infamous charlatan, Balbillus, took advantage of the impression which these events sometimes made on the emperor, to excite his suspicions against the most illustrious, and to draw from him the cruellest orders.

The plagues of the period, besides, justified up to a certain point these madnesses. Blood ran in floods on all sides. The death of Nero, which was a deliverance in many points of view, began a period of civil wars. The battle of the legions of Gaul under Vindex and Virginius had been frightful; Galilee was the theatre of an unexampled extermination; the war of Corbulon among the Parthians had been most murderous. There was still worse than that in the future; the fields of Bedriac and Cremona soon exhaled an odour of blood. Punishments made the amphitheatre like hell. The cruelty of the military and civil manners had banished all pity from society. Withdrawing themselves trembling to their humble abodes, the Christians doubtless again repeated the words they attributed to Jesus: "When ye hear of wars and rumours of wars, be not troubled, for this must be; but the end is not yet. Nation shall be seen rising against nation, kingdom against kingdom; there shall be great earthquakes, shakings, famines, pestilences on all sides, and great signs in the heavens. These are the beginnings of sorrows."

Famine, indeed, was added to the massacres. In the year 68 the arrivals from Alexandria were insufficient. At the beginning of March, 69, an inundation of the Tiber was most disastrous. The wretchedness was fearful; a sudden eruption of the sea covered Lycia with mourning. In the year 65, a horrible pestilence afflicted Rome; during the autumn the dead were reckoned at 30,000. In the same year everybody spoke of the fearful fire at Lyons. And the Campagna was ravaged by water-spouts and cyclones, whose outbreaks were heard even at the gates of Rome. The order of nature seemed reversed; fearful storms spread terror in all directions.

But what struck people most was the earthquakes. The globe underwent a convulsion parallel to that of the moral world; it seemed as if the world and the human race had fever at the same time. It is a peculiarity of popular movements to mix together all that excites the imagination of the crowds, at the time when they are carried out. A natural phenomenon, a great crime, a crowd of things accidental or without apparent connection, are linked together in the grand rhapsody which humanity composes from age to age. It is thus that the history of Christianity is incorporated with everything which at different periods has shaken the people. Nero and the Solfatara had as much importance there as theological argument; a place must be given to geology, and the Solfatara and the catastrophes of the planet. Of all natural phenomena besides earthquakes are those which most cause men to abase themselves before unknown forces. The countries where they are frequent, Naples and Central America, have superstition in an endemic condition; there must be said as much for the ages in which they raged with a peculiar violence. Now never were they more common than in the first century. No time could be remembered when the surface of the old continent had been so greatly agitated.

Vesuvius was preparing for its terrible eruption of 79. On the 5th February, 63, Pompeii was nearly engulfed by an earthquake. A great number of the inhabitants would not re-enter it. The volcanic centre of the Bay of Naples at the time of which we speak was near Pouzzoles and Cuma. Vesuvius was still silent, but that series of little craters which constitute the district to the west of Naples and which are called the Phlegrean Fields, shewed everywhere the mark of fire. Avernus, the Acherusia palus (the lake Fusaro), the lake Aguano, the Solfatara, the little extinct volcanoes of Astroni, Camaldoli, Ischia, and Nisida, present to-day something squalid; the traveller takes away an impression of them rather more pleasant than frightful. Such was not the sentiment of antiquity. These stoves, these deep grottoes, these thermal springs, those bubblings up, those miasmas, those hollow sounds, those yawning mouths, (bocche d'inferno) vomiting out sulphur and fiery vapours, inspire Virgil. They were likewise one of the essential factors in the Apocalyptic literature. The Jew who disembarked at Pouzzoles to proceed to business or intrigue at Rome, saw this ground smoking in all its pores, shaking without ceasing, as if its bowels were peopled by giants and agonies. The Solfatara especially appeared to him the pit of the abyss, the airhole scarcely shutting out hell. Was the continuous jet of sulphurous vapour which escapes through this opening not in his eyes the manifest proof of a subterranean lake of fire destined plainly, like the lake of Pentapolis, for the punishment of sinners? The moral spectacle of the country did not astonish him less. Baïa was a town of waters and baths, the centre of luxury and pleasure, the favourite residence of light society. Cicero aid himself harm among grave people by having his villa in the midst of this kingdom of brilliant and dissolute manners. Propertius only wished his mistress dwelt there; Petronius placed there the debauches of Trimalcion, Baïa, Bauli, Cuma, Misena, saw, in fact, all follies and all crimes. The basin of azure blue waves included in the contour of this delicious bay was the bloody naumachia, into which they cast thousands of victims in the fêtes of Caligula and Claudius. What a reflection would arise in the mind of the pious Jew, of the Christian who called with fervour for the conflagration of the world at sight of this nameless spectacle, the absurd construction, in the midst of the waves, those baths, the object of horror to the puritans? Only one. "Blind that they are," they would say, "their future dwelling is under these; they dance over the hill which is to swallow them up."

Nowhere is such an expression which is applied to Pouzzoles or other places of the same character more striking than in the book of Enoch. According to one of the authors of that bizarre Apocalypse, the residence of the fallen angels is a subterranean valley situated in the west near the "mountain of metals." This mountain is filled with flames of fire, it breathes an odour of sulphur; there go forth from it bubbling and sulphurous streams (thermal waters) which are used to cure diseases and near which the kings and great men of the earth gave themselves up to all sorts of pleasures. The fools! they see every day the chastisement which they are preparing for themselves, and nevertheless they do not pray to God. This valley of fire is perhaps the valley of Gehenna, to the east of Jerusalem, bounded at the depression of the Dead Sea by the Quadi en-nâr (the valley of fire), then there are the springs of Callirrhoe, the pleasure place of the I3erods, and the entire demoniacal region of Machero, which is in the neighbourhood. But thanks to the elasticity of the apocryphal topography the baths can also be those of Baïa and Cuma. In the valley of fire there can be recognised the Solfatara of Pouzzoles or the Phlegrean fields in the mountain of metals, Vesuvius, such as it was before the eruption of 79. We shall soon see these strange places inspiring the author of the Apocalypse, and the pit of the abyss revealing itself to him ten years before nature, by a singular coincidence, reopened the crater of Vesuvius. For the people, that was no chance occurrence. It caused that the most tragic country in the world, that which was the theatre of the great reigns of Caligula, Claudius, and Nero, was found at the same time the country par excellence of phenomena, which nearly the whole world then considered as infernal. could not be without result.

It was besides not only Italy, it was the eastern regions of the Mediterranean which trembled. For two centuries Asia Minor was in one continual quake. The towns were unceasingly occupied in reconstructing themselves; certain places like Philadelphia experienced shocks every day. Tralles was in a condition of perpetual falling down; they were obliged to invent for the houses a system of mutual support. In the year 17 he destruction of fourteen towns in the district of Timolus and Messogis took place; it was the most terrible catastrophe of which mention had ever been made till then. In the years 23, 34, 37, 46, 51 and 53 there were partial misfortunes in Greece, Asia and Italy. Thera tans in a condition of active labour, Antioch was incessantly shaken. From the year 59, indeed, there was scarcely a year which was not marked by some disaster. The valley of the Lycus in particular, with its Christian cities of Laodocea and Colosse, was engulfed in the year 60. When we reflect that exactly there was the centre of the millenarian ideas, we are persuaded that a close connection existed between the revelation of Patmos and the overturnings in the globe, so much so that there is here one of the rare examples which can be quoted of a reciprocal influence between the material history of the planet and the history of mental development. The impression of the catastrophes in the valley of the Lycus is found likewise in the Sibylline poems. These earthquakes in Asia spread terror everywhere; people spoke about them over the world, and the number of those who did not see in those accidents the signs of an angry divinity was very small

All this made a sort of gloomy atmosphere, in which the imagination of the Christians found a strong excitement. Now, in view of the commotion of the physical and moral world, would not the believers cry with more assurance than ever, Maranatha, Maranatha! "Our Lord is coming, our Lord is coming." The earth appeared to them to be crumbling, and already they believed they saw the kings and powerful men and the rich fleeing as they cried "Mountains, fall upon us, bills, conceal us." A constant habit of mind of the old prophets was to take occasion by some natural plague to announce the near approach of the "day of Jehovah." A passage in Joel which was applied to Messianic times gave as certain prognostications of the great day signs in heaven and on the earth, prophets arising from all parts, rivers of blood, fire, pillars of smoke, the sun darkened, the moon bloody. They believed likewise that Jesus had announced earthquakes, famines, and pestilences as the overtures to the great day; then, as foregoing indexes of his coming, eclipses, the moon obscured, the stars falling from the firmament, the whole heaven troubled, the sea foaming, the people flying despairing, without knowing on which side was safety or death. Fear became thus an element of the whole Apocalypse; the idea of persecution was associated with it. It was admitted that the Evil one before being destroyed would redouble his rage and give proof of a skilful art in order to exterminate the saints.

CHAPTER XV

TUE APOSTLES IN ASIA

The province of Asia was that most agitated by those terrors. The church at Colosse had received a mortal blow by the catastrophe of the year 60. Hierapolis, although built in the midst of the most bizarre dejections of a volcanic eruption, did not suffer, it seems. It was perhaps there that the Colossian believers took refuge. Everything shows us from that time Hierapolis as a city apart. The profession of Judaism was public there. Some inscriptions still existing among the wonderfully preserved ruins of that extraordinary city mention the annual distributions which should be made to some corporations of workmen, from "the feast of unleavened bread," and from "the feast of Pentecost." Nowhere were good works, charitable institutions, and societies for mutual help among people following the same trade of so much importance. Kinds of orphanages, créches or children's homes, evidence philanthropic cares singularly developed. Philadelphia presents an analogous aspect; the state bodies there became the basis of political divisions. A peaceful democracy of workmen, associated among themselves and not occupied with politics, was the social form of almost all those rich towns of Asia and Phrygia. Far from being forbidden to a slave, virtue was considered to be the special portion of the man who suffers. About the time we are writing of, was born at Hierapolis an infant even so poor that they sold it in its cradle, and never knew it except under the name of the "bought slave," Epictetus, a name which, thanks to him, has become the synonym of virtue itself. One day there shall come forth from his instructions, the wonderful book, a manual for strong souls who reject the supernatural of the Gospel, and who believe that duty is falsified by creating in it any other charm than that of its austerity.

In the eyes of Christianity Hierapolis had an honour which far surpassed that of having given birth to Epictetus. It gave hospitality to one of the few survivors of the first Christian generation, to one of those who had seen Jesus, the Apostle Philip. We may suppose that Philip came into Asia after the crises which rendered Jerusalem uninhabitable for peaceful people, and expelled the Christians from its midst. Asia was the province where the Jews were most at peace; thither flowed the others. The relations between Rome and Hierapolis were likewise easy and regular. Philip was a priestly personage and belonged to the old school, very analogous to James. It was pretended that he wrought miracles, even the raising of the dead. He had four daughters, who were prophetesses. It appears that one of these died before Philip came into Asia. Of the three others, two grew old in their virginity; the fourth married during her father's life, prophesied like her sisters, and died at Ephesus. These strange women were very famous in Asia. Papias, who was bishop of Hierapolis about the year 130, had known them, but he had never seen the Apostle himself. He heard from these old enthusiastic women some extraordinary facts and marvellous recitals of their father's miracles. They also knew many things as to the other Apostles or Apostolic personages, especially a Joseph Barnabus, who, according to them, had drank a deadly poison without being harmed.

Thus, on John's side, there was constituted in Asia a second centre of authority and Apostolic tradition. John and Philip elevated the countries which they had chosen to reside in nearly to the level of Judea. "These two great stars of Asia," as they were called, were for some years the lighthouse of the church, deprived of its other pastors. Philip died at Hierapolis and was buried there. His virgin daughter arrived at a very advanced age and was laid near him; she that was married was interred at Ephesus; all the graves, it was said, were visible in the second century. Hierapolis had thus Apostolic tombs, rivals of those at Ephesus. The province would appear to be ennobled by those holy bodies, which they imagined they could see rising from the dead on the day in which the Lord should come, full of glory and majesty, to raise his elect from the dead.

The crisis in Judea, by dispersing, about 68, the apostles and apostolic men, would yet bring to Ephesus and into the valley of the Meander, other considerable personage in the nascent Church. A very great number of disciples, in any ease, who had seen the Apostles at Jerusalem, were found in Asia, and appear to have led that wandering life from town to town which was much to the taste of the Jews. Perhaps the mysterious personages called Presbyteros Johannes and Aristion were among the emigrés. Those listeners to the Twelve spread throughout Asia the tradition of the Church of Jerusalem, and succeeded in giving Judeo-Christianity the preponderance there. They were eagerly questioned as to the sayings of the apostles and the authentic words of Jesus. Later on those who had seen them were so proud of having drunk from the pure source, that they despised the little writings which claimed to report the discourses of Jesus.

There was something very peculiar about the state of mind in which these churches lived buried in the depths of a province whose peaceful climate and profound heaven appeared to lead to mysticism. In no place did the Messianic ideas so much preoccupy men's attention. They gave themselves up to extravagant imaginations, the most absurd parabolic language, coming from the traditions of Philip and John, were propagated. The gospel which was formed on this coast had something mythical and peculiar about it. It was imagined generally that after the resurrection of the bodies which was nigh at hand there would be a corporeal reign of Christ upon the earth which should last a thousand years. The delights of this paradise were described in a thoroughly materialistic way; they actually measured the size of the grapes and the strength of the ears of corn under Messiah's reign. The idealism which gave to the simplest words of Jesus such a charming velvety aspect was for the most part lost.

John at Ephesus strengthened daily. His supremacy was recognised throughout the whole province, except perhaps at Hierapolis, where Philip lived. The churches of Smyrna, Pergamos, Thyatira, Sardis, Philadelphia, and Laodocea had adopted him as their head, listening with respect to his statements, his councils, and his reproaches. The Apostle, or those whom he gave the right to speak for him, generally assumed a severe tone. A great rudeness, an extreme intolerance, a hard and gross language against those who thought otherwise than he did appeared to have been a part of John's character. It is, it was said, in regard him that Jesus promulgated this principle, "whosoever is not for us is against us." The series of anecdotes which were told of his sweetness and indulgence seem to have been invented agreeably to the model which is visible in the Johannine epistles, epistles whose authenticity is very doubtful. Features of an opposite kind, and which show much violence, accord better with the evangelical records and with the Apocalypse, and prove that the hastiness which had gained him the surname of Son of Thunder had only grown greater with age. It may be, however, that these qualities and contradictory defects might not be so exclusive of each other as one might think. Religious fanaticism often produces in the same person the extremes of harshness and goodness; just as an inquisitor of the middle ages, who made thousands of unfortunates burn for insignificant subtleties, was at the same time the gentlest, and in one sense the humblest, of men. It was especially against the little conventicles of the disciples of him whom they called the new Balsam that the animosity of John and his followers appeared to have been lively and deep. Such was the injustice inherent in all parties, such was the passion which filled these strong Jewish natures, that probably the disappearance of the "Destroyer of the law" was hailed with cries of joy by his adversaries. To many the death of this blunderer, this mar-plot, was a relief. We have seen that Paul at Ephesus felt himself to be surrounded by enemies; the last discourses which are attributed to him in Asia are full of sad forebodings. At the beginning of the year 69, we find the hatred against him bitter still; then the controversy shall grow calm, silence shall fall around his memory. At the point we have reached no one appears to have upheld him, and there is precisely in this what vindicated him later on. The reserve, or if it must be said, the weakness of his partisans, brought about a reconciliation: the boldest thoughts finished by gaining acceptance on condition that they yielded a long time without reply to the objections of the conservatives.

Rage against the Roman empire, delight in the misfortunes which befel it, the hope of soon seeing it dismembered, were the innermost thoughts of all the believers. They sympathized with the Jewish insurrection, and were persuaded that the Romans had not quite reached their end. The time was distant since Paul, and perhaps Peter, preached the acceptance of the Roman authority, attributing even to that authority a sort of divine character. The principles of the enthusiastic Jews in the refusal to pay taxes, as to the diabolic origin of all profane power, as to the idolatry implied in acts of civil life according to the Roman usages, carried them away It was the natural consequence of persecution; moderate principles had ceased to be applicable. Without being so violent as in 64, persecution continued secretly. Asia was the province where the fall of Nero had made the deepest impression. The general opinion was that the monster, cured by Satanic power, kept himself concealed somewhere and was about to re-appear. One could imagine what kind of effect these rumours would produce among the Christians. Many of the faithful at Ephesus, beginning perhaps with their head, had escaped from the great butchery of 64. What! The horrible beast saturated with luxury, fatuity, going to return! The thing was clear, those continued to think who still supposed that Nero was Anti-Christ. See him, this mystery of iniquity who would appear to be assassinated, making everybody martyrs before the luminous advent. Nero is that Satan incarnate who shall accomplish the slaughter of the saints, A little time yet and the solemn moment shall comb! The Christians adopted this idea so much the more willingly that the death of Nero had been too mean for an Antiochus; persecutors of that species usually perished with greater éclat. It was concluded that the enemy of God was reserved for a more splendid death which should be inflicted on him in sight of the whole world and the angels gathered together by the Messiah.

This idea, which gave birth to the Apocalypse, took every day more distinct forms; the Christian conscience had arrived at the height of its enthusiasm when a matter which took place in the neighbouring isles of Asia gave body to what up till then had been only imagination. A false Nero appeared and inspired in the provinces of Asia and Achaia, a lively sentiment of either curiosity, hope, or fear. He was, it would appear, a slave from Pontus, according to others an Italian of servile rank. He much resembled the deceased emperor; he had his large eyes, his strong hair, his haggard look, his theatrical and fierce face; he knew like him how to play the guitar, and to sing. The impostor found around him a first nucleus composed of deserters and vagabonds, and attempting to reach by sea Syria and Egypt, was cast by a tempest on the island of Cythnos, one of the Cylades. He made that island the centre of a propaganda, increased his band by enrolling some soldiers who were returning from the east, did some bloody deeds, pillaged the merchants and armed the slaves, The excitement was great, especially among the kind of people who from their credulity were open to the most absurd reports. From the month of December, Asia and Greece had no other subject of talk. The waiting and the terror increased every day. That name whose fame had filled the world turned heads anew, and made people believe that what they had seen was nothing like to what they would see.

Other things which took place in Asia or in the Archipelago, and whose date we cannot fix for want of sufficient indications, increased the agitation still more. An ardent Neronian who joined to political passion some marks of a sorcerer, declared himself loudly for either the Cythnian impostor or for Nero, who was thought to have taken refuge among the Parthians. He apparently forced peaceable people to recognise Nero. He re-established his statues and ordered them to be honoured; we are sometimes even tempted to believe that a coin was struck with the legend Nero redux. What is certain is, that the Christians imagined they would be forced to honour Nero's statues, the money, token, or stamp in the name of "the beast" "without which one could neither sell nor buy," and thus caused them insurmountable scruples; the gold marked with the sign of the great head of idolatry burned their fingers. It appears that rather than lend themselves to such acts of apostasy some of the believers in Ephesus were exiled; we can suppose that John was of that number. This incident, obscure for us, plays a large part in the Apocalypse, and was perhaps its prime origin. "Attention" said the seer, "there is here the end of the patience of the saints who keep the commandments of God and the faith of Jesus." The occurrences in Rome and Italy gave reason for this feverish expectancy. Galba did not succeed in establishing himself, up till Nero, the title of dynastic legitimacy created by Julius Cæsar and by Augustus, had stifled the thought of a competition for Empire among the generals; but since that title had been barred by limitation, every military chief could aspire to the heritage of Cæsar. Vindex was dead, Virginius had loyally submitted; Nymphidius Lavinus, Macer, Fonteius, Capito, had expiated by death their revolutionary ideas; nothing was done, however. On the 2nd January, 69, the legions of Germany proclaimed Vetillius, on the 10th Galba adopted Piso, on the 15th Otho was proclaimed at Rome. For some hours there were three emperors; in the evening Galba was killed. Faith in the empire was terribly shaken, people did not believe that Otho could manage to reign alone; the hopes of the partisans of the false Nero of Cythnos and those who imagined every day to see the emperor's so much regretted return from beyond the Euphrates, could not be concealed. It was then, at the end of January, in the year 69, that there was spread among the Christians of Asia a symbolic manifesto representing itself as a revelation of Jesus Christ himself. Did the author know of the death of Galba or had he only foreseen it? It is as much more difficult to say that a feature of the Apocalypses is that the writer puts forward sometimes, to the profit of his pretended foresight, some recent news which, he believes, he alone knows. Thus the publicist, who composed the book of Daniel, appears to have had a hint of the death of Antiochus. Our Seer appears to be possessed of special information on the political condition of his time. It is doubtful if he knew Otho; he believed that the restoration of Nero would immediately follow the fall of Galba. This latter appears to him already condemned. The eve of the Beast's return is, therefore, reached. The ardent imagination of the author then appears to him a collection of views "upon what must arrive in a little while," and thus the successive chapters of a prophetic book are unrolled, the object of which is to make clear the conscience of the believers in the crisis through which they are passing, and reveal to them the meaning of a political situation which disturbed the strongest spirits, and especially to reassure them as to the fate of their brethren already slain. It must be remembered that the credulous sectaries, whose sentiments we seek to discover, were a thousand miles from the ideas of the immortality of the soul, which have come forth from Greek philosophy. The martyrdoms of the last year were a terrible crisis for a society which trembled artlessly when a saint died, and asked if that one would see the Kingdom of God. People showed an unconquerable need to represent the faithful already passed into rest and blessed, although with a provisory in the midst of the plagues which struck the earth. Their cries of vengeance were heard; they considered their saints impatient, they called for the day on which God would arise and avenge his own elect.

The form of "Apocalypse" adopted by the author was not new in Israel. Ezekiel had already inaugurated a considerable change in the old prophetic style, and we may in a sense regard it as the creator of the Apocalyptic class. To fervent preaching, accompanied sometimes by extremely allegorical acts, he had substituted, doubtless under the influence of Assyrian art, the vision, that is to say, a complicated symbolism, where the abstract idea was presented by means of chimerical beings conceived outside of all reality. Zachariah continues to walk in the same path; a vision becomes the necessary framework of all prophetic instruction. Indeed, the author of the book of Daniel, by the extraordinary popularity he obtained, fixed absolutely the rules of the class. The book of Enoch, the Assumption of Moses and certain sibylline poems were the fruit of his powerful initiative. The prophetic instinct of the Semites, their tendency to group facts in view of a certain philosophy of history, and to present their individual thought ender the form of s divine absolute, their aptitude for seeing the great lines of the future, finding in this fantastic framework some singular facilities. In every critical situation of the people of Israel, they, in fact, demanded an apocalypse. The persecution by Antiochus, the Roman occupation, the profane reign of Herod had excited some ardent visionaries. It was inevitable that Nero's reign and the siege of Jerusalem should have their apocalyptic protest, as later on had the severities of Domitian, Hadrian, Septimus Severus, Decius, and the invasion of the Goths in 250 called forth for themselves.

The author of this bizarre writing, which a still more bizarre fate destined to such different interpretations, laid down in it the whole weight of the Christian conscience, then addressed it under the form of an epistle to the seven principal Churches of Asia. He asked that it should be read, as was the custom with all apostolic epistles, to the assembled faithful. There was perhaps in that an imitation of Paul, who preferred to act by letters than personally. Such communications in any case were not rare, and it was always the coming of the Lord which was their object. Some pretended revelations on the nearness of the last day circulated under the name of different apostles, so much so that Paul was obliged to warn his churches against the abuse which might be made of his writing to support such frauds. The work begins by a title which was worthy of its origin and its lofty theme:--

The Revelation of Jesus Christ which God gave him to show unto his servants, even the things which must shortly come to pass: and he sat and signified it by his angel unto his servant John, who bare witness of the word of God, and of the testimony of Jesus Christ, even of all things that he saw. Blessed is he that readeth, and they that hear the words of the prophecy and keep the things which are written therein, for the time is at hand.

John, to the seven churches which are in Asia, Grace to you, and peace from him which is, and which was, and which is to come, and from the seven spirits which are before his throne: and from Jesus Christ, who is the faithful witness, the first born of the dead, and the ruler of the kings of the earth. Unto him that loveth us, and loosed us from our sins by his blood: and he made as to be a kingdom to be priests unto his God and Father, to him be the glory and the dominion for ever and ever, Amen.

Behold he cometh with the clouds, and every eye shall see him, and they which pierced him; and all the tribes of the earth shall mourn over him, even so, Amen. I am the Alpha and the Omega, saith the Lord God, which is and which was, and which is to come, the Almighty.

John, your brother and partaker with you in the tribulation and kingdom and patience which are in Jesus, was in the isle that is called Patmos, for the word of God and the testimony of Jesus. I was in the Spirit on the Lord's day, and I heard behind me a great voice, as of a trumpet, saying, What thou seest write in a book, and send it to the seven churches, unto Ephesus and unto Smyrna, and unto Pergamum, and unto Thyatira, and unto Sardis, and unto Philadelphia, and unto Laodicea. And I turned to see the voice which spake unto me, and having turned I saw seven golden candlesticks, and in the midst of the candlesticks one like unto a son of man, clothed with a garment down to the foot, and girt about at the breasts with a golden girdle. And his head and his hair were white as white wool, white as snow, and his eyes were as a flame of fire, and his feet like unto burnished brass, as if it had been refined in a furnace, and his voice as the voice of many waters, and he had in his right hand seven stars, and out of his mouth proceeded a sharp two-edged sword, and his countenance was as the sun shineth in his strength. And when I saw him I fell at his feet as one dead. And he laid his right hand upon me, saying, Fear not; I am the first and the last and the living one. And I was dead, and behold I am alive for evermore, and I have the keys of death and of Hades Write therefore the things which thou sawest and the things which are and the things which shall come to pass hereafter; the mystery of the seven stars which thou rawest in my right hand, and the seven golden candlesticks. The seven stars are the angels of the seven churches, and the seven candlesticks are seven churches.

In the Jewish conceptions, among the Gnostics and Cabbalists who were dominant about this time, every person, and indeed every moral being, such as death or grief, has its angel; there was thus the angel of Persia and the angel of Greece; the angel of the waters, the angel of fire, and the angel of the abyss. It was therefore natural that each church should have thus its heavenly representative. It is to this kind of fervour or genius of each community that the Son of Man addresses his statements one after the other:--

To the angel of the church of Ephesus;

These things saith he that holdeth the seven stars in his right hand, who walketh in the midst of the seven golden candlesticks I know thy works and thy labour, and thy patience, and how thou can et not bear them which are evil, and thou hast tried them which say they are apostles, and are not, and hast found them liars. And hest borne and had patience, and for my name's sake hast laboured and hast not fainted. Nevertheless I have somewhat against thee, because thou hest left thy first love. Remember therefore from whence thou art fallen, and repent and do the first works; or else I will tome unto thee quickly, and will remove thy candlestick out of his place, except thou repent. But this thou hast, that thou hatest the deeds of the Nicolaitanes, which I also hate. He that hath an ear let him hear what the spirit saith unto the churches; to him that overcometh will I give to eat of the tree of life which is in the midst of the paradise of God.

And unto the angel of the church of Smyrna:

These things saith the first and the last, which was dead and is alive. I know thy works and tribulation, and poverty, (but thou art rich) and I know the blasphemy of them which say they are Jews and are not, but are the synagogue of Satan. Fear none of those things which thou shalt suffer, behold the devil shall cast some of you into prison that ye may be tried, and ye shall have tribulation ten days. Be thou faithful unto death, and I will give thee a crown of life. He that hath an ear let him hear what the Spirit saith unto the churches. He that overcometh shall not be hurt of the second death.

And to the angel of the church of Pergamum:

These things saith he which hath the sharp sword with two edges: I know thy works and where thou dwellest, even where Satan's seat is; and thou holdest fast my name, and hast not denied my faith, even in those days wherein Antipas was my faithful martyr who was slain among you, where Satan dwelleth. But I have a few things against thee, because thou hast there them that hold the doctrine of Balsam, who taught Balak to cast a stumbling block before the children of Israel, to eat things sacrificed unto idols and to commit fornication. So hast thou also them that hold the doctrine of the Nicolaitanes, which thing I hate. Repent, or else I will come unto thee quickly and will fight against them with the sword of my mouth. He that hath an ear let him hear what the Spirit saith unto the churches; to him that overcometh will I give to eat of the hidden manna, and will give him a white stone, and in the stone a new name written, which no man knoweth saving he that receiveth it.

And unto the angel of the church of Thyatira:

These things saith the son of God, who hath his eyes like unto a flame of fire, and his feet are like fine brass. I know thy works, and charity, and service, and faith, and thy patience and thy works; and the last to be more than the first. Notwithstanding, I have a few things against thee, because thou sufferest that woman Jezebel, which calleth herself a prophetess, to teach and to seduce my servants to commit fornication and to eat things sacrificed unto idols. And I give her space to repent of her fornication, and she repented not. Behold I will cast her into a bed and them that commit adultery with her into great tribulation, except they repent of their deeds. And I will kill her children with death; and all the churches shall know that I am he which searcheth the reins and hearts; and I will give unto every one of you according to your works. But unto you I say, and unto the rest in Thyatira, as many as have not this doctrine and which have not known the depths of Satan as they speak, I will put upon you none other burden. But that which ye have already hold fast till I come. And he that overcometh and keepeth my works unto the end, to him will I give power over the nations. And he shall rule them with a rod of iron; as the vessels of a potter shall they be broken to shivers, even as I received of my father. And I will give him the morning star. He that hath an ear let him hear what the Spirit saith unto the churches.

And unto the angel of the church of Sardis:

These things saith he that hath the seven Spirits of God and the seven stars: I know thy works, that thou hast a name, that thou livest, and art dead. Be watchful and strengthen the things which remain that are ready to die; for I have not found thy works perfect before God. Remember therefore how thou hast received and heard, and hold fast and repent. If therefore thou shalt not watch, I will come on thee as a thief, and thou shalt not know what hour I will come upon thee. Thou hast a few names even in Sardis which have not defiled their garments, and they shall walk with me in white, for they are worthy. He that overcometh, the same shall be clothed in white raiment, and I will not blot out his name out of the book of life, but I will confess his name before my Father, and before his angels. He that hath an ear let him hear what the Spirit saith unto the churches.

And to the angel of the church of Philadelphia:

These things saith he that is holy, he that is true, he that hath the key of David, he that openeth and no man shutteth, and shutteth and no man openeth. I know thy works; behold I have set before thee an open door, and no man can shut it; for thou hast a little strength and hast kept my word, and hast not denied my name. Behold, I will make them of Satan, which say they are Jews and are not, but do lie; behold I will make them to come and worship before thy feet, and to know that I have loved thee. Because thou hast kept the word of my patience, I also will keep thee from the hour of temptation, which shall come upon all the world, to try them that dwell upon the earth. Behold I come quickly, hold that fast which thou hast, that no man take my crown. Him that overcometh will I make a pillar in the temple of my God, and he shall go no more out; and I will write upon him the name of my God, and the name of the city of my God, which is new Jerusalem; which cometh down out of Heaven from my God, and I will write upon him my new name. He that hath an ear let him hear what the Spirit saith unto the churches.

And unto the angel of the church of Laodicea:

These things saith the Amen, the faithful and true witness, the beginning of the creation of God. I know thy works, that thou art neither cold nor hot. I would thou wert cold or hot. So then because thou art lukewarm and neither cold nor hot, I will spew thee out of my mouth. Because thou sayest I am rich, and increased with goods, and have need of nothing, and knowest not that thou art wretched, and miserable, and poor, and blind, and naked. I counsel thee to buy of me gold tried in the fire that thou mayest be rich, and white raiment that thou mayest be clothed, and that the shame of thy nakedness do not appear, and anoint thine eyes with eye-salve that thou mayest see. As many as I love I rebuke and chasten: if any man hear my voice and open the door I will come in to him and will sup with, him and he with me. To him that overcometh will I grant to sit with me in my throne, even as I also overcame, and am set down with my Father in his throne. He that hath an ear let him hear what the Spirit saith unto the churches.

Who is this John who dares to make himself the interpreter of these celestial mandates, who speaks to the Churches of Asia with such authority, who boasts that he has passed through the same persecutions as his readers? It is either the Apostle John or a homonym of the Apostle John, or some one who has a desire to pass for the Apostle John. It is scarcely admissible that in the year 69, during the apostle's life or a little after his death, some one had usurped his name without his consent for such searching counsels and reprimands. Among the apostle's homonyms, no one would have dared to take up such a position. The Presbyteros Johannes (the only person who is alleged to have done so), if he ever existed, was, it would seem, of a later generation. Without denying the doubts which rest on nearly all these questions as to the authenticity of the apostolic writings, seeing the emit scruple which is made in attributing to apostles and holy persons the revelations to which they wished to give authority, we regard it as probable that the Apocalypse is the work of the Apostle John, or at least that it was accepted by him and addressed to the Churches of Asia under his patronage The prong impression of the massacres of the year 64, the feeling of the dangers through which the author has run, the horror of Rome, appear to us to point to the apostle who, according to our hypothesis, had been at Rome and could say, in speaking of those tragic events: Quorum pars magna fui. Blood stifled him, filled his eyes, and prevented him from seeing nature. The images of the monstrosities of Nero's reign take hold of him as a fixed idea. But some grave objections here render the task of criticism very difficult. The taste for mystery and apocrypha which the first Christian generations possessed has covered with an unpenetrable mystery all the questions of literary history relating to the New Testament. Fortunately the soul shines out in those anonymous and pseudonomic writings in accents which cannot lie. The part of each man, in popular movements, it is impossible to discern--it is the sentiment of all which constitutes the true creator spirit.

Why did the author of the Apocalypse, whoever he was, choose Patmos for the place of his vision? It is difficult to say. Patmos or Pathos is a little island about four leagues in length, but very narrow. It was in the antiquity of Greece, flourishing and very populous. In the Roman period, it kept all the importance which its smallness warranted, thanks to its fine port, formed in the centre of the island by the isthmus which joins the massive rocks of the north to those of the south. Patmos was, according to the habits of the coasting trade then, the first or the last station for the traveller who went from Ephesus to Rome or from Rome to Ephesus. It is wrong to represent it as a rock or a desert, Patmos was and will become again one of the most important maritime stations of the Archipelago: for it is at the branching off of many lines. If Asia should renew its youth, Patmos would be for it something analagous to what Syra is for modern Greece, to what Delos and Rhenia among the Cyclades, a sort of emporium in the eyes of the merchant marine, a point of "correspondence" useful to travellers.

It was probably this which caused this little island to be selected--a selection from which has resulted later on such a high Christian celebrity to the spot. Whether the apostle had retired thither to escape some persecuting measure of the Ephesian authorities; or whether, returning from a voyage to Rome, or on the eve of seeing his faithful people again, he had prepared, in one of the cauponæ which would be on the shore of the port; the manifesto he wished to precede him in Asia; or whether, taking a kind of step backward to strike a heavy blow, and being of opinion that the place for the vision could not be made Ephesus itself, he had chosen the island in the Archipelago which, removed by about a day's journey, was connected with the metropolis of Asia by a daily sailing; or whether he desired to keep the recollection of the last stoppage on the voyage, full of emotions, which he made in 64; or whether it was a simple accident of the sea which had obliged him to spend several days in this little port. Those navigations of the Archipelago are full of danger; the crossing of the ocean cannot give any idea of it: for in our seas there are constant winds ruling which help us, even when they are contrary. There, there are one after another dull calms, and when the narrow straits are being sailed through, violent winds. One has no control over one's movement: he stops where he can and not where he will.

Men so ardent as those bitter and fanatical descendants of the old prophets of Israel carried their fancies wherever they went, and that imagination was so completely shut in within the circle of the old Hebrew poetry that the nature which surrounded them did not exist for them. Patmos resembles all the islands of the Archipelago: an azure sea, limped air, a serene sky, rocks with jagged peaks, only occasionally clad with a light downy verdure. The aspect is naked and sterile; but the forms and colour of the rock, the living blue of the sea, pencilled by beautiful white birds, opposed to the reddish tints of the rocks, are something wonderful. Those myriads of isles and islets of the most varied forms which emerge like pyramids or shields on the waves, and dance an eternal rondo around the horizon, resemble a fairy world in a circle of marine gods and oceanides, leading a brilliant life of love, youth and sadness, in grottoes of a glaucous green, on shores without mystery, alternately sweet and terrible, luminous and sombre. Calypso and the Sirens, the Tritons and the Nereides, the dangerous charms of the sea, its caresses at once voluptuous and sinister, all these fine sensations which have their inimitable expression in the Odyssey, escaped the dark visionary. Two or three peculiarities, such as the great preoccupation of the sea, the image of "a mountain burning in the midst of the sea," which seem borrowed from the Thera, have alone some local reference. From a small island, used as the basis of the picture in the delicious romance of Daphnis and Chloe, or of pastoral scenes like those of Theocistus and Moselms, he makes a black volcano, belching forth ashes and fire. Yet he must have tasted more than once upon these waves the silence full of serenity, of nights on which one hearing nothing but the groaning of the halycon and the dull whisper of the dolphin. For whole days he was facing Mount Mycale, without thinking of the victory of the Greeks over the Persians, the finest which has ever been accomplished after Marathion and Thermopylæ. At this central point of all the great Greek creations, at some leagues from Samos, Cos, Miletus, Ephesus, he was dreaming of something else than the prodigious genius of Pythagoras, Hippocrates, Thales, and Heraclitus: the glorious memories of Greece had no existence for him. The poem of Patmos ought to have been some Hero and Leander, or rather a pastoral in the style of Longus, telling of the play of beautiful children on the threshold of love. The gloomy enthusiast, thrown by chance on these Ionian shores, never quitted his Biblical recollections. Nature for him was the living chariot of Ezekiel, the monstrous cherub, the deformed Nineveh bull, an uncouth zoology, setting statuary and painting at defiance. This strange defect, which the eye of the Orientals has for altering the images of things, a defect which made all the pictured representations coming from their hands appear fantastic and bereft of the spirit of life, was with him at its height. The disease which had possession of his entrails tinged everything with its hues; he saw with the eyes of Ezekiel, with those of the author of the Book of Daniel, or rather he saw nothing but himself, his sufferings, his hopes, and his anger. A vague and dry mythology, already cabalistic and gnostic, wholly founded upon the transformation of abstract ideas in the divine hypostases, put him beyond the plastic conditions of art. Never has anyone been more isolated from his surroundings; never has anyone denied more openly the tangible world to substitute for the harmonies of reality the contradictory chimera of a new earth and a new heaven.

CHAPTER XVI

THE APOCALYPSE

After the message to the seven churches, the course of the vision unrolls itself. A door is opened in heaven; the Seer is wrapped in spirit, and through this opening his look penetrates to the very heart of the heavenly court. All the heaven of the Jewish cabala reveals itself to him. A single throne exists, and upon that throne, around which is the rainbow, is seated God himself, like a colossal ruby, darting forth its fires. Around the throne are twenty-four secondary seats, upon which are seated four-and-twenty elders clothed in white, having upon their heads crowns of gold. It is humanity represented by a senate of its élite, who form the permanent court of the Eternal; in front burn seven lamps, which are the seven spirits of God (the seven gifts of the divine wisdom). Behind are four monsters, composed of features borrowed from the cherubs of Ezekiel, and seraphs of Isaiah. These are: the first in the form of a lion, the second in the form of a calf, the third in the form of a man, the fourth in the form of an eagle with outspread wings These four monsters in Ezekiel formerly represented the attributes of the divine being: wisdom, power, omniscience, and creation. They have six wings and are covered with eyes over their whole bodies. The angels, creatures inferior to the great supernatural personifications which had been spoken of, a sort of winged servants, surround the throne in thousands of thousands and myriads of myriads. An eternal rolling of thunder comes forth from the throne. In the foreground there stretches an immense azure surface, like crystal (the firmament). A sort of divine liturgy proceeds without end. The four monsters, organs of universal life (nature), never sleep, and sing night and day the heavenly trisagion, "Holy, holy, holy, is the Lord God Almighty, who was, and is, and shall be." The four-and-twenty elders (humanity) unite in this canticle by prostrating themselves and casting their crowns at the feet of the throne of the creator.

Christ has not figured up till now in the court of heaven; the Seer makes us assist at the ceremony of his enthronement. At the right of him who is seated on the throne there is seen a book in the form of a roll, written on both sides and sealed with seven seals. It is the hook of the divine secrets, the great Revelation. No one either in earth or heaven has been found worthy to open it or even to look upon it. John then begins to weep; the future, the only consolation of the Christian, is not there to be revealed to him. One of the elders encourages him. In fact he who should open the book is soon found. It may be divined without difficulty that it is Jesus, for in the very centre of the great assembly at the foot of the throne in the midst of the animals and elders upon the crystalline altar appears a slain lamb. It was the favourite image under which the Christian imagination loved to picture Jesus to itself; a lamb slain became a Paschal victim and always with God. He has seven horns and seven eyes, symbols of the seven spirits of God, whose fulness Jesus has received, and who are through him about to be spread over the whole world. The Lamb rises, goes right up to the throne of the Eternal, and takes the Book. A wondrous emotion then fills heaven. The four animals, the four-and-twenty elders fall on their knees before the Lamb. They hold in their hands harps and vials of gold full of incense (the prayers of saints) and sing a new song: "Thou, thou alone art worthy to take the book and to open its seals; for thou hast been slain and with thy blood hast thou gained unto God a company of elect out of every tribe and tongue and people and race, and thou hast made of them a kingdom of priests, and they shall reign on the earth. The myriads of angels join in this canticle and discern in the Lamb the seven great prerogatives (power, riches, wisdom, strength, honour, glory, and blessing); all the creatures who are in heaven, on the earth, or under the earth, and in the sea, join in this heavenly ceremony and cry: "To him who is seated upon the throne and to the Lamb be blessing, and honour, and glory, and strength through the ages of ages." The four animals representing nature, with their deep voice say Amen; the elders fall down and worship.

Thus is Jesus introduced in the highest rank of the celestial hierarchy. Not only the angels, but also the four-and-twenty elders, and the four animals who are superior to the angels, prostrate themselves before him. He has mounted the steps of the throne of God and has taken the book placed at the right hand of God, which no one could even look upon. He opens the seven seals of the book and the grand drama begins. The début is brilliant. According to a conception of the most righteous people, the author places the origin of the Messianic agitation at the moment in which Rome extends its empire to Judea. At the opening of the first seal a white horse comes forth. The rider who is mounted on him carries a

84

bow in his hand, a crown surrounds his head, he gains victory everywhere. This is the Roman Empire, which up till the time of the Seer none could resist, but this triumphal prologue is of short duration; the signs coming before the brilliant appearance of Messiah shall be unheard-of plagues, and it is by the most terrific images that the celestial tragedy is carried out. We are at the beginning of what is called "the period of the sorrows of the Messiah." Each seal which is opened henceforth brings upon humanity some horrible misfortunes.

At the opening of the second seal a red horse comes forth. To him who rides upon it is given power to take away peace from the earth and to make men slay each other; there is put into his hand a great sword. It is War. Since the revolt of Judea, and especially since the insurrection of Vindex, the world was in fact nothing but a field of carnage, and peaceable men knew not where to flee.

At the opening of the third seal a black horse leaps forth. His rider holds a balance. In the midst of the four animals the voice which tariffs in heaven the prices of commodities for poor mortals, says to the horseman, "A bushel of wheat for a penny, three bushels of barley for a penny, and touch not the oil or the wine." That is famine, not to speak of the great dearth which took place under Claudius; the scarcity in the year 68 was extreme.

At the opening of the fourth seal a yellow horse comes forth. His rider was called Death. Sheol followed him, and there was power given to him to kill the quarter of the world by the sword, pestilence, and wild beasts.

Such are the great plagues which announce the approaching advent of the Messiah. Justice wills it that immediately the divine wrath shall be lit against the world. In fact at the opening of the fifth seal the Seer is witness of a touching spectacle. He recognises under the altar the souls of those who have been slain for their faith, and for the witness they have rendered to Christ (certainly the victims of the year 64). These holy souls cry out to God, and say to Him, "How long, Ω Lord, holy and true. Wilt Thou not do justice and demand our blood from those that dwell upon the earth?" But the time is not yet come, the number of the martyrs who should fill up the overflowing of wrath has not yet been reached. To each one of the victims who are under the altar, is given a white robe, a pledge of future justification and triumph, and they are told to wait a little while until their fellow-servants and brethren who should be slain like them should bear witness in their turn.

After this fine interlude, we do not return to the period of precursory plagues, but the phenomena of the last judgment. At the opening of the sixth seal a great shaking of the universe takes place. The heaven becomes black like sackcloth of hair, the moon takes the colour of blood, the stars fall from heaven to earth like the fruit of a fig tree shaken with the wind. The sky draws itself back like a book that is rolled up, the mountains and hills are hurled from their places. The kings and the great men of the earth, the military tribunes, and the rich and the strong, slaves and free men, hide themselves in the caves and among the rocks saying to the mountains, "Fall upon us, and save us from the glance of Him who sits upon the throne and from the wrath of the Lamb!"

The great execution is then to be accomplished. The four angels of the winds are placed at the four corners of the earth; they have only to give bridle to the elements which are entrusted to them, that these, following their natural fury, should destroy the world. All power is given to these four actors. They are at their posts; but the fundamental idea of the poem is to show the great judgment adjourned without ceasing till the moment it appears it must take place. An angel bearing in his hand the seal of God (a seal which has for a legend, like all royal seals, the name of him to whom it belongs, Iyhvh), comes forth from the east. He cries to the four angels of the destroying winds to keep back for some time yet the forces which they wield, until the elect, who presently live, are marked in the forehead, by the stamp, by which, as was done by the blood of the Paschal Lamb in Egypt, they should be preserved from these plagues. The angel impresses then the divine signet upon a hundred and forty-four thousand persons belonging to the twelve tribes of Israel. It is not really said that these hundred and forty-four thousand elect are only Jews. Israel is here certainly the true spiritual Israel, "the Israel of God," as St. Paul calls it, the elect family, embracing all those who are connected with the race of Abraham through faith in Jesus and by the practice of the necessary rites. But there is here a category of the faithful which is already introduced in the time of peace, they are those who have suffered death for Jesus. The prophet sees them under the figure of a numberless crowd, of every race, tribe, people, and tongue, standing before the throne and before the Lamb clothed in white robes and carrying palms in their hands, and singing to the glory of God and the Lamb. One of the elders explains to him what this crowd is: These are the people who have come out of great persecution and they have washed their robes in the blood of the Lamb. Therefore are they before the throne of God, and they adore him night and day in his temple, and he who is seated on the throne shall dwell eternally among them. They shall hunger no more, they shall thirst no more, nor shall they suffer any more from the heat. The Lamb shall lead them to pastures and shall guide them to the waters of life, and God himself shall wipe away all tears from their eyes.

The seventh seal is opened. They are waiting for the grand spectacle of the consummation of time. But, in the poem, as in reality, this catastrophe always recedes; we believed it was coming, but it has not. In place of the final dénoûement which ought to be the effect of the opening of the seventh seal, there is silence in heaven for half-an-hour, indicating that the first act of the mystery has ended, and that another is about to begin.

After the sacramental silence the seven archangels which are before the throne of God, and of whom mention has just been made, enter on the scene. To them are given seven trumpets, which each uses as a signal of other prognostics. John's gloomy fancy was not satisfied; this time it is in the plagues of Egypt that his anger against the world seeks types for punishments. Some natural phenomena occurring about the year 68, and with which popular opinion is preoccupied, affords him apparent justification for such comparisons.

Before the blast of the seven trumpets begins, a silent scene of great effect comes in. An angel advances toward the golden altar which is before the throne, having in his hand a golden censer. Some lumps of incense are turned over the coals of the altar and send up perfumes before the Eternal. The angel then refills his censer with coals from the altar and throws them on the ground. These coals, in striking the surface of the earth, produce thunders and lightnings, voices and earthquakes. The incense, the author himself tells us, are the prayers of saints. The sighs of these pious persons, rising before God, and calling for the destruction of the Roman empire, become burning coals to the profane world, which strikes it, rends it, and consumes it, without knowing whence the attack comes.

The seven angels then prepare to place their trumpets to their lips.

At the sound of the first angel's trumpet a hail mingled with fire and blood falls on the earth. The third of the earth is burned, the third of the trees is burned; all green herbage is burned. In 63 and 68 and 69, there was, in fact, a great terror caused by storms in which men saw something supernatural

At the sound of the second angel's trumpet, a great mountain, incandescent, is thrown into the sea; the third of the sea is turned into blood, the third of all fishes die, the third of ships is destroyed. There is here an allusion to the aspects of the isle of Thera, which the prophet could almost see on the horizon of Patmos, and which resembles an extinct volcano. A new island had appeared in the midst of its crater in the year 46 or 47. In its moments of activity one can see in the neighbourhood of Thera flames on the surface of the sea.

At the blast of the third angel's trumpet, a great star falls from heaven, burning like a faggot; it extinguishes the third of rivers and streams. Its name is "Wormwood;" the third of the waters are turned into wormwood (that is to say, they become bitter and poisonous), and many men die from this. One is led to suppose that there is here an allusion to a certain borealis whose fall was placed in connection with an infection which might be produced in some reservoir of water by altering its quality. We must recollect that our prophet sees nature through the artless stories and popular conversations of Asia, the most credulous country in the world. Phlegon, of Tralles, half a century later, was to pass his life in compiling some absurdities of this kind. Tacitus, on every page, is prepossessed by them.

At the blast of the fourth angel's trumpet the third of the sun, the third of the moon, and the third of the stars are extinguished, so that the third of the world's light is darkened. This may be connected with eclipses which terrified people during those years, or the terrible storm of 10th January, 69.

These plagues are not over yet. An eagle flying in the zenith uttered three cries of misfortune, and announced to men some unheard-of calamities for the three trumpet blasts which remain.

At the sound of the fifth trumpet a star (that is to say, an angel) falls from heaven; the key of the bottomless pit (hell) is given to him. The angel opens the bottomless pit; then comes up from it a smoke like that of a great furnace; the sun and the heavens are darkened. From this smoke come forth locusts, who cover the earth like squadrons of cavalry. These locusts, led by their king, the angel of the abyss, who is called in Hebrew Abaddon, and in Greek Apollyon, torment men during five months (a whole summer). It is possible that the plague of the locusts may about this time have been very intense in some provinces; in any case the imitation of the plagues of Egypt is evident here. The bottomless pit is probably the Solfatara of Pouzzuoli (what is termed the Forum of Vulcan) or the ancient crater of the Somma conceived of as mouths of hell. We have said that the crisis in the suburbs of Naples was then very violent. The author of the Apocalypse, who may be allowed to claim a voyage to Rome, and consequently to Pouzzuoli, may have witnessed such phenomena. He connects the clouds of locusts with volcanic exhalations! for the origin of these clouds being obscure, the people would be led to see there the outcome of hell. At this day, moreover, an analogous phenomena is seen yet at Solfatara. After a heavy rain the water pools which are in the warm portions cause some rapid and abundant spawning of locusts and frogs. That this generation, apparently spontaneous, would be considered by the vulgar as emanations from the infernal mouth itself, was much more natural than that the eruptions, being ordinarily the result of heavy rains which covered the country with marshes, should appear to be the immediate cause of the clouds of insects which came forth from these marshes.

The sound of the sixth trumpet brings another plague: it is the invasion of the Parthians, which everybody believed imminent. A voice comes from the four horns of the altar, which is before God, and orders the release of four angels who are chained on the banks of the Euphrates. The four angels (perhaps the Assyrians, Babylonians, Medes and Persians), who were ready for the day, the hour, the month, and the year, were placing themselves at the head of terrible cavalry amounting to two hundred millions of men. The description of the horses and horsemen is quite fantastical. The horses, which kill with the tail, are probably an allusion to the Parthian cavalry, who shot arrows while flying. A third of humanity is exterminated. Nevertheless those who survive do not repent. They continue to worship devils, idols of gold and silver, who can neither see, nor hear, or walk. They are obstinate in their homicides, their evil deeds, their fornications, their robberies.

They wait for the seventh trumpet to sound; out here, as in the act of the opening of the seals, the Seer appears to hesitate, or rather to place himself in a position to wait the result. He stops himself at the solemn moment. The terrible secret cannot yet be entirely made known. A gigantic angel, his head girt with a rainbow, one foot on the earth, another on the sea, whose voice seven thunders repeat, says certain mysterious words, which a voice from heaven forbids John to write. The gigantic angel then lifts his hands towards heaven and swears by the Eternal that there shall be no more delay, and that at the sound of the seventh trumpet will be accomplished the mystery of God announced by the prophets.

The apocalyptic drama therefore is about to finish. To prolong his book, the author gives himself a new prophetic mission. Rejecting an energetic symbol employed before by Ezekiel, John receives a fatidic book from the gigantic angel, and eats it. A voice says to him: "It is necessary that thou shouldst prophecy still before many races, and peoples, and tongues, and kings." The framework of the vision, which is to be closed by the seventh trumpet, enlarges itself thus, and the author begins a second part, when he will unveil his views on the destinies of the kings and peoples of his time. The first six trumpets, in fact, like the opening of the first six seals, are connected with the facts which had taken place when the author wrote. What follows, on the contrary, is connected for the most part with the future.

It is upon Jerusalem first that the looks of the Seer are cast. By a plain symbolism, he gives it to be understood that the city should be delivered to the Gentiles; to see that in the opening months of 69, needed no great prophetic effort. The portico and the court of the Gentiles shall even be polluted by the feet of the profane; but the imagination of a Jew so fervent cannot conceive of the temple destroyed, the temple being the only place in the world where God can receive a worship (a worship of which that of heaven is but the reproduction). John cannot imagine the earth without the temple. The temple shall therefore be preserved, and the faithful, marked in the forehead by the sign of Jehovah, can continue to adore him there. The temple shall thus be like a sacred space, a spiritual residence of the whole Church; this will last forty-two months, that is to say, three years and a half (a half-schemitta or week of years). This mystic cipher, borrowed from the book of Daniel, will often recur in the sequel. It is the space of time which yet remains for the world to live.

Jerusalem, during this time, shall be a theatre of a partly religious battle analogous to the struggles which have filled history in all times. God will give a mission to "his two witnesses" who shall prophecy during two hundred and sixty days (that is, three years and a half) clothed in sackcloth. These two prophets are compared to two olive trees and to two candles before the Lord. They shall have the powers of a Moses and an Elias; they will be able to shut heaven and keep back the rain, to turn water into blood, and to smite the earth with whatever plague they will. If any one tries to do them harm, a fire shall come out of their mouths and devour their adversaries. When they shall have finished giving their witness, the beast who comes up from the abyss, the Roman power, (or rather Nero reappearing as Antichrist) shall slay them. Their bodies will remain three days and a half stretched out without burial in the streets of the great city which is symbolically called "Sodom" and "Egypt," and where their master was crucified. The worldly shall rejoice, and shall felicitate each other, and send each other presents; for these two prophets had become insupportable by their austere preaching and by their temple miracles. But at the end of three days and a half, behold, the spirit of life shall re-enter the two saints: they shall rise to their feet, and a great terror shall seize all those who see them. Soon they mount heavenwards on the clouds, in the sight of their enemies. A fearful earthquake takes place at this moment; the tenth of the city falls; 7,000 men are killed; the others, terrified, are converted.

We have already often met this idea that the solemn hour shall be preceded by the appearance of the two witnesses, who are most often believed to be Enoch and Elias in prison. These two friends of God passed, indeed, for not being dead. The first was reported to have uselessly predicted the deluge to his contemporaries, who would not listen to him. He was the type of a Jew preaching repentance among the heathen. Sometimes also, the witnesses seem to resemble Moses, whose death was equally uncertain, and Jeremiah. Our author appears, moreover, to consider the two witnesses two important personages in the church of Jerusalem, two apostles of a great holiness, who shall be slain, then raised again, and shall ascend to heaven like Elias and Jesus. It is not impossible that the vision had for its first portion a retrospective value and is connected with the murder of the two Jameses, especially with the death of James, the Lord's brother which was considered by many at Jerusalem as a public misfortune, a fatal event and a sign of the times. Perhaps also one of these preachers of repentance is John the Baptist, the other Jesus. As to the persuasion that the end shall not take place till the Jews shall be converted, it was general among the Christians; we find it likewise in St. Paul.

The remainder of Israel having come to the true faith, the world has only to end. The seventh angel places his trumpet to his lips. At the sound of that last trumpet great voices cry out: "Behold! the hour has come when our Lord with his Christ shall reign over the world to all eternity." The four-and-twenty elders fall on their faces and worship. They thank God for having inaugurated his kingdom, in spite of the powerless rage of the Gentiles, and proclaim the hour of recompense for the saints, and of extermination for those who pollute the earth. Then the gates of the heavenly temple open: there is perceived in the centre of the temple the bow of the new covenant. This scene is accompanied by earthquakes, thunders and lightnings.

All is finished; the believers have received the great revelation which should comfort them. The judgment is at hand; it shall be held in a sacred half-year, equivalent to three years and a half. But we have already seen the author, little careful as to the unity of his work, reserving to himself the means of continuing it, when it should be finished. The book, in fact, is only half of the course; a new series of visions is about to be unrolled before us.

The first is one of the finest. In the midst of heaven appears a woman (the Church of Israel) clothed with the sun, having the moon under her feet, and around her head a crown of twelve stars (the twelve tribes of Israel). She cries as if she was in the throes of labour, pregnant as she is with the ideal Messiah. Before her is set an enormous red dragon, with seven crowned heads and ten horns, and whose tail, sweeping the sky, draws down a third of the stars and casts them on the earth. It is Satan, in the features of the most powerful of his incarnations, the Roman empire, the red pictures the imperial purple. The seven crowned heads are the seven Cæsars who have reigned up till the time the author writes: Julius Cæsar, Augustus, Tiberius, Caligula, Claudius, Nero and Galba; the ten horns are the ten pro-consuls who govern the provinces. The dragon waits for the birth of the child to devour it. The woman brings into the world a son, destined "to rule the nations with a rod of iron"--a feature characteristic of the Messiah. The child (Jesus) is raised to heaven by God. God places him at his side upon his throne. The woman flees into the desert, where God has prepared a retreat for her for 1,260 days. There is here an evident allusion either to the flight of the Church from Jerusalem or to the peace which it should enjoy within the walls of Pella during the three years and a half which remain until the end of the world, or to the residence which the Judaizing Christians and some Apostles had in the province of Asia. The image of the "desert" agrees better with the former explanation than with the latter. Pella, beyond Jordan, was a peaceable country, bordering upon the deserts of Arabia, and where the sound of war scarcely ever came.

Then a great battle takes place in heaven. Up till then Satan, the Katigor, the malevolent critic of the creation, had his entrées into the divine court. He profits by them, according to an old habit which he had not lost since the age of the patriarch Job, to hurt pious men and especially the Christians, and to bring upon them frightful troubles. The persecutions of Rome and Ephesus have been his work. Now he will lose this privilege. The archangel Michael (the guardian angel of Israel) with his angels, gives battle to him. Satan is defeated, chased from heaven, cast to the earth as well as his supporters; a song of victory arises, when the celestial beings see precipitated from height to depth the caluminator, the detractor of all good, who does not cease day and night to accuse and to blacken their brethren dwelling on the earth. The church of heaven and that below fraternize over the defeat of Satan. That defeat is due to the blood of the Lamb and also to the courage of the martyrs who have carried their sacrifice even up to death. But woe to the profane world The Dragon has descended to his own place, and they can all wait for his despair; for he knows that his days are numbered.

The first object against which the Dragon cast on the earth turns his rage, is the woman (the church of Israel) who has brought into the world this divine fruit whom God has made to sit at his right hand. But protection from on high covers the woman; there are given to her the two great wings of an eagle, bearing herself on which she goes to the place prepared for her, that is Pella. She is nourished there three years and a half, far from the sight of the Dragon. His fury is now at its height. He vomits out of his mouth after the woman a river to hurt her and stop her, but the earth comes to the help of the woman; it opens and absorbs the river (an allusion to some circumstance of the flight to Pella which is unknown to us). The Dragon, seeing his powerlessness against the woman (the mother-church of Israel) turns his anger against "the rest of her race," that is, against the churches of the Dispersion who keep the precepts of God and are faithful to the testimony of Jesus. There is here an evident allusion to the persecutions of the last days, and especially to that of the year 64.

Then the prophet sees coming up from the sea a beast which in many points resembles the Dragon. It has ten horns, and seven heads and diadems on its ten horns, and on each of its heads a blasphemous name. Its general aspect is that of the leopard; his feet are those of a bear, his mouth that of a lion. The Dragon (Satan) gives him his strength, his throne and his power. One of his heads has received a mortal blow; but the wound has been healed. The whole earth falls in wonder before this powerful animal, and all men begin to worship the Dragon because he has given power to the beast; they also worship the beast, saying: "Who is like the beast, and who can fight against him?" And there is given to him a mouth speaking words full of blasphemy and pride, and the duration of his omnipotence is fixed at forty-two months (three years and a half). Then the beast begins to vomit forth blasphemies against

God, against his name and the tabernacle, and against those who dwell in heaven. And it was given to him to make war on the saints and to conquer them, and power was ceded to him over every tribe and tongue and race. And all men worshipped him except those whose name is written from the beginning of the world in the book of life of the lamb who has been slain: "Let him hear who hath ears, he who makes captive shall be made captive in his turn, he who takes the sword shall perish by the sword. This is the secret of the patience and the faith of the saints."

This symbolism is very clear. Already in the Sibylline poem, composed in the second century B.C., the Roman power is qualified by having "numerous heads." The allegories drawn from polycephalous beasts were very much in vogue; the principal interpretation of these emblems was to consider each head as signifying a sovereign. The monster of the Apocalypse, is besides, composed by the reunion of the attributes of the four empires of Daniel, and that alone shows it concerns a new empire, absorbing in itself the former empires. The beast which comes forth from the sea is therefore the Roman empire, which, to the people of Palestine, appeared to come from beyond the seas. This empire is only a form of Satan (the dragon) or rather, it is Satan himself with all his attributes; he holds his power to cause Satan to be adored, that is, to maintain idolatry, which, to the authors mind, is nothing but the worship of demons. The ten crowned are the ten provinces, whose pro-consuls are real kings; the seven heads are the seven emperors who have succeeded each other from Julius Cæsar to Galba; the blasphemous name written on each head is the title of Σεβαστός, or Augustus, which appeared to the seven Jews to imply an injury to God. The whole world is given up by Satan to this empire, in return for the homage which the said empire procures Satan; the greatness and the pride of Rome, the imperium which it has decreed, its divinity, an object of a special and public worship, are a perpetual blasphemy against God, sole real sovereign of the world. The empire in question is naturally the enemy of the Jews and Jerusalem. He made a fierce war with the saints (the author appears on the whole favourably to the Jewish revolt): he will conquer them; but he has only three and a-half years to last. He with the head wounded to death, but whose wound has been healed, is Nero, lately overthrown, saved miraculously from death, and who was believed to have taken refuge with the Parthians. The adoration of the beast is the worship of "Rome and Augustus," so much spread over all the province of Asia, and which was made the basis of the religion of the country.

The symbol which follows is far from being as transparent to us. Another beast goes forth from the earth; it has two horns like those of a lamb, but it speaks like the Dragon (Satan). It exercises all the power of the first beast in its presence and under its eyes; it fills in its turn the rôle of delegate, and employs all its authority to cause the inhabitants of the earth to worship the first beast, "whose mortal hurt has been cured." This second beast works great miracles; it goes so far as to bring the fire of heaven upon the earth in presence of numerous spectators; it seduces the world by the prodigies which it executes in the name and for the service of the first beast (of that beast, adds the author, which has received a stroke of the sword and nevertheless lives). And there was given (to the second beast) to put the breath of life into the image of the first beast, so that that image spoke. And it had the power to cause after this that all those who refused to adore the first beast should be put to death. And it established as a law that all, small and great, rich and poor, free and slaves, should bear a mark on their right hand or on their forehead. And it commanded besides that no one should be able to buy or sell if he did not bear the sign of the beast, or his name in all its letters, that is, the number made up by the letters of his name added together like figures. "Here is wisdom!" cries the author. "Let him who has understanding calculate the number of the beast. It is the number of a man This number is 666."

In reality, if we add together the letters of the name of Nero, transcribed in Hebrew nrrn qsv (Νέρων Καῖσαρ) according to their numerical value we obtain the number 666. Neron Kesar was indeed the name by which the Christians of Asia designated the monster; the coins of Asia bore as a legend: ΝέΡΩΝ ΚΑῖΣΑΡ. Those kinds of reckonings were familiar to the Jews, and made a cabbalistic puzzle which they called ghematria; the Greeks of Asia even were no longer strangers to it; in the second century the Gnostics affected it.

Thus the Emperor, who was represented by the head wounded to death, but not killed (the author himself tells us), is Nero--Nero who, according to a popular opinion widespread in Asia, still lived. But who is this second beast, this agent of Nero, who has the manners of a pious Jew, and the language of Satan, who is the alter ego of Nero, toils for his profit, and even causes a statue of Nero to speak, persecutes the believing Jews who do not wish to render Nero the same honour as the heathen, nor to bear the mark of affiliation to his party, renders life impossible, and forbids them to do the most necessary things, to buy and sell? Certain peculiarities would apply to a Jewish functionary, such as Tiberius Alexander, devoted to the Romans and held by his compatriots as an apostate. The mere fact of paying the impost to the empire might be called "an adoration of the beast," tribute in the eyes of the Jews having the character of a religious offering, and implying a worship of the sovereign. The sign or mark of the beast (Neron Kaisar) that it would be needful for him to enjoy the common law, must have been either the brevet of a Roman citizenship, without which in some countries life was difficult, and which for the enthusiastic Jews constituted the crime of association with a work of Satan; or the coin with the effigies of Nero, a coin held by the revolted Jews as execrable because of the images and blasphemous inscriptions they found there, so that they hastened, when they were free at Jerusalem, to Substitute an orthodox coin for it. The partisan of the Romans who is in question, by maintaining the money with Nero's stamp as having a forced course in transactions, would appear to have been held to be wicked. Money with Nero's stamp alone passed in the market, and those who by religious scruple refused to touch it were put outside the law.

The pro-consul of Asia at this time was Fonteius Agrippa, a grave functionary, to whom we cannot look to take us out of our embarrassment. A high priest of Asia, zealous for the worship of Rome and Augustus, and accustomed to vex the Jews and the Christians by the delegation of civil power which was granted him, meets some of the exigencies of the problem. But the features which the second beast presents as a seducer and a wonder-worker do not agree with such a personage. These features lead us to think of a false prophet, an enchanter, notably Simon the Magician, imitator of Christ, become in the legend the flatterer, the parasite and the wizard of Nero, or to Balbillus of Ephesus, or to the Antichrist, of whom Paul speaks obscurely in the second epistle to the Thessalonians It is probable that the personage seen here by the author of the Apocalypse is some impostor of Ephesus, a partisan of Nero, probably an agent of the false Nero or the false Nero himself. The same personage, in fact, is later on called "the False Prophet" in the sense that he is the proclaimer of a false god who is Nero. It is necessary to take account of the importance held at this time by the Magi, the Chaldean and "Mathematicians," pests of whom Ephesus was the principal home. We recall also that Nero dreamed once of "the kingdom of Jerusalem," that he was much mixed up with the astrological movements of his age, and that, nearly alone of all the emperors, he was worshipped while he lived, which was the sign of the Antichrist. During his travels in Greece, especially, the adulation of Achaia and Asia went beyond all conceivable bounds. Lastly, we cannot forget the seriousness which in Asia and the islands of the Archipelago attached to the movement of the false Nero. The circumstance that the second beast came from the earth, and not like the first from the sea, shows that the incident spoken of took place in Asia or Judea, not at Rome. All this is not sufficient to remove the obscurities of this vision, which no doubt would have in the mind of the author the same material precision as the others, but which, connecting itself with a provincial fact which the historians have not mentioned, and which has only an importance in the personal impression of the Seer, remains a puzzle to us.

In the midst of the waves of wraths there now appears a grassy islet. In the most violent of the frightful struggles of the last days, it shall be a place of refreshment: it is the church--the little family of Jesus. The prophet sees, resting on Mount Sion, the 144,000 sealed out of the whole world, bearing the name of God written on their foreheads. The Lamb dwells peacefully in the midst of them. Some celestial chords of harps descend on the assembly; the musicians sing a new song, which no ether than the 144,000 elect can repeat. Chastity is the sign of those blessed ones; all are virgin, without stain; their mouth has never uttered a lie: they also follow the Lamb whithersoever he goes, as firstfruits of the earth and the nucleus of the future world.

After this brief glance at a residence of innocence and peace, the author returns to his terrible visions. Three angels rapidly cross the sky. The first flies in the zenith holding the everlasting Gospel. He proclaims in the face of all nations the new doctrine, and announces the day of judgment. The second angel celebrates in advance the destruction of Rome. "She has fallen, she has fallen, the great Babylon which has made all nations drunk with the wine of her fornication." The third angel forbids the adoration of the beast and the images of the beast borne by the false prophet. "Those who shall worship the beast or his image, who shall receive the mark of the beast on their forehead or hand, shall drink of the burning wine of God, of the pure wine pressed within the cup of his anger; and they shall be tormented in the fire and brimstone before the angels and before the Lamb; and the smoke of their torments shall mount through the ages of ages, and they shall have no rest day nor night, those who adore the beast or his image, and who receive on them the sign of his name." It is here that the patience of the saints, those who keep the commandments of God and the faith of Jesus, shines forth. To reassure the faithful as to a doubt which sometimes relatively torments them as to the lot of the brethren who die every day, a voice orders the prophet to write: "Blessed from henceforth are the dead who die in the Lord, yea, saith the Spirit, they rest from their labours and their works follow them."

Pictures of the great judgment present themselves to the imagination of the Seer. A white cloud comes from the sky: on this cloud is seated like a Son of Man an angel like the Messiah having on his bead a golden crown and in his hand a sharp sickle. The harvest of the earth is ripe. The Son of Man puts forth his sickle and the earth is reaped. Another angel comes to the vintage; he throws it all into the great winepress of the wrath of God. The winepress is trodden under-foot outside the city; the blood which comes forth from it rises up to the horse bridles, over a space of six hundred stadii.

After these different episodes, a celestial ceremony, analogous to the two mysteries of the opening of the seals and the trumpet unrolls itself before the Seer. Seven angels are charged to quiet the earth with seven different hurts, by which the wrath of God may be exhausted. But first we are reassured as to what concerns the fate of the elect. Upon a vast crystalline sea, mingled with fire, are seen the conquerors of the beast, that is, those who have refused to adore his image and the number of his name, holding in their hands the harps of God, singing the song of Moses after the passage of the Red Sea and the song of the Lamb. The door of the heavenly tabernacle is opened and seven angels are seen coming out of it clothed in linen and their bosoms girt with girdles of gold. One of the four living creatures gives them seven cups of gold full to the brim of the wrath of God. The temple is then filled with the smoke of a divine majesty, and no one can enter till the seven cups are emptied.

The first angel empties his cup on the earth and a pernicious ulcer strikes all men who bear the mark of the beast and who adore his image.

The second empties his cup upon the sea and it is changed into blood, and all the animals living in its bosom die.

The third angel empties his cup upon the rivers and streams and they are changed into blood. The angel of the waters does not complain of the loss of his element. He says: "Thou art just, oh Lord, and art holy, who art and who west, thou shalt do whatsoever is right. They have shed the blood of the saints and the prophets, and thou hast given them blood to drink; they are worthy of it." The altar says from its side: "Yea, Lord God Almighty, thy judgments are true and just." The fourth angel empties his cup upon the sun and the sun burns men like a fire. Men, far from being penitent, blaspheme God, who has power to smite them with such plagues.

The fifth angel empties his cup upon the throne of the beast (the city of Rome) and all the kingdom of the beast (the Roman empire) is plunged into darkness. Men gnaw their tongues in pain; in place of repenting they insult the God of heaven.

The sixth angel empties his cup into the Euphrates, which dries up at once to prepare the way for the king's coming from the East. Then, from the mouth of the dragon (Satan), from the mouth of the beast (Nero), and from the mouth of the False Prophet (?) proceed three unclean spirits like frogs. These are the spirits of devils, working miracles. These three spirits would find the kings of the whole earth, and assemble them for the battle of the great day of God. ("I come as a thief," cries the voice of Jesus in the midst of all this. "Blessed is the man who watches and keeps his garments lest he should need to go naked and men should see his shame.") They gather together, and say, in the place which is called in Hebrew, Armageddon. The general thought of all this symbolism is clear enough. We have already formed with the Seer the opinion universally adopted in the province of Asia that Nero, after having escaped from Phaon's villa, had taken refuge among the Parthians, and that from thence he would return to crush his enemies. It is believed, not without apparent grounds, that the Parthian princes, friends of Nero during his reign, maintained him yet, and it is the fact that the court of the Arsacides was for more than twenty years the refuge of the false Neros. All this seems to the author of the Apocalypse an infernal plan, conceived between Satan, Nero, and this counsellor of Nero, who has already figured under the form of the second beast. These condemned creatures are occupied in forming in the East a league, whose army shall soon pass the Euphrates and crush the Roman empire. As to the special puzzle in the name Armageddon, it is to us undecipherable.

The seventh angel empties his vial into the air; a cry comes forth from the altar, "It is done'" And there were lightnings, and voices, and thunderings, and an earthquake such as has never been seen, while the great city (Jerusalem) is broken into three parts; and the cities of the Decapolis are destroyed, and the great Babylon (Rome) comes up in remembrance before God, who is prepared at length to make her drink of the cup of His wrath. The islands fled, and the mountains disappeared: hail of the weight of a talent fell on men, and men blasphemed because of this plague.

The cycle of the preludes is completed, and there remains nothing more but to see the judgment of God unroll itself. The Seer makes us first look on at the judgment of the greatest of all the culprits, the city of Rome. One of the seven angels who has emptied the vials approaches God and says to him: "Come, and I will show thee the judgment of the great whore who sits on the great waters, with whom the kings of the earth have committed fornication." John then saw a woman seated on a beast like that which, coming forth from the sea, figured in its entirety the Roman empire, by one of its heads, Nero. The beast is scarlet, covered with names of blasphemy, it has seven heads and ten horns. The prostitute wears the dress of her profession; clothed in purple, covered with gold, pearls, and precious stones, she holds in her hand a cup full of the abomination and impurities of her fornication. And upon her forehead is written a name, a mystery, "Babylon the great, the mother of harlots, and the abomination of the earth."

And I saw the woman drunken with the blood of the saints and with the blood of the martyrs of Jesus. And when I saw her, I wondered with a great wonder, and the angel said unto me, Wherefore didst thou wonder? I will tell thee the mystery of the woman, and of the beast that carrieth her, which hath the seven heads and the ten horns. The beast that thou sawest was, and is not, and is about to come out of the abyss, and to go into perdition. And they that dwell on the earth shall wonder, they whose name hath not been written in the book of life from the foundation of the world, when they behold the beast, how that he was, and is not and shall come. Here is the mind which hath wisdom. The seven heads are seven mountains on which the Roman sitteth: and they are seven kings, the five are fallen, the one is, the other is not yet come; and when he cometh he must continue a little while. And the beast that was, and is not, is himself also an eighth, and is of the seven; and he goeth into perdition. And the ten horns that thou sawest are ten kings, which have received no kingdom as yet; but they receive authority as kings, with the beast for one hour. These have one mind, and they give their power and authority unto the beast. These shall war against the Lamb, and the Lamb shall overcome them, for he is Lord of lords, and King of kings; and they also shall overcome that are with him, called and chosen and faithful. And he saith unto me, the waters which thou sawest where the harlot sitteth, are peoples, and multitudes, and nations, and tongues. And the ten horns which thou sawest, and the beast, these shall hate the harlot, and shall make her desolate, and naked, and shall eat her flesh, and shall burn her bitterly with fire. For God did put in their hearts to do his mind, and to come to one mind, and to give their kingdom unto the beast, until the words of God should be accomplished; and the woman whom thou sawest is the great city, which reigneth over the kings of the earth.

This is quite clear. The harlot is Rome, who has corrupted the world, who has employed her power to propagate and to uphold idolatry, who has persecuted the saints, and who has made the blood of the martyrs to flow in streams. The beast is Nero, who was believed to be dead; who shall return, whose second reign shall be ephemeral and be followed by complete destruction. The seven heads have two meanings; they are the seven hills on which Rome is set; but they are especially the seven emperors: Julius Cæsar, Augustus, Tiberius, Caligula, Claudius, Nero and Galba. The first five are dead. Galba reigns for the moment; but he is old and feeble; he soon falls. The sixth, Nero, who is at once the beast and one of the seven kings, is not really dead; he will reign still, but for a short time; he will be thus the eighth king, and then perish. As to the ten horns; these are the pro-consuls and the imperial legates of the ten principal provinces who are not real kings, but who receive power from the emperor for a limited time, ruling agreeably to one thought, that which is conveyed to them from Rome, and are perfectly submissive to the empire, from whom they derive their power. These partial kings are all as malevolent against the Christians as Nero himself. Representing provincial interests, they will humble Rome, and take from her the right of conducting the empire, which she has enjoyed till then, maltreating her, setting her on fire, and sharing in her ruins. Yet God will not allow the dismemberment of the empire yet; he inspires the generals, commandants of the provincial armies, and all those who should have one by one the fate of the empire in their hands (Vindex, Virginius, Nymphidius, Sabinus, Galba, Macer, Capito, Otho, Vitellius, Mucian, and Vespasian), to act in harmony for the reconstitution of the empire, and instead of establishing it under independent sovereigns, which appears to the Jewish author the most natural position, to do homage for their kingdom to the beast.

We see at what point the pamphlet by the head of the churches of Asia enters into the life of a position which, for an imagination so easily struck as that of the Jews, would appear strange; in fact, Nero by his wickedness and folly of a special kind, had thrown reason out of doors. The empire at his death was as if escheat. After the assassination of Caligula, there was still a republican party; besides, the adopted family of Augustus had all his prestige; after Nero 's assassination, there was no longer a republican party, and the family of Augustus was extinct. The empire fell into the hands of eight or ten generals who held high commands. The author of the Apocalypse, not understanding anything as to the Roman matters, is astonished that ten leaders, who appeared to him as kings, should not be declared independent and form a concert, and has attributed this result to an act of the divine will. It is clear that the Jews of the east, oppressed by the Romans for two years back, and who feel themselves feebly compact since July 68, because Mucian and Vespasian were absorbed by general affairs, believed that the empire was about to be dissolved, and triumphed for a while. There was in this not such a superficial view as we might believe. Tacitus, beginning the recital of the events of the year on the threshold of which the Apocalypse was written, calls it annum reipublicæ prope supremum. It was to the Jews a great astonishment when they saw the "ten kings" come before the "beast" and put their kingdoms at his feet. They had hoped that the result of the independence of the "ten kings" would be the ruin of Rome; antagonistic to a great central State organisation they thought the pro-consuls and the legates would hate Rome, and judging them according to themselves, they supposed that these powerful leaders might act like the satraps, or indeed like the Hyrcani kings exterminating their enemies. They had relished at least like spiteful provincials the great humiliation which the city had endured, when the right of making the sovereigns passed to the provinces, and Rome received within her walls masters whom she had not first called to power.

Such was the relation of the Apocalypse with the singular episode of the false Nero, who just at the moment when the Seer of Patmos wrote filled Asia and the islands of the Archipelago with emotion. Such a coincidence is assured by the most singular facts. Cythnos and Patmos are only forty leagues from each other, and news circulates quickly in the Archipelago. The days of the Christian prophet were those when most was spoken of the impostor, hailed by some with enthusiasm, looked upon with terror by others. We have shown that he established himself at Cythnos in 69, or perhaps in December 68. The centurion Sisenna who touched at Cythnos in the first days of February, coming from the East and bringing to the Pretorians of Rome some pledges of agreement on the part of the army of Syria, had much difficulty in escaping from them. A few days after, Calpurnius Asprenas, who had received from Galba the government of Galatia and Pamphylia, and who was accompanied by two galleys of the fleet of Misena, arrived at Cythnos. Some emissaries of the pretender tried the magical effect of the name of Nero on the commanders of the ships; the knave, affecting a sorrowful air, appealed to those who were formerly "his soldiers." He begged them at least to conduct him to Syria or Egypt, countries on which he founded his hopes The commanders, whether from cunning or whether they were moved by this, asked for time. Asprenas, having heard of everything, took the impostor by surprise and caused him to be killed. His body was taken to Asia, then brought to Rome, so as to refute those of his partisans who would have wished to raise doubts as to his death. Would it be to this wretch that allusion is made in these words: "The beast thou sawest was and is no more, and it is coming forth from the abyss, and it hastens to its destruction . . . the other being is not yet, and when he shall come, he will remain a little?" It is possible. The monster rising from the abyss would be a lively image of ephemeral power which the sagacious writer saw coming forth from the sea in the horizon of Patmos. One cannot pronounce on this with certainty, for the opinion that Nero was among the Parthians was sufficient to explain everything; but this opinion did not exclude belief in the false Nero of Cythnos, since it could be supposed that his reappearance might be the return of the monster, coinciding with the passage of the Euphrates of his Eastern allies. In any case, it appears to us impossible that these lines had been written after the murder of the false Nero by Asprenas. The sight of the impostor's corpse carried from city to city, the contemplation of his features marked by death, would have spoken very plainly against the apprehensions of the beast's return, by which the author is possessed. We admit therefore willingly that John, in the isle of Patmos, had cognisance of the events in the isle of Cythnos, and that the effect produced upon him by some strange rumours was the principal cause of the letter he wrote to the Churches of Asia, to convey to them the great news of Nero risen again.

Interpreting the political events to the taste of his hatred, as a fanatic Jew, he predicted that the commandants of the provinces, whom he believed full of rancour against Rome, and up to a certain accord with Nero, should ravage the city and burn it Taking the fact now as accomplished, he sings of the ruin of his enemy. He has for that only to copy the declamations of the ancient prophets against Babylon and Tyre. Israel has marked the history of its curses. To all the great profane States he said: "Blessed is he who shall render thee for the evil which thou hest done us!" A bright angel descends from heaven, and with a strong voice: "Fallen, fallen," said he, "is the great Babylon, and it is no longer anything but a dwelling for devils, a place for unclean spirits, a refuge for abominable birds, because that all the nations have drunk of the wine of her fornication, with whom the kings of the earth have polluted themselves, and by whom the merchants of the earth have been enriched by her wealth." Another voice was heard from heaven saying:

Come out of her, my people, lest be ye partakers of her crimes and be struck by the plagues which will fall on her. Her abominations have come up even to heaven, and God has remembered her iniquities. Render her what she has done to others; pay her back double for her works; return her the double of the cup she has poured out to others. For as much glory and wealth as she had, so give her as much torment and affliction. I sit as a queen, said she in her heart; and shall never know sorrow. Behold why her chastisements shall come all in the same day: death, desolation, famine and fire; for powerful is the God who judges her. And there shall be seen weeping over her the kings of the earth who have partaken of her uncleanness and her debaucheries. At the sight of the smoke of her burning; "Woe woe!" shall her companions in debauchery exclaim, keeping at a distance, struck with terror. "What! the great, the powerful Babylon! In one hour her judgment has come!" And the merchants of the earth shall bewail her, for no one longer buys their merchandise. Vessels of gold and silver, precious stones, pearls, fine linen, purple, silk, scarlet, thyinewood, ivory, brass, iron, marble, incense, wine, oil, flour of wheat, corn, beasts, sheep, horses, chariots, bodies and souls of men; . . . the merchants of all these things, who were enriched by her, standing at a distance in fear of her torments: "Woe! Woe!" they will say, "What! is that great city which was clothed in scarlet, purple, and fine linen, and adorned with gold, precious stones and pearls destroyed? In one hour have so much riches perished?" And the sailors who came to her and all those who traffic at sea, standing at a distance, at sight of the smoke of her burning, throwing ashes on their heads, give forth cries, weeping and lamentations. "Woe Woe!" they say, "The great city which enriched with its treasures all those who had vessels on the sea, behold in an hour has been changed into a desert."

Rejoice over her ruin, Ω heaven; rejoice, ye saints, apostles and prophets; for God has judged your cause and has avenged you of her."

Then an angel of strong power seized a great stone, like n millstone, and cast it into the sea, saying:

Then shall Babylon be thrown down, and there shall be found no longer a trace of her; and the voice of the harp players and the musicians, the sound of the flute and the trumpet shall be heard no more at all in thee, and the light of a lamp shall shine no more at all in thee, and the voice of the bridegroom and of the bride shall be heard no more at all in thee, for thy merchants were the princes of the earth, for with thy sorcery were all the nations deceived. And in her was found the blood of prophets and of saints, and of all that have been slain upon the earth.

The ruin of this chief enemy of the people of God is the object of great festival in heaven. A voice like that of an innumerable multitude makes itself heard and cries "Alleluia! salvation, and glory and power to our God; for his judgments are righteous, and he has judged the great whore who has polluted the earth by her whoredom, and he has revenged the blood of his servants shed by her." And another chorus replies: "Alleluia! the smoke of her burning shall ascend in the ages of ages." Then the four-and-twenty elders and the four beasts prostrate themselves and adore God, seated on the throne, saying: "Amen! Alleluia!" A voice comes forth from the throne chanting the inaudible song of the new kingdom, "Praise our God all ye who are his servants and who fear him small and great;" a voice like that of a crowd or like that of great waters, or like the sound of a mighty thunder replied, "Alleluia, it is now that the Lord God Almighty reigns; let us rejoice and free ourselves quickly and render him the glory, for behold the hour of the Lamb's marriage is come, and the garments of his bride are ready; and it has been given her to be clothed in a robe of fine linen of brightness sweet and pure. "The fine linen," adds the author, "is the virtuous acts of the saints." Delivered in fact from the presence of the great whore (Rome) the earth is ripe for the heavenly marriage, for the reign of Messiah. The angel says to the Seer, write: "Blessed are those invited to the festival of the marriage of the Lamb." Then the heaven opens, and Christ, called there for the first time by his mystic name "The Word of God," appears as a conqueror, mounted upon a white horse. He comes to trample with pressure the grapes of the wrath of God, to inaugurate for the heathen the reign of the sceptre of iron. His eyes sparkle. His garments are tinged with blood; he wears upon his head many crowns with an inscription in mysterious characters. From his mouth goes forth a sharp sword to strike the Gentiles; upon his thigh is written his title, King of Kings, Lord of Lords. The whole army of heaven follows him on white horses and clothed in white linen. They look for his peaceful triumph, but it is not yet time. Although Rome may be destroyed, the Roman world, represented by Nero the Antichrist, is not annihilated. An angel above the sun cries with a strong voice to all the birds which fly in the zenith: "Come, assemble yourselves for the great festival of God, come and eat the flesh of kings and the flesh of tribunes, and the flesh of the strong, and the flesh of horses and their riders, and the flesh of free men and slaves, of great and small." The prophet then sees the beast (Nero) and the kings of the earth (the provincial generals, almost independent) and their armies banded together to make war upon him who is seated upon the horse. And the beast (Nero) is seized and with him the false prophet who works miracles before him; both are thrown alive into the brimstone pit, which burns eternally. Their armies are exterminated by the sword which comes forth from the mouth of him who is seated on the horse, and the birds are satiated with the flesh of the dead.

The Roman armies, the grand instrument of the power of Satan, are conquered; Nero, the Antichrist, their last head, is shut up in hell; but the dragon, the old serpent, Satan, exists still. We have seen how he was cast from heaven to the earth; the earth must now in turn be delivered from him. An angel descends from heaven holding the key of the abyss and having in his hand a great chain. He seizes the dragon, binds him for a thousand years, precipitates him into the abyss, closes with his key the opening of the gulf and seals it with a seal. For a thousand years the devil remains chained; moral and physical evil, which are his productions, are suspended, not destroyed. Satan cannot any longer seduce the peoples, but he is not destroyed for all eternity.

A tribunal is established to proclaim those who should take part in the reign of a thousand years. This reign is reserved for the martyrs. The first place there belongs to the souls which have been smitten by the axe to render testimony to Jesus and to the word of God (the Roman martyrs of 64); then come those who have refused to worship the beast and his image, and who have not received his mark upon their foreheads nor in their hands (the confessors of Ephesus, of whom the Seer was one). The elect of this first kingdom are raised from the dead and reign upon the earth with Christ for a thousand years. It is not that the rest of humanity had disappeared, nor even the whole world had become Christian; the millenium is in the centre of the earth like a little paradise. Rome no longer exists; Jerusalem has replaced it in its position as the capital of the world, the faithful constitute there a kingdom of priests; they serve God and Christ, there is no longer a great profane empire of civil power hostile to the church; the nations come to Jerusalem to render homage to the Messiah who maintains them by terror. During these thousand years the dead who have not had part in the first resurrection do not live, they wait. The participants in the first kingdom are therefore the privileged; beyond eternity, in the infinite, they shall have the millenium on the earth with Jesus. No death shall touch them.

When the thousand years shall have been accomplished, Satan shall be loosed from his prison for some time; evil shall begin again upon the earth. Satan unchained shall wander anew among the nations, shall drive them from one end of the world to the other by frightful wars; Gog and Magog, mythical personages of the barbarian invasions, lead to battle armies as numerous as the sand of the seashore. The church shall be as if drowned in this deluge. The barbarians shall besiege the camp of the saints, the beloved city, that is to say this Jerusalem, terrestrial still, but entirely holy, where the faithful friends of Jesus are; the fire of heaven shall fall upon them and devour them. Then Satan, who has seduced them, shall be cast into the flaming brimstone furnace, where are already the beast (Nero) and the false prophets (?) and where all the cursed go thenceforth to be tormented night and day through the ages of ages.

Creation has now accomplished its task. There remains nothing more but to proceed to the last judgment. A throne shining with light appears, and upon this throne the supreme judge. At sight of him the heaven and the earth fled away, there was no more place found for them. The dead, great and small, are raised again. Death and Sheol give up their prey; the sea on its side gives up the drowned, which, devoured by it, had not regularly descended into Sheol. All appear before the throne. The great books are opened, and in them there is a rigorous account kept of the actions of every man. They open also another book, "the Book of Life," wherein are written the names of those fore-ordained. Then all are judged according to their works. Those whose names are not found written in the Book of Life are cast into the furnace of fire. Death and hell are likewise cast into it.

Evil being destroyed without recovery, the reign of absolute good begins. The old earth and the old heaven have disappeared; a new earth and a new heaven succeed them, and "there was no more sea." That earth and that heaven are nothing, nevertheless, but a regeneration of the present earth and heaven, and even Jerusalem, which was the pearl, the gem of the whole earth, this same Jerusalem shall still be the radiant centre of the new. The apostle saw this new Jerusalem ascending out of heaven from God, clothed like a bride prepared for her husband. A great voice comes forth from the throne, "Behold the tabernacle of God will dwell with men." Men shall be still henceforth his people and he shall be present always in the midst of them, and he shall wipe away all tears from their eyes, and death shall be no more, neither shall there be any more grief, nor cries, nor sorrows, for all that has passed away. Jehovah himself takes the word to promulgate the law of this eternal world. "It is done, behold, I make all things new, I am the A and Ω, I am the beginning and the end. To him who is athirst I will give to drink freely of the water of life. The conqueror shall possess all these good things and I will be his God, and he shall be my son. As to the fearful, the unbelieving, the abominable, murderers, fornicators, authors of wicked deeds, idolaters, and liars, their part shall be in the lake of brimstone and fire." An angel approached the Seer and said to him, "Come I will shew thee the bride of the Lamb," and he led him in spirit to a high mountain from which he shewed him in detail the ideal Jerusalem, permeated and clothed with the glory of God. His appearance was that of a crystalline jasper Its form is that of a perfect square, of three thousand stadia each side, orientated according to the four winds of heaven, and surrounded by a wall forty-four cubits high, pierced by twelve gates. At each gate watches an angel, and above is written the name of one of the twelve tribes of Israel. The foundation of the wall has twelve settings of stones; upon each of the foundations shines the names of the twelve apostles of the Lamb. Each of these foundations is ornamented with precious stones, the first of jasper, the second sapphire, the third chalcedony, the fourth emerald, the fifth sardonyx, the sixth cornelian, the seventh chrysolite, the eighth aquamarine, the ninth topaz, the tenth chrysoprasus, the eleventh jacinth, the twelfth an amethyst. The wall itself is of jasper, the city is of pure gold like transparent glass, the gates are composed of a single large pearl. There was no temple in the city; for God himself and the Lamb serve as a temple. The throne which the prophet at the opening of his revelation has seen in heaven is now in the midst of the city: that is to say, in the centre of a regenerated and harmoniously organized humanity. Upon this throne are seated God and the Lamb. From the base of the throne flows the river of life, brilliant and transparent as crystal. On its banks grows the tree of life, bearing twelve kinds of fruits, a kind for each month; these fruits appear reserved for the Israelites; the leaves have medicinal virtues for the healing of the Gentiles. The city has no need of either the sun or the moon to shine on it; for the glory of God lightens it, and its light is the Lamb. The nations walk in its light; the kings of the earth do homage to him with their glory, and its gates are not shut either day or night, so great shall be the wealth of those who shall come to bring their tribute there. Nothing impure, nothing that defiles shall enter there; all those who are written in the Lamb's book of life shall find a place there. There shall exist no longer any religious division or curse; the pure worship of God and the Lamb shall gather together the whole world. At every moment its servants shall enjoy his presence and his name shall be written in their foreheads. This reign of good shall last through the ages of ages.

CHAPTER XVII

THE FORTUNE OF THE BOOK

The work then closes with this epilogue:

And I John am he that heard and flaw these things. And when I heard and saw I fell down to worship before the feet of the angel which shewed me these things. And he saith unto me, see thou do it not; I am a fellow servant with thee and with thy brethren the prophets, and with them which keep the words of this book; worship God. And he saith unto me, seal not up the words of the prophecy of this book. For the time is at hand. He that is unrighteous, let him do unrighteousness still: and he that is filthy, let him be made filthy still: and he that is righteous, let him do righteousness still: and he that is holy let him be made holy still.

A distant voice, the voice of Jesus himself, is supposed to reply to these promises and to guarantee them.

Behold I come quickly, and my reward is with me to render to each man according as his work is. I am the Alpha and the Omega, the first and the last, the beginning and the end. Blessed are they that wash their robes, that they may have the right to come to the tree of life and may enter in by the gates into the city. Without are the dogs, and the sorcerers, and the fornicators, and the murderers, and the idolaters, and everyone that loveth and maketh a lie. I Jesus have sent mine angel to testify unto you these things for the churches. I am the root and the offspring of David, the bright, the morning star.

Then the voices of heaven and those of earth cross each other and arrive moriendo in a finale of complete sympathy:

And the spirit and the bride say come, and he that heareth, let him say, come. And he that is athirst let him come: he that will, let him take the water of life freely.

I testify unto every man that heareth the words of the prophecy of this book. If any man shall add unto them, God shall add unto him the plagues which are written in this book. And if any man shall take away from the words of the book of this prophecy, God shall take away his part from the tree of life, and out of the holy city which are written in this book.

He which testifieth these things saith, Yea, I come quickly, Amen. Come, Lord Jesus. The grace of the Lord Jesus be with you all, Amen.

There is no doubt that, presented under cover of the most venerated name in Christianity, the Apocalypse made upon the Churches of Asia a very deep impression. A crowd of details now become obscure, were clear to his contemporaries. His bold announcement of an approaching convulsion was not all surprising. Discourses, not less formal, attributed to Jesus, were spread abroad every day and accepted. For a year, besides, the events of the world would present a marvellous confirmation of the Book. About the 1st February the death of Galba and the accession of Otho became known in Asia. Then each day brought some apparent indication of the breaking up of the empire; the powerlessness of Otho became known through all the provinces; Vitellius maintaining his title against Rome and the Senate, the two bloody battles of Bedriac, Otho deserted in his turn, the accession of Vespasian, the battle in the streets of Rome, the fire in the Capitol lit by the combatants, a fire from which many concluded that the destinies of Rome were drawing to a close; everything would appear astonishingly conformable to the gloomy predictions of the prophet. The deceptions did not begin till the taking of Jerusalem, the destruction of the temple, and the final termination of the Flavian dynasty But religious faith is never cast down in its hopes; the work besides was obscure and susceptible in many passages of different interpretations. Thus a few years after the publication of the book a different meaning was attached to many chapters from that which the author had intended. The author had announced that the Roman empire would not be reconstituted, and that the temple of Jerusalem would not be destroyed. It was necessary on these two points to find some way of escape. As to the reappearance of Nero, that was not renounced so readily; even under Trajan, a certain class of people obstinately believed that he would return. For a long time they kept up the idea of the number of the beast. A variant was spread abroad even in Western countries for the accommodation of that number to Latin latitudes: Certain copies bear 616 instead of 666. Now 616 answers to the Latin form, Nero Cæsar (the Hebrew noun counting fifty).

During the three first centuries the general meaning of the book was preserved at least for some initiated persons. The author of the Sibylline poem, which is dated a little before the year 80, if he had not read the prophesy of Patmos, had heard it spoken of. He sees in it quite an analagous order of ideas; he knows what the sixth vial signifies. For him Nero is the Anti-Messiah: the monster has fled beyond the Euphrates; he will return with thousands of men. The author of the apocalypse of Esdras, (a work dating from certainly the year 96, 97, or 98), notoriously imitates the apocalypse of John, employs his symbolic process, his notations, and his language. We can say as much of the Ascension of Isaiah (a work of the second century), where Nero, the incarnation of Belial, plays a rôle which proves that the author knew the number of the beast. The authors of the Sibylline poems, which date from the time of the Antonines, penetrate likewise the enigmas of the apostolic manifesto, and adopted their utopias, even those which, like the return of Nero, were decidedly smitten with decay. St. Justin and Melito appear to have had a nearly complete knowledge of the book. We can say as much of Commodian who (about 250) mingled with his interpretation some elements from another source, but who does not for an instant doubt that Nero, the Anti-Christ, will be raised from hell to carry on a final conflict against Christianity, and who conceived the destruction of Rome-Babylon exactly as it was conceived of two hundred years before. Lastly, Victorinus of Pettau (died 303) comments upon the Apocalypse with a very correct sentiment. He knew perfectly that Nero raised again was the real Anti-Christ. As to the number of the beast it was lost probably before the beginning of the second century. Ironæus (about 190) deceives himself grossly upon this point, as also upon some others of major importance and opens the series of chimerical commentaries and arbitrary symbolisms. Some subtle peculiarities, such as the meaning of the false prophet and Armageddon, were lost at an early date.

After the reconciliation of the empire and the church, in the fourth century, the fortune of the Apocalypse was gravely compromised. The Greek and Latin doctors, who no longer separated the future of Christianity from that of the empire, could not admit as inspired a book whose fundamental basis was hatred of Rome and a prediction of the end of its ruler. Nearly every enlightened portion of the Eastern church which had received a Hellenic education, full of dislike to the Millenarian and Judeo--Christian writings--declared the Apocalypse apocryphal. The book had taken in the Greek and Latin New Testament such a strong position that it was impossible to expel it; men had recourse, to disembarrass themselves of the objections which it raised, to feats of exegetical power. Yet the evidence was crushing The Latins, less opposed than the Greek to millenarianism, continued to identify Anti-Christ with Nero. Up to the time of Charlemagne, there was a sort of tradition of that kind. St. Beat of Liebana, who commented on the Apocalypse in 786, affirms, by mixing up, it is true, more than one inconsequence, that the beast of chapters xiii. and xvii., which should reappear at the head of ten kings to destroy the City of Rome, is Nero, the Anti-Christ. For a moment even there are two elements of the principle which, in the nineteenth century, shall lead the critics to the true computation of the Emperors and the fixing of the date of the book.

It was not till about the twelfth century, when the Middle Ages threw themselves into the path of a scholastic rationalism, little concerned with the tradition of the Fathers, that the meaning of the vision of John was at all compromised. Joachim of Flores may be considered as the first who carried the Apocalypse boldly into the field of boundless imagination, and sought, under the bizarre figures of a circumstantial writing, which limited its horizon to three and a-half years, the secret of the entire future of humanity.

The chimerical commentaries to which this false idea gave rise have thrown on the book an unjust discredit. The Apocalypse has taken again in our days, thanks to a sounder exegesis, the high place which belongs to it in the sacred writings. The Apocalypse is, in a sense, the seal of prophecy, the last word of Israel. When we read in the ancient prophets, in Joel, for example, the description of "the day of Jehovah," that is of the grand assize which the supreme judge of human things holds from time to time, to restore the order constantly disturbed by men, we find there the germ of the Patmos vision. Every historic revolution or convulsion became, to the fancy of the Jew, determined to pass from the immortality of the soul and to establish the reign of justice on the earth, a providential force, the prelude of a judgment much more solemn and final still. At each event a prophet rose, crying, "Sound, sound the trumpet in Zion; for the day of Jehovah comes; it is near." The Apocalypse is the sequel and the crown of this strange literature, which is the proper glory of Israel. Its author is the last great prophet: he Is only inferior to his predecessors because he imitates them; it is the same soul, the same mind The Apocalypse presents the nearly unique phenomena of a pastiche of genius, of an original cento. If we except two or three inventions peculiar to the author and of marvellous beauty, the entire poem is made up of features borrowed from the earlier prophetic and apocalyptic literature, especially from Ezekiel, from the author of the books of Daniel and the two Isaiahs. The Christian Seer is the true disciple of these great men; he knows their writings by heart, and draws from them the last results. He is the brother (less the serenity and harmony) of that marvellous poet of the time of the captivity of that second Isaiah, whose luminous soul appears as if impregnated (six hundred years in advance) with all the dew and all the perfumes of the future.

Like the larger number of people who possess a brilliant past literature, Israel lived in pictures consecrated by its old and wonderful literature. They were not composed of much else than scraps from the ancient texts; Christian poetry, for example, knew no other literary process. But when passion is sincere the form, even the most artificial, takes from the beauty. The Words of a Believer are in regard to the Apocalypse what the Apocalypse is in regard to the ancient prophets, and yet the Words of a Believer is a book of real effect; one never can re-read it without lively emotion.

The dogmas of the time present, like the style, some-thing artificial; but they correspond to a deep feeling. The process of theological elaboration consists in a bold transposition, applying to the reign of Messiah and to Jesus every phrase of the ancient writings which appears susceptible of a vague relation with an obscure ideal. As the exegesis which presides over these Messianic combinations was thoroughly mediocre, the singular formations of which we speak imply often grave contradictions. That is seen especially in the passages of the Apocalypse concerning Gog and Magog, if we compare these with the parallel passages in Ezekiel. According to Ezekiel, Gog, king of Magog, shall come "in the end of the time" when the people of Israel shall have returned from the captivity and are established in Palestine, to make a war of extermination with them. Already, about the time of the Greek translators of the Bible and of the composition of the book of Daniel, the expression which marks simply in the classical Hebrew an unfixed future signifies "at the end of the time," and is no longer applied except to the time of the Messiah. The author of the Apocalypse is led from this to connect chapters xxxviii. and xxxix. of Ezekiel with the Messianic times, and to look on Gog and Magog as the representatives of the barbarian and heathen world which shall survive the ruin of Rome, and shall co-exist with the millennial reign of Christ and his saints.

This method of creation by the outer way, if I may say so, this fashion of combining by means of an exegesis of appropriation--phrases taken from here and there, and of constructing a new theology by this arbitrary play--is found again in the Apocalypse in everything that regards the mystery of the end of time. The theory of the Apocalypse on this point is distinguished by essential features from that which we find in St. Paul, and from that which the synoptical gospels place in the mouth of Jesus. St. Paul seems, it is true, sometimes to believe in the reign of Christ during the time which should be before the last end of all things, but he never becomes so precise as our author. In fact, according to the Apocalypse, the coming of the future reign of Christ is very near--it ought to follow closely on the destruction of the Roman empire The martyrs shall alone be raised again in this first resurrection: the rest of the dead shall not rise yet. Such absurdities were the result of the slow and incoherent manner in which Israel formed its ideas on the other life. We may say that the Jews have only been led to the dogma of immortality by the necessity of such a dogma to give a meaning to martyrdom. In the second book of the Maccabees, the seven young martyrs and their mother are strong in the belief that they shall rise again, while Antiochus shall not rise. It is in connection with these legendary heroes that we find in Jewish literature the first clear affirmations of an eternal life, and in particular this fine formula: "Those who die for God live in God's sight." We even see a certain tendency leaning towards the creation for them of a sort of special outer tomb, and for ranging themselves near the throne of God, "from then to the present," without awaiting the resurrection. Tacitus, on his side, made the remark that the Jews did not claim immortality but for the souls of those who had died in the combats or in the punishments.

The reign of Christ with his martyrs takes place on the earth, at Jerusalem, doubtless in the midst of nations not converted, but bound in respect towards the saints. It will last a thousand years. After these thousand years there shall be a new reign of Satan over the barbarous nations, whom the Church would not have converted; he shall make horrible wars, and be on the point of crushing the Church itself. God will exterminate them, and then there will come "the second resurrection," that is the general, and the last judgment, which shall be followed by the end of the world. It is the doctrine which has been styled "millenarianism," a doctrine spread soon in the first three centuries, which never could become dormant in the Church, but which has re-appeared constantly at different periods in her history, and is supported by texts much more ancient and formal than those which support many other dogmas universally accepted. It was the result of a materialistic exegesis, ruled by the need of finding true both the phrases in which the kingdom of God was presented as being to endure "through the age of ages," and those in which, to express the indefinite length of the Messianic reign, it was said that it should last "a thousand years." According to the rule of the interpreters, who are called harmonists, they put end to end in a clumsy manner the data which can be made to coincide quite properly. They were guided in the choice of the number thousand by a combination of passages from Psalms, whence there appears to result "that a day of God equals a thousand years." Among the Jews is also found the thought that the reign of Messiah shall not be the blessed eternity, but an era of felicity during the ages which precede the end of the world. Many rabbis hold, like the author of the Apocalypse, the duration of this reign of a thousand years. The author of the epistle attributed to Barnabas declares that, just as the creation took place in six days, in the same way the accomplishment of the destiny of the world shall be completed in six thousand years (a day for God being equivalent to a thousand years), and that after-wards, even as God rested on the seventh day, so also, "when His son shall come, and he shall abolish the age of iniquity and judge the impious and change the sun and moon and all the stars, he shall rest again on the seventh day." This is equivalent to saying he shall reign a thousand years, the reign of the Messiah being always compared to the Sabbath, which ends by rest the gradual agitations of the development of the universe. The idea of the eternity of individual life is so little familiar to the Jews that the era of future rewards is, according to them, confined to a number of years, doubtless considerable, but yet coming to an end.

The Persian aspect of these dreams can be perceived at the first glance. Millenarianism, and, if it can be so expressed, apocalypticism have flourished in Iran for a very long time back. At the bottom of the Zoroastrian ideas there is a tendency to number the ages of the world, to reckon the periods of universal life by hazars, that is by millions of years, to conceive of a reign of salvation which shall be the final crowning of the trials of humanity. These ideas, joined to the statements as to the future which fill the ancient Hebrew prophets, became the soul of Jewish theology in the ages which preceded our era. The Apocalypses especially were penetrated by this; the revelations attributed to Daniel, Enoch, and Moses are nearly all from Persian books, from their style, doctrine, and images. Is that to say that the authors of these extraordinary books had read the Zend writings, such as existed in their time? Not at all. These borrowings were indirect: they arose from what the Jewish fancy had tinged with the colours of Iran. It was the same with the apocalypse of John. The author of this apocalypse had no direct connection with Persia any more than any other Christian; the foreign data which he brought into his book were already incorporated with the traditional midraschim; our Seer takes them film the atmosphere in which he lived. The fact is that since Hoschedar and Hoschedar-mah, the two prophets who preceded Sosiosch, up to the plagues which smote the world on the eve of the great days, up to the wars of the kings with each other, which shall be signs of the last struggle, all the elements on the apocalyptic stage are found again in the Parsi theory as to the end of the world. The seven heavens, the seven angels, the seven Spirits of God, who recur constantly in the vision of Patmos, transport us into full Parsiism, and even beyond that. The hieratic and apostolic meaning of the number seven appears indeed to have its origin in the Babylonian doctrine of the seven planets ruling the fate of men and of empires. Some resemblances more striking still are to he noted in the mystery of the seven seals. Just as, according to the Assyrian mythology, each of the seven tables of fate was dedicated to one of the planets; in the same way the seven seals have singular relations to the seven planets, with the days of the week, and with the colours which the Babylonians associated with the planets. The white horse, indeed, answers to the Moon, the red horse to Mars, the black horse to Mercury, and the yellow horse to Jupiter.

The defects of such a system are manifest, and it was attempted in vain to hide them. Some hard and glaring colours, a complete absence of all plastic sentiment, harmony sacrificed to symbolism, something crude, bitter, and inorganic, made the Apocalypse the perfect antipodes of the Greek chef d'oeuvre, whose type is the living beauty of the body of the man or woman. A sort of materialism lessens the most ideal conceptions of the author. He piles up gold: he has, like the Orientals, an immoderate taste for precious stones. His heavenly Jerusalem is awkward, puerile, impossible, in contradiction to all the good rules of architecture, which are those of reason. He makes it brilliant to the eyes, and he does not dream of having it sculptured by a Phidias. God, likewise, is for him "a smargdine vision," a sort of huge diamond, flashing a thousand fires on a throne. Assuredly Jupiter Olympus was a symbol much superior to that. The error which too often has led away Christian art towards rich decoration finds its root in the Apocalypse. A temple of Jesuits, in gold or in lapis-lazuli, is more beautiful than the Parthenon, if we were to admit this idea, that the liturgical use of a precious article glorifies God.

A most troublesome feature was this gloomy hatred of the profane world, which is common to our author and to all the makers of apocalypses, especially the author of the book of Enoch. His harshness, his passionate and unjust judgments on Roman society, shock us, and justify to a certain extent those who summed up the new doctrine as odium humani generis. The virtuous poor man is always a little inclined to look on the world which he does not know as more wicked than that world is in reality. The crimes of the rich and of people at court appear to him peculiarly gross That sort of virtuous anger, which certain barbarians, such as the Vandals, showed four hundred years later against civilisation, the Jews of the prophetic and apocalyptic school had in a very high degree. They feel among them a remainder of the old spirits of the nomads, whose ideal is patriarchal life, a profound aversion to the great cities regarded as the focus of corruption, and an ardent jealousy against the powerful States, founded on a military principle of which they are incapable, and which they do not admit.

This is what has made the Apocalypse a dangerous book in some points of view. It is the book par excellence of the proud Jew. According to its author, the distinction between Jews and heathens will continue even in the kingdom of God. While the twelve tribes eat of the fruit of the tree of life, the Gentiles must be content with a medicinal concoction of its leaves. The author looks on the Gentiles, even believing in Jesus, even martyrs of Jesus, as strangers introduced into the family of Israel, as plebeians admitted by grace to connect themselves with an aristocracy. His Messiah is essentially the Jewish Messiah; Jesus is for him beyond everything the good David, a product of the Church of Israel, a member of the holy family which God had chosen; it is the Church of Israel which works the saving work by this elect coming forth from its bosom. Every practice capable of establishing a bond between the pure race and the heathen (eating ordinary food, the practice of marriage in the ordinary conditions) appeared to him an abomination. The heathen, as a whole, are, in his eyes, wretches, polluted by all crimes, and who can only be governed by terror. The real world is the kingdom of devils. The disciples of Paul are disciples of Balsam and Jezebel. Paul himself has no place among "the twelve apostles of the Lamb," the only foundation of God's Church; and the Church of Ephesus, the creation of Paul, is praised for having tried those who say they are apostles without being so, and to have found out that they are only liars.

All this is very far from the Gospel of Jesus. The author is too passionate, he sees everything through the veil of a sanguine apoplexy, or the gleam of a fire. What was most lugubrious at Paris on the 25th May, 1871, was not the flames, it was the general colour of the city, when seen from an elevated position: a yellow and false tone, a sort of flat paleness. Such is the light with which our author colours his vision. Nothing resembles it less than the pure sun of Galilee. We feel from the present time that the apocalyptic species, no more than the species of the epistles, shall not be of the literary form which shall convert the world. There are these little collections of sentences and parables which are disdained by exact traditionists, that memory-help by which the less educated and the least well instructed set forth for their own personal use what they know of the acts and words of Jesus, who are destined to be the reading--the charm of the feature. The simple framework of the anecdotal life of Jesus has manifestly done more to enchant the world than the painful piling up of apocalypses and the touching exhortations in the letters of apostles. So true is that Jesus, Jesus only, had in the mysterious work of the Christian growth, always the great, the triumphant, and decisive part. Each book, each Christian institution is valued in proportion to what it contains of Jesus. The synoptical gospels, where Jesus is alone, and of which it may be said he is the true author, are par excellence the Christian book, the eternal book.

Yet the Apocalypse occupies in the sacred canon a legitimate place in many points of view. A book of menaces and terror, it gives a body to the gloomy antithesis which the Christian conscience, moved by a deep aesthetic, would oppose to Jesus. If the Gospel is the book of Jesus, the Apocalypse is the book of Nero. Thanks to the Apocalypse, Nero has for Christianity the importance of a second founder. His odious face has been inseparable from that of Jesus. Increasing century by century, the author coming forth from the nightmare of the year 64, has become the bugbear of the Christian conscience, the gloomy giant of the world's night. A folio book of 500 pages has been composed on its birth and education, its vices, riches, caskets, perfumes, women, doctrines, miracles, and festivals.

Antichrist has ceased to frighten us, and the book of Malvenda has no longer many readers. We know that the end of the world is not so near as the illummati of the first century believed it, and that that end shall not be a sudden catastrophe. It shall take place calmly, in millions of years, when our system shall not repair its losses sufficiently, and when the earth shall have used up the treasure of the old sun warehoused like a provision for the journey in its depths. Before this exhaustion of planetary capital, will humanity attain to perfect knowledge--which is nothing else than the power of mastering the forces of the world, or even the earth--an experience wanting among so many millions of others; will it freeze before the problem which shall kill death has been solved? We know not. But, with the Seer of Patmos, beyond changing alternatives, we shall discover the ideal, and we affirm that this ideal shall be realised some day. Across the clouds of a universe in their state of embryo, we perceive the laws of the progress of life, the consciousness of going on increasing unceasingly, and the possibility of a condition in which all shall be in a definitive being (God) what the innumerable boughs of the tree are in the tree, what the myriads of cells of the living being are in the living being--in a condition, I say, in which the life of everything shall be complete, and in which the persons who have been revived in the life of God, shall see, shall enjoy in Him, singing in Him an eternal Alleluia. Whatever may be the form under which each of us may conceive of this future event of the absolute, the Apocalypse cannot fail to please us. It expresses symbolically that fundamental thought that God is, but especially that He shall be. The features are heavy there, and the contour paltry; it is the thick pencil of a child tracing, with a tool it cannot use, the design of a city it has never seen. His naïve picture of the city of God, a grand toy of gold and pearls, remains no less an element of our dreams. Paul has better said no doubt when he sums up the final goal of the universe in these words: "That God may be all in all." But for a long time humanity yet shall have need of a God to dwell with them, have compassion on their trials, take account of their struggles, and "wipe away all tears from their eyes."

CHAPTER XVIII

THE ACCESSION OF THE FLAVII

The spectacle of the world, as we have already said, only answered too well to the dreams of the Seer of Patmos. The government of the military Coups d'Etat, bore its fruits. Politics were in the camps, and the empire was at auction. There had been some assemblies during Nero's time, where there could be seen gathered together seven future emperors and the father of an eighth. The real republican, Virginius, who wished the empire for the senate and the people, was only a Utopian. Galba, an old honest general, who refused to lend himself to these military orgies, was soon destroyed. The soldiers for a moment had the idea of killing all the senators, to make the government easy. Roman unity appeared on the point of being broken up. It was not only among the Christians that such a tragical situation inspired sinister predictions. Men spoke of a child with three heads, born at Syracuse in 68, and in whom people saw the symbol of the three emperors who ruled for less than a year, and who existed together all three for many hours.

Some days after the prophet of Asia had written his strange work, Galba was killed, and Otho proclaimed (15th January, 69). That was like a resurrection of Nero. Grave, economic, and disagreeable, Galba was in everything the contrary of him whom he replaced. If he had succeeded in making good his adoption of Piso, he would have been a sort of Nerva, and the series of the philosophic emperors would have begun thirty years sooner; but the detestable school of Nero prevailed. Otho resembled that monster; the soldiers and all those who had loved Nero made him their idol. They had seen him by the side of the deceased emperor, playing the part of first of his minions, and rivalling him by his affectation of ostentatious debaucheries, his vices and mad prodigalities. The lower classes gave him from the first day the name of Nero, and it appears as if he took it himself in some letters. He allowed them in any case to set up statues to the Beast; he re-established the Neronian coterie in the great places, and announced loudly as before to continue the principles inaugurated by the last reign. The first act he signed was to secure the completion of the Golden House.

What is sadder is that the political lowering which had taken place did not give security. The ignoble Vitellius had been proclaimed some days before Otho (2nd January, 69) in Germany. He did not desist. A horrible civil war, such as had not been since that between Augustus and Antony, appeared inevitable. The public imagination was much excited; people only saw frightful prognostics; the crimes of the soldiery spread terror everywhere. Never had such a year been seen; the world sweated blood. The first battle of Bedriac, which left the empire to Vitellius alone, (about 15th April) cost the lives of 80,000 men. The disbanded legionaries pillaged the country, and fought among themselves. The people mixed themselves up with them; one would have imagined it was the breaking up of society. At the same time the astrologers and the charlatans of all sorts swarmed; the city of Rome was theirs; reason appeared confounded in presence of a deluge of crimes and follies, which defied all philosophy. Certain words of Jesus which the Christians repeated quite low, kept them in a sort of continual fever; the fate of Jerusalem was especially with them the object of an ardent pre-occupation.

The East, indeed, was not less troubled than the West. We have seen that at the opening of the month of June of the year 68, the military operations of the Romans against Jerusalem were suspended. Anarchy and fanaticism did not diminish for that matter among the Jews. The violent acts of John of Gischala and some zealots rose to their height, John's authority existed chiefly over a corps of Galileans who committed all imaginable excesses. The Jerusalemites often rose and forced John with his brigands to take refuge in the temple; but they feared him so much that, to preserve themselves from him, they believed themselves obliged to oppose a rival to him. Simon, son of Gioras, originally from Gerasa, who was distinguished from the commencement of the war, had filled Idumea with his acts of brigandage. Already he had had to struggle with the zealots, and twice he had appeared threateningly at the gates of Jerusalem. He came back there for the third time when the people called him, believing thus to put themselves under the shelter of a moan offensive to John. This new master entered Jerusalem in the month of March, of the year 69. John of Gischala remained in possession of the temple. The two chiefs sought to surpass each other in ferocity. The Jew is cruel, when he is master. The brother of the Carthaginians at the last hour, shows himself in his natural state. This people has always included an admirable minority; there lies its greatness; but never has there been seen in a group of men so much jealousy, so much ardour in the extermination of each other. Arrived at a certain degree of exasperation, the Jew is capable of everything, even against his religion. The history of Israel shows us people enraged against each other. We can say of this race the good we wish and the evil which we wish, without ceasing to be right; for, let us repeat it, the good Jew is an excellent being, and the bad Jew a detestable being. It is this that explains the possibility of this phenomenon, apparently inconceivable, that the gospel idyll and the horrors recounted by Josephus have been realities in the same land, among the same people, about the same time.

Vespasian, during this time, remained inactive m Cesarea. His son Titus had succeeded in engaging him in a network of intrigues, cunningly combined. Under Galba, Titus had hoped to see himself adopted by the old emperor. After the death of Galba, he saw that he could not arrive at the supreme power except as successor to his father. With the art of the most consummate policy he knew how to turn the chances in favour of a grave, honest general, without distinction, without personal ambition, who did nearly nothing to aid his own fortune. All the East contributed to it. Mucian and the legions of Syria impatiently endured the sight of the legions of the West disposing alone of the empire; they pretended to make him emperor in their turn. Now Mucian, a sort of sceptic more zealous in disposing of the power than in exercising it, did not wish the purple for himself. In spite of his old age, his middle-class birth, his second-rate intelligence, Vespasian found himself designated thus. Titus, who was twenty-eight years of age, raised besides by his merits, his address, his activity, what the talent of his father had obscured. After Otho's death, the legions of the east took only with regret the oath to Vitellius. The insolence of the soldiers of Germany revolted them. They had made them believe that Vitellius wished to send his favourite legions into Syria, and to transport over the borders of the Rhine the legions of Syria, beloved in this country, and to which many alliances had attached them.

Nero, besides, although dead, continued to hold the die of human things, and the fable of his resurrection was not without some truth, as a metaphor. His party survived him. Vitellius, after Otho, placed himself to the great joy of the little people as a declared admirer, imitator, and avenger of Nero. He protested that, in his opinion, Nero had given the model of the best government of the republic. He made him magnificent funeral obsequies, ordered some pieces of his music to be played, and at the first note, rose transported, to give the signal for applause. Reasonable and honest people, fatigued by these miserable parodies of an abhorred reign, wished for a strong reaction against Nero, against his men, against his buildings; they demanded especially the rehabilitation of the noble victims of tyranny. They knew that the Flavii conscientiously played this rôle. In fine, the indigenous princes of Syria pronounced strongly for a chief in whom they saw a protector against the fanaticism of the revolted Jews. Agrippa II. and Berenice, his sister, were body and soul with the two Roman generals. Berenice, although forty years of age, gained Titus by some secrets against which an ambitious young man, a worker, a stranger to the great world, only preoccupied up till now with his own advancement, could not protect himself. She succeeded also with the old Vespasian by her amiabilities and her presents. The two roturier leaders, up till then poor and simple, were seduced by the aristocratic charm of a woman wonderfully beautiful, and by the exterior of a brilliant world they knew nothing of. The passion which Titus conceived for Berenice did not in any wise injure his concerns; everything indicates, on the contrary, that he found in this woman, accomplished in the intrigues of the east, one of the most useful agents. Thanks to her the little kings of Emesa, Sophena, and Comagena, all relatives or allies of the Herods, and more or less converted to Judaism, were gained over by this complot. The Jewish renegade, Tiberius Alexander, prefect of Egypt, entered fully into it. The Parthians even declared themselves ready to uphold Titus.

What was most extraordinary in this is that the moderate Jews, such as Josephus, adhered to him also, and wished with all their strength to apply to the Roman general the ideas by which they were prepossessed. We have seen that the Jewish surroundings of Nero had succeeded in persuading him that, dethroned at Rome, he would find at Jerusalem a new kingdom, which would make him the greatest potentate on the earth. Josephus pretends that from the year 67, at the time when he was made prisoner by the Romans, he predicted to Vespasian the future which awaited him according to certain texts in his sacred scriptures. By dint of repeating their prophecies, the Jews had made a great number of people believe, even some who were not connected with their sect, that the East would gain, and that the master of the world would soon come from Judea. Already Virgil had lulled to sleep the vague sadnesses of his melancholy imagination by applying to his time a Cumæum carmen, which appears to have had some relation to the oracles of the second Isaiah. The Magi, the Chaldeans, and astrologers also talked of the belief in a star of the East; the messenger of a king of the Jews reserved for high destinies. The Christians took these chimeras quite seriously. Prophecy had a double meaning like all oracles; it appeared sufficiently justified if the heads of the legions of Syria, established some leagues from Jerusalem, obtained the empire in Syriain consequence of Assyrian movements. Vespasian and Titus, surrounded by Jews, lent an ear to this discourse, and were pleased by it. While exercising their military talent against the fanatics of Jerusalem, the two generals had a considerable liking for Judaism, studied it, and shewed a deference towards the Jewish books. Josephus had penetrated some time before into their familiar society, especially that of Titus, by his gentle, facile, and insinuating character. He boasted to them of his law, related to them old Biblical stories which he often put in Greek, and spoke mysteriously of the prophecies. Some other Jews entered into the same sentiments, and made Vespasian accept a sort of Messianic position. Some miracles were joined to this; there is mention of cures very analogous to those described in the Gospels wrought by this Christ of a new kind. The heathen priests of Phenicia did not wish to remain behind in this flattering concourse. The oracle of Paphos and the oracle of Carmel maintained that they had announced the advancement of the fortunes of the Flavii. The consequences of all this developed themselves at a later date. Having had the help of Syria, the Flavian emperors were much more open than the disdainful Cæsars to Syrian ideas. Christianity penetrated to the very heart of this family; some adherents were reckoned there, and thanks to this it shall enter on a phase of its destinies quite new. Toward the end of the Spring of 69 Vespasian appeared to wish to leave the military idleness in which policy held him. On the 29th of April he took the field and appeared with his cavalry before Jerusalem. During this time Cerealis, one of his lieutenants, burned Hebron. All Judea submitted to the Romans except Jerusalem and the three castles of Masada, Herodium, and Machero, occupied by the brigands. These four places needed arduous sieges. Vespasian and Titus hesitated to enter on that work in the precarious state in which they then were, on the eve of a new civil war in which they would have need of all their forces. Thus was prolonged for a year the revolution, which, for three years back, had held Jerusalem in the condition of the most extraordinary crisis of which history has preserved the recollection.

On the 1st July, Tiberius Alexander proclaimed Vespasian at Alexandria, and caused the oath to be taken to him; on the 3rd, the army of Judea saluted him as Augustus at Cesarea; Mucian, at Antioch, caused him to be recognised by the Syrian legions, and on the 15th all the East submitted to him. A congress was held at Beyrout, at which it was decided that Mucian should march upon Italy, while Titus continued the war against the Jews, and that Vespasian should await the issue of events at Alexandria. After a bloody civil war (the third which had taken place within eighteen months) power remained definitively with the Flavii. A middle-class dynasty, industrious in business, moderate, not having the energy of the Cæsar race, but exempt also from their errors, was thus substituted for the inheritors of the title erected by Augustus. The prodigals and the fools had so abused their privilege of spoiled children, that people hailed with gladness the accession of a brave man, without distinction, who had slowly risen by merit, in spite of his little absurdities, his vulgar air, and lack of habit. The fact is that the new dynasty conducted business for ten years with sense and judgment, saved the Roman unity, and gave a complete contradiction to the predictions of Jews and Christians who already saw in their dreams the empire dismantled and Rome destroyed. The fire at the Capitol on 19th December, the terrible massacre which took place in Rome the next day, would for the moment make them believe that the great day was drawing nigh. But the undisputed establishment of Vespasian (at the beginning of 20th December) made them feel that they must live still, and forced them to find some shift for adjourning their hopes to a more distant future.

The wise Vespasian, much less shaken than those who fought with him to conquer the empire, spent his time at Alexandria, with Tiberius Alexander. He only revisited Rome in the month of July of the year 70, a little before the total destruction of Jerusalem. Titus, instead of pushing the war in Judea, had followed his father into Egypt; he remained beside him until the early days of March.

The struggles in Jerusalem only increased. Fanatical movements are far from excluding from them those who are actors in their hatred, jealousy, and defiance; banded together, men who are very self-opinionated and passionate usually suspect each other, and there is in that a power; for this reciprocal suspicion creates a terror among them, binds them together as by a chain of iron, and prevents defection and moments of weakness. It is policy, artificial and without conviction, which proceeds with the appearances of concord and civility. Interest creates the coterie; while principles create division, and inspire temptation to decimate, expel and kill their enemies. Those who judge human things by middle-class conceptions believe that the revolution is lost when the revolutionaries "eat each other." There is thereon the contrary, a proof that revolution has all its energy, and that an impersonal ardour guides it. We never see this more clearly than in that terrible drama of Jerusalem. The actors appear to have among them a covenant of death. Like these infernal rondos, in which, as the superstition of Middle Ages taught, men saw Satan forming the chain to draw to a fancied whirlpool files of men dancing and holding each other by the hand; so revolution permits no one to escape from the dance it leads. Terror is behind the conspirators; in turn exalting some, and then they, exalted by others, go on to the abyss; nothing can keep them back, for behind everyone is a hidden sword, which at the moment they wish to stop, compels them to march forward.

Simon, son of Gioras, commanded in the city; John of Gischala with his assassins was master of the temple. A third party was formed, under the conduct of Eleazar, son of Simon, of priestly race, who detached a party of the zealots from John of Gischala and established himself in the inner enceinte of the temple, living on the consecrated provisions they found there, and of those which still continued to be brought to the priests, as first fruits. These three parties were at continual warfare with each other;

they walked over heaps of corpses; they no longer buried the dead. Immense provisions of barley had been made, and this would permit them to exist for years. John and Simon burned these in order to keep each other from them. The situation of the inhabitants was fearful; peaceable people made prayers that order might be re-established by the Romans, but all the exits were guarded by the terrorists, they could not escape. Yet, strange indeed! from the end of the world people still came to the temple. John and Eleazar received the proselytes and profited by their offerings. Often the pious pilgrims were slain in the midst of their sacrifices, with the priests who read the liturgy for them, by the arrows and stones from John's machines. The rebels worked with activity beyond the Euphrates, to obtain help either from the Jews of these countries or from the king of the Parthians. They believed that all the Jews of the East would take up arms. The civil wars of the Romans inspired them with foolish hopes; like the Christians, they believed that the empire was about to be dismembered. Jesus, son of Hanan, had traversed the city, calling for the four winds of heaven to destroy it; on the eve of their extermination the fanatics proclaimed Jerusalem the capital of the world, in the same manner as we have seen Paris invested, hungered, and maintaining all the time that the world was in it, working through it, and suffering with it.

The oddest thing in all this was that they were not altogether wrong. The enthusiasts of Jerusalem, who declared that Jerusalem was eternal, while it was burning, were much nearer the truth than the people who saw in them nothing but assassins. They deceived themselves on the military question, but not on the distant religious result. These disturbed days, indeed, well marked the moment in which Jerusalem became the spiritual capital of the world. The Apocalypse, the burning expression of love which it inspires, has made sacred the image of "the beloved city." Ah! who is able to say beforehand what shall be in the future, holy or wicked, foolish or wise? A sudden change in the course of a vessel makes a progress a retreat, and turns a contrary into a favourable wind. In view of these revolutions, accompanied by thunders and earthquakes, let us place ourselves among the blessed, who sing "Praise ye God," or among the four creatures, spirits of the universe, who after each act of the heavenly tragedy, say Amen.

CHAPTER XIX

DESTRUCTION OF JERUSALEM

At last the circle of fire had wound itself around the unfortunate city, never more to relax its hold. As soon as the season permitted, Titus left Alexandria, reached Cesarea, and from that city, at the head of a formidable army, advanced towards Jerusalem. He had with him four legions, the 5th, Macedonian, the 10th, Fretensis, the 12th, Fulminata, the 15th, Apollinaris, not to speak of the numerous auxiliary troops furnished by his Syrian allies, and many Arabs who had come to pillage. All the Jews who had rallied to him, Agrippa, Tiberius Alexander, now prefect of the prætorium, Josephus the future historian, accompanied him; Berenice doubtless waited at Cesarea. The military valour of the captain corresponded with the strength of the army. Titus was a remarkable soldier, and especially an excellent officer of genius, while he was also a very sensible man, a profound politician, and considering the cruelty of the manners of the age, very humane. Vespasian, irritated by the satisfaction the Jews showed in seeing the civil wars, and the efforts they were making to bring about an invasion by the Parthians, had ordered great severity. Gentleness, according to him, was always interpreted as weakness by haughty races, persuaded that they were fighting for God and with God.

The Roman army arrived at Gabaoth-Saul, a league and a half from Jerusalem, in the early days of April. They were just on the eve of the feast of the Passover; an enormous number of Jews from all countries had assembled in the city; Josephus gives the number of those who perished during the siege at 1,100,000; it appeared as if the whole nation had made a rendezvous in order that they might be exterminated. About the 10th April, Titus established his camp at the angle of the tower of Psephina (Kasr-Djalond of the present day). Some partial advantages gained by surprise, and seven wounds Titus received at first, gave the Jews an exaggerated confidence in their strength, and shewed the Romans with what care they must guard themselves in this war with furious people.

The city could be reckoned among the strongest in the world. The walls were a perfect type of those constructions in enormous blocks which were always affected in Syria; in the interior, the enceinte of the temple, that of the high city, and that of Acra formed as if partition walls, and appeared to be so many ramparts. The number of the defenders was very great; provisions, although diminished by the fires, abounded still The parties in the interior of the city continued to fight still; but they combined for defence. At the beginning of the days of the Passover, Eleazar's faction nearly disappeared and merged itself in John's. Titus conducted the operations with consummate skill; never had the Romans shown such a skilful poliorcétique. In the closing days of April, the legions had forced the first enceinte from the north side and were masters of the northern portion of the city. Five days after the second wall, the wall of Acra, was taken, the half of the city was thus in the power of the Romans. On the 12th May, they attacked the fortress Antonia. Surrounded by Jews who all, Tiberius Alexander excepted, desired the preservation of the city and the temple, ruled more than he would confess by his love for Berenice, who appears to have been a pious Jewess and much devoted to her nation, Titus sought, it is said, a means of reconciliation, and made acceptable offers; all was useless. The besieged replied to the propositions of the conqueror only by sarcasm.

The siege then assumed a character of horrible cruelty. The Romans displayed instruments of the most hideous tortures; the audacity of the Jews only increased. On the 27th and 29th of May they burned the machines of the Romans, and even attacked them in their camp. Discouragement fell on the besiegers. Many were persuaded that the Jews spoke the truth, and that Jerusalem was impregnable; desertion began. Titus, giving up the hope of carrying the place by sheer force, blockaded it closely. A wall of countervallation, raised rapidly (in the beginning of June) and doubled on the side of Perea by a line of castella, crowning the heights of the mount of Olives, totally separated the city from without. Up till then vegetables were procured from the neighbourhood; famine now became fearful. The fanatics, provided with necessaries, cared little for this. Rigorous perquisitions, accompanied by tortures, were made to discover concealed grain. Whoever wore a certain look of strength at once passed as culpable in hiding provisions. Pieces of bread were torn from people's mouths. The most fearful diseases developed in the heart of this huddled-up, enfeebled, fevered mass. Some terrible stories were circulated and redoubled the terror.

From that moment hunger, rage, despair, and madness inhabited Jerusalem. It was a cage of wild madness, a city of shrieks, of cannibals, a hell. Titus, on his side, was cruel; five hundred unfortunates per day were crucified with odious refinements in sight of the city. There was not sufficient wood to make crosses, and there was no room to place them.

In this excess or evils, the faith and fanaticism of the Jews shewed themselves more ardently than ever. They believed the temple to be indestructible. The greater number were persuaded that, the city being under the special protection of the Eternal, it was impossible to take it. Prophets spread themselves among the people, announcing approaching succour. The confidence on this point was such that many who could have escaped, remained to see this miracle of Jehovah. The frenzied people, nevertheless, ruled as masters. They slew all those who were suspected of advising capitulation. Thus perished, by order of Siomon, son of Gioras, the hight priest Matthias, who had caused this brigand to be received into the city. His three sons were executed before his eyes. Many people of distinction were likewise put to death. The mere fact of weeping together or holding a meeting was a crime. It was forbidden from the smallest assembly. Josephus, from the Roman camp, tried vainly to have some spies in the place; he was suspected by both sides. The position had been reached in which reason and moderation have no longer any chance of being heard.

Yet Titus became weary of these delays; he longed only for Rome: its splendours and its pleasures. A city taken by famine appeared to him an exploit insufficient to inaugurate brilliantly a dynasty. He then caused to be constructed four new aggeræ for a sharp attack. The trees of the gardens in the suburbs of Jerusalem were cut down a distance of four leagues. In twenty-one days everything was ready. On the 21st July the Jews attempted the operation in which they had succeeded on the former occasion; they went out to burn and sap the tower Antonia. On the 5th July Titus was master of it, and caused it to be almost entirely demolished, to open a large passage for his cavalry and his machines, at the point where all his efforts converged, and where the last struggle must take place.

The temple, as we have said, was by its peculiar method of construction the strongest of fortresses. The Jews who had entrenched themselves with John of Gischala prepared themselves for battle. The priests themselves were under arms. On the 17th the perpetual sacrifice ceased for want of ministers to offer it. That made a great impression upon the people. It became known outside the city. The interruption of the sacrifice was for the Jews a phenomenon as grave as a stop in the progress of the universe. Josephus seized this occasion to try anew to conquer John's obstinacy. The fortress Antonia was only about 60 yards from the temple. From the parapets of the tower Josephus cried out in Hebrew by order of Titus (unless the story of the Wars of the Jews is false) that John could retire with as great a number of his men as he wished, that Titus would charge himself with having the legal sacrifices continued by the Jews, that he would allow John even the choice of those who should offer them. John refused to listen. Those whom fanaticism had not blinded escaped at this moment to the Romans. Everyone who remained chose death.

On the 12th July Titus began his works against the temple. The struggle was most bloody. On the 28th the Romans were masters of the whole gallery of the north from the fortress Antonia up to the vale of Kedron. The attack commenced then against the temple itself. On the 2nd August the most powerful machines were put to assail the walls wonderfully constructed with porticos which surrounded the inner courts. The effect was scarcely felt; but on the 8th of August the Romans succeeded in setting the gates on fire. The stupor of the Jews was then inexpressible; they had never believed that this was possible. At sight of the flames which leapt up they poured upon the Romans a flood of curses. On the 9th August Titus gave orders that the fire should be extinguished, and held a council of war at which there were present Tiberius Alexander, Cerealis, and his principal officers. The question was as to whether the temple should be burned. Many were of opinion that so long as the edifice remained the Jews would never be quiet. As to Titus, it is difficult to know what he meant, for on this point we have two opposing stories. According to Josephus, Titus was of opinion that such an admirable work should be spared, as its preservation would do honour to his reign and prove the moderation of the Romans. According to Tacitus, Titus insisted upon the necessity of destroying an edifice with which two superstitions equally fatal were associated, that of the Jews, and that of the Christians. "These two superstitions," he is said to have added, "although contrary to one another are of the same source; the Christians come from the Jews, the root torn up, the shoot will perish quickly."

It is difficult to decide between two versions so absolutely irreconcilable, for the opinion attributed to Titus by Josephus may very well be regarded as an invention by that historian, jealous of shewing the sympathy of his patron for Judaism, cleansing himself in the eyes of the Jews of the crime of having destroyed the temple and of satisfying the ardent desire of which Titus had to pass for a very moderate man. It cannot be denied that the brief discourse put by Tacitus in the mouth of the victorious captain may be, not only for the style but for the order of ideas, an exact reflex of the sentiments of Tacitus himself. We have a right to suppose that the Latin historian, full of spite against the Jews and the Christians, and of that bad temper which characterizes the age of Trajan and the Antonines, had made Titus speak like a Roman aristocrat of his time, while in reality the middle-class Titus had more complacence for oriental superstitions than the high noblesse who succeeded the Flavii had for them.

Living for two or three years with Jews who had boasted to him of their temple as the wonder of the world, won by the caresses of Josephus, Agrippa, and still more of Berenice, he might very well desire the preservation of a sanctuary whose worship many of his friends represented to him as being quite peaceable. It is therefore possible that, as Josephus has it, some orders had been given that the fire lit the evening before should be extinguished, and that in the frightful tumult which they foresaw, some measures should be taken against fire There was in the character of Titus, besides real goodness, much pose and a little hypocrisy. The truth is doubtless that he did not order the fire, as Tacitus says; did not countermand it, as Josephus says, but allowed it to go on, presenting some appearances for all the theories which people may be allowed to maintain in the different regions of probability, whatever may be on this point difficult to ascertain. A general assault was decided against the building, which had already lost its gates; as to military work, what remained to be done was an effort, bloody perhaps, but whose issue could not be doubtful.

The Jews anticipated the attacks. On the 10th of August in the morning they delivered a furious attack without success. Titus retired into the Antonia to rest and to prepare for the assault next day. A detachment was left to prevent the fire from being relit. Then took place, according to Josephus, the incident which led to the ruin of the sacred pile. The Jews threw themselves with rage upon the detachment which watched near the fire; the Romans repulsed them, entering pell-mell into the temple with the fugitives. The irritation of the Romans was at its height. A soldier "without any one commanding him, and as if impelled by a supernatural movement," took a joist which was in flames, and having raised it, with one of his companions, threw the brand through a window which opened upon the porticos of the north side. The flame and the smoke rose rapidly. Titus was resting at that moment in his tent. They ran to call him. Then, if Josephus must be believed, a sort of struggle was begun between him and his soldiers; Titus with voice and gesture ordered the fire to be extinguished; but the disorder was such that they did not understand him; those who might doubt his intentions affected not to hear him. In place of stopping the fire the legionaries stirred it up. Drawn by the wave of invaders, Titus was borne into the Temple itself--the flames had not reached the central building. He saw intact this sanctuary of which Agrippa, Josephus, and Berenice had spoken to him so often with admiration, and found it much superior to what they had told him. Titus redoubled his efforts, made them evacuate the interior, and gave even an order to Liberalos, a centurion of his guards, to strike those who refused to obey. All at once a jet of flame and smoke rose from the gate of the Temple. At the moment of the tumultuary evacuation a soldier had set fire to the interior. The flames gained on all sides; the position was no longer tenable. Titus retired.

This recital of Josephus includes more than one probability. It is difficult to believe that the Roman legions could have shown themselves so disobedient to a victorious leader. Dion Cassius declares, on the contrary, that Titus needed to employ force to make the soldiers penetrate into a place surrounded by terrors, and of which all the profaners were believed to be struck dead. One thing only is certain--that Titus some years afterwards would have been glad if in the Jewish world they had told the same thing as Josephus did, and that they should have attributed the burning of the Temple to the discipline of his soldiers, or rather to a supernatural movement of some agent, unconscious of a superior will. The history of the war of the Jews was written about the end of the reign of Vespasian, in 76, or rather sooner, when Titus already aspired to be "the delight of the human race," and wished to pass as a model of gentleness and goodness. In the preceding years, and that of another world than that of the Jews, he would surely have received eulogia of a different kind. Among the tableaux which were borne in the triumph of the year 71 was the image of "the fire set to the Temple," in which certainly they would not seek to represent that fact otherwise than as glorious. About the same time the court poet, Valerias Flaccus, proposed to Domitian, as the finest employment of his poetical talent, to sing the war of Judea, and to represent his brother scattering burning torches everywhere--

Solymo ingrantem pulvere fratrem,
Spargentemque faces et in omni turre furentem?

The struggle during this time was hot in the court and parvis. A frightful carnage was made round the altar, a sort of truncated pyramid, surmounted by a platform, which was raised in front of the Temple; the corpses of those whom they killed upon the platform rolled over upon the steps and reached to the feet. Rivers of blood flowed on all sides, nothing was heard but the piercing cries of those whom they killed and who died adjuring heaven. There was time still to take refuge in the high city; many liked rather to go to be killed, regarding as a lot to be envied dying for their temple; others threw themselves into the flames; others still precipitated themselves upon the swords of the Romans, while some slew themselves or each other. Some priests who had succeeded in gaining the crest of the Temple roof, tore the points which they found there with their leaden sockets and threw them upon the Romans; they continued this up till the time the flames enveloped them. A great number of Jews had assembled around the holy place, upon the word of a prophet, who had assured them that the very moment had come when God was about to shew them the signs of salvation. A gallery where it is said six thousand of these wretches had retired (nearly all women and children) was burned. Two gates of the Temple and a part of the enceinte reserved for the women were only preserved for the moment. The Romans planted their ensigns upon the place where the sanctuary had been, and offered the worship to which they had been accustomed. The old Zion remained; the high town, the strongest part of the city, having its ramparts still intact, and which still gave safety to John of Gischala, Simon son of Gioras, and a great number of combatants who had succeeded in forcing a way through the conquerors. This stand of madmen demanded a new siege. John and Simon had established the centre of their resistance in the palace of the Herods, situated near the, site of the present citadel of Jerusalem, and covered by the three enormous towers of Hippicus, of Phasaël, and Mariamne. The Romans were obliged, to carry this last refuge of Jewish obstinacy, to construct some aggerae against the western wall of the city, opposite the palace. The four legions were occupied in this work for the space of eighteen days (from 20th August to 6th September). During this time Titus made them set fire to the parts of the town which were in his power. The low town especially, from Ophel up to Siloam, were systematically destroyed. Many of the Jews belonging to the middle classes were able to escape. As to, the people of inferior condition, they were sold at a very low price. This was the origin of a multitude of Jewish slaves who, coming down upon Italy and upon the other countries of the Mediterranean, took from thence the elements of a new ardour of propagandism. Josephus reckons the number at 97,000. Titus gave pardon to the princes of Adiabene; the pontifical dresses, the precious stones, the tables, the cups, the candelabra, and the hangings were brought to him. He ordered that they should be preserved carefully, that they might be used in the triumph he was preparing, and to which he wished to give a particular mark of foreign pomp, by exhibiting there the rich material of the Jewish worship.

The aggeræ being finished, the Romans began to batter the wall of the high tower. At the first attack, 7th September, they overturned a part as well as some of the tower. Attenuated by famine, undermined by fever and rage, the defenders were nothing more than skeletons. The legions passed in without difficulty; up till the end of the day, the soldiers burned and slew; the greater part of the houses into which they went to pillage were full of corpses. The wretches who could escape fled to Acra, which the Roman force had nearly evacuated, and to those vast subterranean cavities, which mark the subsoil of Jerusalem. John and Simon grew weaker at this time. They possessed still the towers of Hippicus, of Phasaël, and Mariamne, the most astonishing marks of military architecture in antiquity. The ram had been powerless against enormous blocks, collected with unequalled perfection, and bound together by iron cramps. Amazed and lost, John and Simon quitted these impregnable works, and sought to force the line of countervallation on the side of Siloam. Not succeeding, they went to rejoin those of their partisans who were concealed in the sewers.

On the 8th all resistance was over; the soldiers were fatigued--they killed the weak who couldn't march. The remainder, women and children, were pushed like a flock towards the enceinte of the Temple, and enclosed in the inner court which had escaped the fire. Of this multitude set aside for death or slavery, they made lists. Everyone who had fought was massacred. Seven hundred people, the finest in figure and the best made, were reserved to follow the triumph of Titus. Among the others, those who had passed the age of 17, were sent into Egypt, their feet in irons, for the forced works, or divided among the provinces to be slain in the amphitheatres. Those who were less than 17 were sold. The sorting of the prisoners occupied many days, during which there died thousands, it is said, some because they gave them no food, others because they refused to accept it.

The Romans employed the following days in burning tits rest of the city, overturning the walls, and rumaging in the sewers and subterranean passages. They found there great riches and many of the insurrectionists living, whom they killed at once, and more than two thousand corpses, without speaking of prisoners whom the Terrorists had shut up. John of Gischala, constrained by hunger to come forth, demanded quarter from the conquerors, who condemned him to perpetual imprisonment. Simon, son of Gioras, who had some provisions, remained concealed till the end of October. His food failing then, he took a singular step. Clothed in a white cloth with a mantle of purple, he came forth unexpectedly from under the earth to the place where the Temple had been. He imagined by this to astonish the Romans, and to pretend that he had been raised from the dead--perhaps to make himself pass as the Messiah. The soldiers were, in fact, a little surprised at first. Simon would only name himself to their commandant, Terentius Rufus. He made them put him in chains, sent the news to Titus, who was at Paneas, and caused the prisoner to be taken to Cesaræa.

The Temple and the great constructions were demolished to the very foundations. The sub-basement of the Temple was, however, preserved, and constitutes what is called at this day Naramesch-scherif. Titus wished also to preserve the three towers of Hippicus, Phasaël, and Mariamne, to make posterity know against what walls he had had to fight. The wall of the western side was left standing to shelter the camp of the 10th legion Fretensius, which was sent to hold guard over the ruins of the fallen city. Lastly, some houses on the extremity of Mount Sion escaped the destruction, and remained in the condition of isolated ruins. All the rest disappeared. From the month of September, 70, to the year 122, when Hadrian re-built it under the name of Ælia Capitolina, Jerusalem was nothing but a field of rubbish, in a corner of which the tents of a legion always on guard were set up. They believed they saw at every instant the fire re-lit which lay under these calcined stones. They trembled lest the spirit of life should come into the corpses which appeared still at the depths of their charnel-house, to raise their arms and declare that they had with them the promises of eternity.

CHAPTER XX

CONSEQUENCES OF THE DESTRUCTION OF JERUSALEM

Titus appears to have remained about a month in the neighbourhood of Jerusalem, offering sacrifices and rewarding his soldiers; the spoils of the captives were sent to Cesaræa. The season, already far advanced, prevented the young captain from leaving for Rome. He employed the winter in visiting different cities of the East and giving fêtes. He took with him bands of Jewish prisoners, who were delivered to the beasts, burned alive, or forced to fight against each other. At Paneas, on the 24th October, the birthday of his brother Domitian, more than 2,500 Jews perished in the flames, or in these horrible games. At Beyrout, on the 17th November, the same number of captives perished, to celebrate the birthday of Vespasian. Hatred of the Jews was the dominant sentiment in Syrian cities. These hideous massacres were hailed with joy. What was perhaps most frightful was that Josephus and Agrippa did not quit Titus during this time, and were witnesses of these monstrosities.

Titus made after this a long voyage into Syria going as far as the Euphrates. At Antioch he found the people exasperated against the Jews--they accused them of a fire which would have consumed the city. Titus contented himself with suppressing the bronze tables on which were engraved their privileges. He made a present to Antioch of the veiled Cherubim which covered the ark. This singular trophy was placed before the great western gates of the city, which took from that the name of the Gate of the Cherubim. Near that he dedicated a guadriga to the moon, for the help which she had given him daring the siege. At Daphne, he caused a theatre to be erected upon the site of the synagogue; an inscription indicated that this monument had been constructed with the booty obtained in Judea. From Antioch Titus returned to Jerusalem; he found there the Tenth Fretensis, under the orders of Terentius Rufus, still occupied in searching the caves by the destroyed city. The appearance of Simon, son of Gioras, coming out of the sewers when they believed that no one was to found there, had caused the subterranean fights to be be commenced; in fact, every day they discovered some wretch and some new treasures. In looking on the solitude which he had created, Titus was unable, it is said, to restrain a motion of pity. The Jews who were near him exercised upon him a cross influence; the phantasmagoria of an Oriental Empire, which they had caused to glitter before the eyes of Nero and Vespasian, reappeared around him, and went so far as to excite umbrage at Rome. Agrippa, Berenice, Josephus and Tiberius Alexander were more in favour than ever, and many augured for Berenice the rôle of a new Cleopatra. On the morning of the defeat of the rebels, men were irritated at seeing people of such a kind honoured and all powerful. As to Titus, he accepted more and more the idea that he was fulfilling a mission in providence. He was pleased to hear them quote the prophecies which they said referred to him. Josephus claims that he connected this victory with God, and recognised that he had been the object of a supernatural power. What is striking is that Philostratus, 120 years after, admits clearly these data and makes them the basis of an apocryphal correspondence between Titus and Apollonius. To believe him, Titus would have refused the crowns which were offered him, alleging that it was not he who had taken Jerusalem--that he had done nothing but lend his services to an irritated God. It is scarcely to be admitted that Philostratus had known the passage in Josephus. He drew the legend, which had become common, from the moderation of Titus. Titus returned to Rome in the month of May or June, 71. He held essentially a triumph which would surpass all that had been seen up till then. Simplicity, seriousness, the somewhat common manners of Vespasian, were not of a nature to give him prestige with a population which had been accustomed to ask before everything from its sovereigns prodigality and a grand style. Titus thought that a solemn entry would have a grand effect, and managed to surmount the repugnances of his old father on that point. The ceremony was organised with all the skill of the Roman decorators of that time. What distinguished it was the choice of local colour and historical truth. It pleased them also to reproduce the simple rites of the Roman religion as if they had the desire to oppose it to the conquered religion. At the opening of the ceremony Vespasian appeared as pontiff, his head more than half veiled in his toga, and made solemn prayers, and after him Titus prayed also according to the same rite. The procession was a marvel. All the curiosities, all rarities, the precious products of Oriental art, besides works achieved by the Græco-Roman art, figured there. It appears as if on the day after the greatest danger which the Empire encountered, they should make a pompous exhibition of their wealth. Some moving scaffolding, rising to the height of three or four tiers, excited universal wonder. All the episodes of the war were represented there; each series of tableaux terminated with the living representation of the strange appearance of Bar-Gorias and his capture--the pale visage and the haggard eyes of the captives disguised by the superb garments with which they clothed them In the midst was Bar-Gorias being led with great pomp to death; then came the spoils of the temple, the golden table, the golden seven-branched candlestick, the veil of the holy of holies, and to conclude, the series of trophies, the captive, the conquered one, the culprit par excellence, the book of the Torah. The conquerors closed the procession. Vespasian and Titus were mounted on two separate oars. Titus was radiant; as to Vespasian, who saw nothing in all this but a day lost for business, he did not seek to dissimulate his vulgar appearance as a business man, because the procession did not move rapidly enough, and said in a low voice, "It is well done. I have deserved it . . . Have I been foolish enough at my age, too!" Domitian, who was robed and mounted on a magnificent horse, caracoled near his father and elder brother. They arrived thus at the Sacred way. At the temple of Jupiter Capitolinus the ordinary termination of a triumph was reached. At the Clivus Capitolinus they made a halt to disembarrass themselves of the gloomy portion of the ceremony--the execution of the chief enemies. This odious custom was observed from point to point. Bar-Gorias, drawn out of the band of captives, was seen led away with a cord round his neck, amid most ignoble insults, to the Tarpeian rock, where they slew him. When a cry announced that Rome's enemy was no more, an immense applause burst out and the sacrifices commenced. After the customary prayers the princes retired to the Palatine; the rest of the day was passed by the whole city in joy and festivity.

The volume of the Thora and the hangings of the sanctuary were taken into the imperial palace, the articles of gold, especially the table of the shew bread and the candlestick, were deposited in a great edifice, which Vespasian caused to be built opposite the Palatine on the other side of the Sacred way under the name of the Temple of Peace, and which was in some sort the Museum of the Flavii. A triumphal arch of Pentelic marble, which exists to this day, kept up the memory of this extraordinary pomp, and the representation of the principal objects which were borne in it. The father and son assumed that day the title of Imperatores but they refused the epithet of Judaic, either because they attached to the name of Judæi something odious or ridiculous, or to indicate that this war in Judea had been not a war against a foreign people, but a simple revolt of slaves put down, or in consequence of some secret thought analogous to that whose exaggerated expressions Josephus and Philostratus have transmitted to us. A coinage, in which Judea chained weeping under a palm tree, figured with the legend Ivdæa Capta Ivdæa Devicta, kept the remembrance of the fundamental exploit of the dynasty of the Flavii. They continued to strike pieces of this type until the days of Domitian. The victory was indeed complete. A captain of our race, of our blood, a man like ourselves, at the head of legions in the position in which we shall encounter if we can read it, many of our ancestors, has crushed the fortress of Semiticism and inflicted upon the theocracy, this redoubtable enemy of civilisation, the greatest defeat which it had ever received. It was the triumph of Roman or rational law, a creation quite philosophic, pre-supposing no revelation, over the Jewish Thora, the result of a revelation. This law, whose roots were partly Greek, but in which the practical genius of the Latins had such a splendid part, was the excellent gift which Rome made to the conquered in return for independence. Every victory of Rome was a progress of reason. Rome brought into the world a better principle in many points of view than that of the Jews; I mean to say the profane State resting upon a purely civil conception of society.

Every patriotic movement is entitled to respect, but the zealots were not only patriots, they were fanatics, assassins, of insupportable tyranny. What they wished was the maintenance of a law of blood which would permit the stoning of the evil thinker. What they rejected was the common law, laic and liberal, which does not interfere with belief in individuals. Liberty of conscience ought to go the length of the Roman law, while that has never gone forth from Judaism. From Judaism nothing can go forth but the synagogue and the church, censure of manners, obligatory morality, the convent, a life like that of the fifth century when humanity would have lost all its vigour, if the barbarians had not relieved it. In fact the reign of the man of war has a better effect than the temporal reign of the priest. For the man of war does not interfere with the mind. People think freely under him, while the priest demands from his subject the impossible, that is, to believe certain things and to bind themselves that they will hold the priest's ways to be true. The triumph of Rome was therefore legitimate in some measure. Jerusalem had become an impossibility; left to themselves the Jews would have demolished it. But a great lacuna was to render this victory of Titus unfruitful. Our Western races, in spite of their superiority, have always shown a deplorable religious nullity. To draw from the Roman or Gallic religion anything analogous to the church was impossible. Now every advantage gained over a religion is useless if it be not replaced by another, satisfying, at least as well as it can, the needs of the heart. Jerusalem will be avenged for her defeat. She shall conquer Rome by Christianity, Persia by Islamism, shall destroy the old fatherland, and shall become for all higher minds the city of the heart.

The most dangerous tendency of its Thora, a law in itself at once moral and civil, giving the advantage to social questions over military and political ones, shall rule in the church. During all the Middle Ages, the individual, censured and overlooked by the community, shall fear the sermon and tremble before excommunication, and that shall be a just return after the moral indifference of heathen societies, a protest against the insufficiency of the Roman institution to improve the individual. It is certainly a detestable principle the saw of coercion which has been accorded to religious communities over their members. It is the worst error to believe that there is a religion which must be exclusively the good; the good religion being for each man what renders him pleasant, just, humble and benevolent. But the question of the government of humanity is difficult. The ideal is very high, the earth is very low. Even only to haunt the desert of philosophy, there one meets at every step madness, folly and passion. The old sages did not succeed in claiming any authority but by impostures which, for want of material force, gave them a power of imagination. Where would civilisation be if during centuries people had not believed that the Brahmin could blast by his glance; if the barbarians had not been convinced of the terrible revenges of St. Martins of Tours. Man has need of a moral pedagogy, for which the care of the family and that of the state do not suffice. In the intoxication of success, Rome scarcely remembered that the Jewish insurrection lived still in the basin of the Dead Sea. Three castles, Herodium, Machero and Masada were still in the hands of the Jews. It needed a man to close his eyes to the evidence to retain any hope after the taking of Jerusalem. The rebels defended themselves with as much passion as if the struggle had but just commenced. Herodium was scarcely anything but a fortified palace; it was taken without great effort by Lucillus Bassus. Machero presented many difficulties. Atrocities, massacres, and the sales of whole bands of Jews recommenced. Masada made one of the most heroic defences that history has recorded. Eleazar, son of Jairus, grand-son of Judas the Ganlonite, had possessed himself of this fortress in the early days of the revolt and made it a haunt of zealots, assassins, and brigands. Masada occupies the platform of an immense rock of nearly fifteen hundred feet high upon the shores of the Dead Sea. To possess himself of such a place it was necessary that Fulvius Sylvia should work positive miracles The despair of the Jews was boundless when they saw to be lost a position which they believed impregnable. At the instigation of Eleazar they killed each other, and set fire to their property which they had heaped up. Nine hundred and sixty persons perished thus. This tragical episode took place on the 15th of April, 72.

Judea after these events was overturned from top to bottom. Vespasian ordered all lands to be sold which were unowned by the death or captivity of their proprietors. The idea was suggested to him which later occurred to Hadrian, to rebuild Jerusalem under another name, and establish a colony there. He did not wish this, and annexed the whole country to the emperor's own domains. He gave only to eight hundred veterans the borough of Emmaus, near Jerusalem, and made of it a little colony, a trace of which is preserved to this day in the name of the pretty village of Kulonia. A special tribute (fiscus) was imposed upon the Jews. In all the empire they were to pay annually to the capital a sum of drachmas which they had been accustomed to pay to their temple at Jerusalem. The little coterie of allied Jews, Josephus, Agrippa, Berenice, and Tiberius Alexander, chose Rome as a residence. We see it continued to play a considerable part, at one time obtaining for Judaism favourable regard at court--at other times pursued by the hatred of the enthusiastic believers; at other times conceiving more than a hope, especially when it seemed to require little for Berenice to become the wife of Titus, and hold the sceptre of the universe.

Reduced to solitude Judea remained tranquil; but the enormous overthrow of which it had been the theatre continued to provoke difficulties in the neighbouring countries. The fermentation of Judaism lasted until the end of the year 73. The zealots who had escaped massacre, the volunteers of the siege, and all the madmen of Jerusalem, spread themselves in Egypt and Cyrenia. The communities of these countries, rich, conservative, and, far removed from the Palestinian fanaticism, felt the danger which these lunatics brought among them. They charged themselves with arresting them and giving them up to the Romans. Many fled into Higher Egypt, where they were hunted like wild beasts. At Cyrene a brigand named Jonathan, a weaver by trade, acted the prophet, and like all Messiahs, persuaded two thousand Ebionim, or poor people, to follow him into the desert, where he promised to let them see prodigies and strange signs. The sensible Jews denounced him to Catullus, the governor of the country, but Jonathan revenged himself by some informations which caused him endless trouble. Nearly all the Jewish community of Cyrene, one of the most flourishing in the world, was exterminated. Its property was confiscated in the name of the Emperor. Catullus, who shewed in this matter much cruelty, was disavowed by Vespasian; he died under frightful hallucinations, which, according to certain conjectures, must have furnished the subject of a theatrical piece of fantastic scenery, the "Spectre of Catullus."

Incredible fact! This long and terrible agony was not immediately followed by death. Under Trajan and under Hadrian we see the national Judaism revived, and still engaging in bloody combats; but the lot was evidently cast. The zealot was conquered beyond recovery. The way traced by Jesus, comprehended instinctively by the church of Jerusalem, who were refugees in Perea, became the way of Israel. The temporal kingdom of the Jews had been hateful, hard and cruel. The epoch of the Asmoneans when they enjoyed independence was their most sorrowful age. Was it Herodianism, Sadduceeism, that shameful alliance of a principality without grandeur with the priesthood, which was to be regretted? No, certainly, that was not the goal of "the people of God." One would need to be blind not to see that the ideal institutions which pursued the Israel of God did not agree with national independence. These institutions, being incapable of making an army, could not exist in the vassaldom of a great empire, leaving much liberty to its rayahs, and disembarassing them of politics and not asking them for military service. The Achemidian empire had entirely satisfied those conditions of Jewish life, later the Caliphate, the Ottoman empire, satisfied them, and shall see developed in their bosom free communities such as those of the Armenian Parsees, the Greeks, nations without fatherland, brotherhood, supplying diplomatic and military autonomy, by the autonomy of the college and the church.

The Roman empire was not flexible, to lend itself to the communities which it united. Of the four empires, this was, according to the Jews, the harshest and most wicked. Like Antiochus Epiphanes, the Roman empire led the Jewish people astray from their true vocation, by causing it through reaction to form a kingdom or separate state. This tendency was not that of men who represented the genius of the race. In some points of view these last preferred the Romans. The idea of Jewish nationality became each day an obsolete idea, an idea of the furious and frenzied, against which the pious men made no scruple to claim the protection of their conquerors. The true Jew, attached to the Thora, making the holy books his rule and his life, as well as the Christian, lost in the hope of his kingdom of God, renounced more and more all nationality. The principles of Judas the Ganlonite, which was the soul of the great revolt, anarchical principles, according to which, God alone being "Master," no man has the right to take that title, could produce bands of fanatics analogous to the Independents of Cromwell, they could found nothing durable. These feverish irruptions were the indication of the deep throes which threatened the heart of Israel, and which, by making it sweat blood for humanity, must necessarily cause it to perish in frightful convulsions.

The nations must choose in fact between the long peaceful and obscure destinies of that which lives for itself, and the trouble and stormy career of that which lives for humanity. The nation which agitates in its bosom social and religious problems is nearly always weak as a nation. Every country which dreams of a Kingdom of God, which looks for general ideas, which pursues a work of universal interest, sacrifices by this its particular destiny, grows feeble and loses its role as a terrestrial country. It was so with Judea, Greece, and Italy. It shall be so with France. One never carries with impunity fire within oneself. Jerusalem, the city of middle-class people, would have pursued indefinitely its mediocre history. It is because it had the incomparable honour of being the cradle of Christianity that it was the victim of the Johns of Gischala, of the Bar Giorases, in appearance plagues of their country, in reality the instruments of their apotheosis. Those zealots, whom Josephus treats as brigands and assassins, were politicians of the lowest order, military men with little capacity, but they lost heroically that which could not be saved. They lost a material city, they opened the spiritual Jerusalem, seated in her desolation much more gloriously than she was in the days of Herod and Solomon.

What did the conservatives and Sadducees desire? They wished something paltry; the continuation of a city of priests like Emesa, Tyana, or Comanus. Certainly they were not deceived when they declared that the rising of enthusiasts was the loss of the nation; but revolution and Messianism were indeed the vocation of this people, that by which it contributed to the universal work of civilisation. We deceive ourselves no longer when we say to France, "Renounce revolution or thou art lost"; but if the future belongs to some ideas which are elaborated obscurely in the heart of the people, it will be found that France will have its revenge by what caused in 1870-1871 its feebleness and its misery. At least of many violent strains given to truth, (everything in this sort is possible) our Bar-Giorases, our Johns of Gischala would never become great citizens, but they would play their part, and we shall perhaps see that more even than sensible people they were in the secrets of fate.

How shall Judaism, deprived of its holy city and its temple, transform itself? How shall Talmudism leave the position which events have made to the Israelite? That is what we shall see in our fifth book. In a sense, after the production of Christianity, Judaism has no longer a raison d'etre. From this moment the spirit of life has gone from Jerusalem. Israel has given all to the son of its sorrow, and it has been exhausted in this childbirth. The Elohim whom they believed they heard murmur in the temple: "Let us go forth, let us go forth!" spoke truly. The law of great creations is that the creator virtually expires in transmitting existence to another. After the complete inoculation of life with that which should continue it, the initiator is nothing but a dry stem, an attenuated being. But it is rare, nevertheless, that this sentence of nature is accomplished at once. The plant which has yielded its flower does not consent to die because of that. The world is full of these walking skeletons who survive the doom which has struck them. Judaism is of this number. History has no spectacle stranger than that of this conservation of a people in the state of a ghost, of a people who, during nearly a thousand years, have lost the sentiment of fact, have not written a readable page, have not transmitted an acceptable instruction. Should one be astonished if, after having thus lived for ages outside of the free atmosphere of humanity, in a cellar, if I may say so, in a condition of partial madness, it should come forth, astonished by the light etiolated?

As to the consequences which resulted for Christianity from the destruction of Jerusalem, they are so evident that one has but to indicate them. Already even many times we have had occasion to remark upon them.

The ruin of Jerusalem and of the temple was for Christianity an unequalled good fortune. If the argument attributed by Tacitus to Titus is exactly reported, the victorious general believed that the destruction of the temple would be the ruin of Christianity, as well as of that of Judaism. Never were men more completely deceived. The Romans imagined to cut away at the same time the shoot, but the shoot was already a bush which lived by its own life. If the temple had survived, Christianity would certainly have been arrested in its development. The temple, surviving, would have continued to be the centre of all Judaic works. They could never have ceased from looking upon it as the most holy place in the world, going there on pilgrimage and bringing tributes thither. The church of Jerusalem, grouped around the sacred parvis, would have continued, by the name of its primacy, to obtain the homages of all the world, to persecute the churches of Paul, demanding that to have the right to to call himself a disciple of Jesus, one must practice circumcision and observe the Mosaic code. Every fertile propaganda would have been forbidden, letters of obedience signed at Jerusalem would have been exacted from the missionary. A centre of indisputable authority, a patriarchate, composed of a sort of college of cardinals, under the presidency of persons analogous to James, pure Jews belonging to the family of Jesus, would have established itself and would have constituted an immense danger for the nascent church. When one sees St. Paul after so much ill-usage remain always attached to the church at Jerusalem, one can conceive what difficulties a rupture with these holy personages would have presented. Such a schism would have been considered an enormity equivalent to the abandonment of Christianity. The separation between it and Judaism would have been impossible; now this separation was the indispensable condition of the existence of the new religion, as the cutting of the umbilical cord is the condition of a new being. The mother will kill the infant. The temple, on the contrary, once destroyed, the Christians thought no more of it; soon they even held it to be a profane place. Jesus shall be everything to them. The church of Jerusalem was by the same blow reduced to a secondary importance. We shall see it reforming itself in the element which makes its strength, the desposyni members of the family of Jesus, the sons of Clopas; but it shall reign no more. This centre of hatred and exclusion, once destroyed, the reconciliation of parties opposed to the church of Jesus shall become easy. Peter and Paul shall be reconciled officially, and the terrible duality of nascent Christianity shall cease to be a mortal wound. Forgotten at the base of Batanea or Hauran, the little group which is connected with the relatives of Jesus, the Jameses, the Clopases, became the Ebionite sect and died slowly through insignificance and unfruitfulness.

The situation much resembles some things in the Catholicism of our days. No religious community has ever had more internal activity, more of a tendency to send forth from its bosom original creations than Catholicism for sixty years back. All these efforts, nevertheless, remain without result for one single reason; that reason is the absolute rule of the court of Rome. It is the court of Rome which has chased from the church Lamennais, Hermes, Döllinger, Father Hyacinthe, and all the Apologists who have defended it with some success. It is the court of Rome which has distressed and reduced to powerlessness Lacordaire and Montalembert, it is the court of Rome which by its Syllabus and its council has cut the whole future from liberal Catholics. When is this sad state of things to be changed? When Rome shall be no more the pontifical city, when the dangerous oligarchy which Catholicism has possessed itself of shall have ceased to exist. The occupation of Rome by the King of Italy will one day be probably reckoned in the history of Catholicism for an event as fortunate as the destruction of Jerusalem has been in the history of Christianity. Nearly all Catholics have groaned over it, just as without doubt the Judeo-Christians of the year 70 looked upon the destruction of the temple as the most sad calamity. But the result will shew how superficial this judgment is. Whilst weeping over the end of Papal Rome, Catholicism will draw from it the greatest advantages. To material uniformity and death we shall see following in its bosom discussion, movement, life, and variety.

APPENDIX

Concerning the Coming of St. Peter to Rome and the Residence of St. John at Ephesus.

All are agreed that, from the end of the second century, the general belief of the Christian churches was that the Apostle Peter suffered martyrdom at Rome, and that the Apostle John lived at Ephesus until an advanced age. Protestant theologians from the sixteenth century have pronounced strongly against the visit of St. Peter to Rome. As to the opinion regarding the residence of John at Ephesus, it is only in our day that it has found contradiction.

The reason why Protestants attach so much importance to the denial of Peter's coming to Rome is easily grasped. During the whole Middle Ages the coming of St. Peter to Rome was the basis of the exorbitant pretentions of the papacy. These pretentions were founded on three propositions which were held to be "of the faith," 1et, Jesus himself conferred on Peter a primacy in the Church; 2nd, that primacy ought to be transmitted to Peter's successors; 3rd, the successors of Peter are the Bishops of Rome. Peter, after having resided at Jerusalem, then at Antioch, having definitively fixed his residence at Rome. To overthrow this last fact, was therefore to overturn from top to bottom the edifice of Roman theology. Men expended much learning on this; they showed that Roman tradition was not supported on direct or very solid evidences; but they treated lightly the indirect proofs; they pointed in a troublesome way to the passage in I. Peter, v. 13. That Βαβυλών in that passage really means Babylon on the Euphrates, is an untenable thesis, first because at that time "Babylon," in the secret style of the Christians, meant Rome; in the second place, because the Christianity of the first century had scarcely left the Roman empire, and spread itself very little among the Parthians.

To us the question has less importance than it had for the first Protestants, and it is easier to solve it impartially. We certainly do not believe that Jesus intended to establish a leader in his church, nor especially, to attach that primacy to the episcopal succession of a fixed city. The episcopate, at first scarcely existed in the thoughts of Jesus; besides, if it was a city of the world, among those whose names Jesus knew, to which he did not think of attaching the series of heads of his church, it was doubtless Rome. They would probably have horrified him if they had told him that this city of perdition, this cruel enemy of the people of God, should one day boast of his Satanic kingdom, to claim the right of inheriting by a new title the power founded by the Son. That Peter had not been at Rome, or that he had been, has therefore for us no moral or political consequence; there is in it only a curious historical question beyond which it is unnecessary to examine farther.

Let us say first that Catholics have exposed themselves to the most weighty objections on the part of their adversaries with their unfortunate theory as to Peter's coming to Rome in the year 42--a theory borrowed from Eusebius and St Jerome, and which limits the duration of the pontificate of Peter to twenty-three or twenty-four years. It is sufficient not to retain any doubt on that point, to consider that the persecution of which Peter was the object at Jerusalem on the part of Herod Agrippa I. (Acts xii.) took place in the very year in which Herod Agrippa tired, that is, in the year 44 (Jos. Ant., xix., viii., 2). Apollonius the Anti-Montanist (at the end of the second century) and Lactantius at the beginning of the fourth did not certainly believe that Peter had been at Rome in 42, the former, when he affirms having heard by tradition that Jesus Christ had forbidden his apostles to leave Jerusalem before twelve years had passed from the time of his death; the latter, when he saw that the apostles employed the twenty-five years which followed the death of Jesus in preaching the gospel in the provinces, and that Peter did not come to Rome till after the accession of Nero. It would be superstitious to combat at length a theory which cannot have a single reasonable defender. We can go much further, indeed, and affirm that Peter had not yet come to Rome when Paul was brought there, that is in the year 61. The epistle of Paul to the Romans, written about the year 58, or at least which had not been written more than two years and a half before the arrival of Paul at Rome, is here a very considerable argument; we can scarcely conceive St. Paul writing to the believers whose leader Peter was, without making the smallest mention of him. What is still more demonstrative is the last chapter of the Acts of the Apostles. That chapter, especially vv. 17-29, is not intelligible if Peter was at Rome when Paul arrived there. Let us hold then as absolutely certain that Peter did not come to Rome before Paul, that is to say before the year 61, or nearly so.

But did he not go there after Paul? This is what Protestant critics have never succeeded in proving. Not only does this late journey of Peter to Rome offer no impossibility, but some strong reasons militate in its favour. I believe that those who read our account with care will find that everything fits in well enough in this hypothesis. Besides that, the testimony of the Fathers of the second and third centuries are not without value in this matter, and here are three arguments, the force of which does not appear to me to be disdained.

1. An incontestable thing is that Peter died a martyr. The evidence of the fourth gospel, Clemens Romans, and of the fragment called the Canon de Muratori, Dionysius of Corinth, Caius and Tertullian, leave no doubt on this matter. That the fourth gospel may be apocryphal, and that the twenty-first chapter has been added at a latter date, is of no consequence. It is clear that we have in the verses where Jesus announces to Peter that he will die by the same penalty as himself, the expression of an opinion established in the churches before the year 120 or 130, and to which allusions are made as to a thing known to all. It was almost alone at Rome, indeed, that Nero's persecution was violent. At Jerusalem or at Antioch, the martyrdom of Peter could be less easily explained.

2. The second argument is drawn from chapter v. verse 13, of the epistle attributed to Peter. "Babylon" in this passage evidently means Rome. If the epistle is authentic, the passage is decisive. It it is apocryphal, the induction to be drawn from this passage is not less strong. In fact the author, whoever he was, wished to have it believed that the work in question is indeed Peter's work. He needed consequently to give probability to his fraud, to dispose the circumstances of the case in a way agreeable to what he knew and to what was believed at his time as to the life of Peter. If, in such a disposition of mind, he dated the letter from Rome, it was because the received opinion at the time when that letter was written was that St. Peter had resided at Rome. Now, in every hypothesis, 1st Peter is a very ancient work and enjoyed very early a high authority.

3. The system which served as the basis for the Ebionite Acts of Peter is also well worthy of consideration. This system shows us St. Peter following Simon Magus everywhere (see on that point St. Paul) to combat his false doctrines. M. Lipsius has brought into the analysis of this curious legend an admirable sagacity of criticism. He has shown that the basis of the different editions which have come down to us was a primitive record, written about the year 130, a writing in which Peter came to Rome to conquer Simon-Paul in the centre of his power, and found it dead, after having confounded this father in all his errors. It seems difficult to believe that the Ebionite author, at a date so remote, should have given so much importance to the journey of Peter to Rome, if that journey had not had some reality. The theory of the Ebionite legend must have a foundation of truth, in spite of the fables mixed up with it. It is indeed admissible that Peter came to Rome as he came to Antioch, following Paul and partly to neutralize his influence. The Christian community in the year 60 was in a state of mind which in no way resembled the tranquil waiting of the twenty years which followed the death of Jesus. The missions of Paul and the facilities which the Jews found for their journey, had put in fashion distant expeditions. The apostle Philip is even pointed out by an ancient and persistent tradition as having become settled at Hierapolis.

I regard then as probable the tradition of Peter's residence at Rome; but I believe that this sojourn was of short duration, and that Peter suffered martyrdom a little time after his arrival in the eternal city. A coincidence favourable to this theory is the record of Tacitus, Annals xv., 44. This record presents a quite natural occasion with which to connect Peter's martyrdom. The apostle of the Judeo-Christians formed part of the list of sufferers whom Tacitus describes as crucibus affixi, and thus it is not without reason that the Seer of the Apocalypse places, "the apostles" among the holy victims of the year 64, who applauded the destruction of the city which slew them.

The coming of John to Ephesus, having a dogmatic value much less considerable than the coming of Peter to Rome, has not excited such lengthened controversies. The opinion generally received up to the present day, was that the apostle John, son of Zebedee, died very old in the capital of the province of Asia, Even those who refused to believe that during his residence the apostle wrote the fourth gospel and the epistles which bear his name, even those who denied that the Apocalypse was his work, continued to believe in the reality of this, journey attended by tradition. The first, Lützelberger, in 1840, raised upon this point some elaborated doubts; but he was little listened to. Some critics who cannot be reproached with an excess of credulousness, Baur, Strauss, Schwegler, Zeller, Hilgenfeld, Volkmar, all by making a large part in the legend in the records as to the sojourn of John at Ephesus, persisted in regarding as historical the very fact of the apostle's coming into these regions. It is in 1867, in the first volume of his Life of Jesus, that M. Keim has directed against this traditional opinion quite a serious attack. The basis of M. Keim's theory is that Presbyteros Johannes has been confounded with John the Apostle, and that the statments of the ecclesiastical writers upon him ought to be listened to first. This was followed by M.M. Wittichen and Holtzmann. More recently M. Scholten, of the University of Leyden, in a lengthened work, was forced to destroy one after another all the proofs of the formerly received theory, and to demonstrate that the Apostle John had never set foot in Asia.

The tractate of M. Scholten is a true chef d'oeuvre of argumentation and method. The author passes in review not only all the evidences which are alleged for or against the tradition, but also all the writings where it can and according to him ought to be mentioned. The learned Professor of Leyden had been formerly of a different opinion. In his long arguments against the authenticity of the fourth gospel, he had strongly insisted on the passage in which Polycrates of Ephesus, about the end of the second century, represents John as having been in Asia, one of the pillars of the Jewish and Quarto-deciman parties. But it is nothing to a friend of truth that it should be necessary in these difficult questions to modify and reform his opinion. M. Scholten's arguments have not convinced me; they have put John into Asia among the number of doubtful facts; they have not put it among the number certainly of apocryphal facts. I believe, indeed, that the chances of truth are still in favour of the tradition. Less probable in my view than Peter's residence at Rome, the theory of the residence of John at Ephesus maintains its probability, and I think that in many cases M. Scholten has given proof of an exaggerated scepticism. As I may permit myself once more to say, a theologian is never a perfect critic. M. Scholten has a mind too lofty to allow himself ever to be ruled by apologetic or dogmatic views; but the theologian is so accustomed to subordinate fact to idea, that rarely does he place himself in the simple point of view of the historian. For twenty-five years back, especially we have seen that the Protestant liberal school have allowed themselves to be carried away by an excess of negativeness in which we doubt whether the laic science which sees in those studies nothing but simply interesting researches, will follow it. Their religious position is come to this point, that they make a defence of supernatural beliefs more easy by "cheapening" the texts and sacrificing them largely, rather then by maintaining their authenticity.

I am persuaded that a criticism unprejudiced by all theological prepossession shall find one day that the liberal theologians of our century have been too much in doubt, and that it will agree not certainly in spirit, but in some results, with the ancient traditional schools.

Among the writings passed in review by M. Scholten the Apocalypse holds naturally the first rank. This is the point where the illustrious critic shews himself weakest. Of three things, one is true either the Apocalypse is by the Apostle John, or it is by a forger who has intended to make it pass for a work of the Apostle John, or it is by a homonym of the Apostle John, such as John Mark or the enigmatical Presbyteros Johannes. On the third hypothesis it is clear that the Apocalypse less nothing to do with the residence of the Apostle John in Asia, but this hypothesis has little plausibility and in any case is not that which M. Scholten adopts. He is for the second hypothesis; he believes the Apocalypse apocryphal in the same way as the Book of Daniel. He thinks that the forger wished, according to a very common proceeding among the Jews of his time, to cover himself with the prestige of a venerated personage, that he has chosen the Apostle John as one of the pillars of the church of Jerusalem, and that he represents himself to the churches of Asia under that venerable name. Such a falsehood scarcely being conceivable during the lifetime of the apostle, M. Scholten declares that John had died before the year 68. But this theory includes downright impossibilities. Whatever may be the authenticity of the Apocalypse, I dare to say that the arguments which are drawn from that writing to establish the truth of a residence of John in Asia are as strong in the second hypothesis set forth here as in the first. There is no question here of a book being produced like the Book of Daniel some centuries after the death of the author to whom it is attributed. The Apocalypse was circulated among the believers in Asia in the winter of 68-69, while the great struggles between the generals for the competition of the empire and the appearance of the false Nero, of Cythnos, kept the whole world in a feverish expectation. If the Apostle John were dead as M. Scholten says, it was shortly before; in any case in M. Scholten's hypothesis the faithful of Ephesus, of Smyrna, &c., knew perfectly at that date that the Apostle John had never visited Asia. What reception would they give to the account of a vision represented as having taken place in Patmos at some leagues from Ephesus, an account which is addressed to the seven principal churches of Asia by a man who is credited to have known the concealed thoughts of their consciences, who distributes to some the hardest reproaches, to others the most exalted praise, who takes with them the tone of an indisputable authority, who represents himself as having been the partaker of their sufferings; if that man had been neither in Patmos nor Asia, if their imagination had always fixed him settled at Jerusalem? The forger must be supposed to have been endowed with little good sense to have created in lightness of heart for his books such reasons of dislike against them. Why does he place the scene of the prophesy at Patmos? That island had never up till then any importance, any significance. People never touched at it except when they went from Ephesus to Rome or from Rome to Ephesus; for such travelling as that Patmos offered a very good part for resting, a small day's journey from Ephesus. It was the first or the last halting-place, according to the rules of the little navigation described in the Acts, and of which the essential principle was to stop as much as was possible every night. Patmos could not be the object of a voyage. A man coming to Ephesus or going from Ephesus alone needed to touch there. Even admitting the non-authenticity of the Apocalypse, the first three chapters of this book constitute therefore a strong probability in favour of the theory of John's residence in Asia, in the same manner as 1st Peter, although apocryphal, is a very good argument for the residence of Peter at Rome. The forger, whatever may be the credulousness of the public whom he addressed, seeks always to create for his writing conditions in which it may be acceptable. If the author of 1st Peter believed himself obliged to date his writing from Rome, if the author of the Apocalypse imagined that he would give a good exordium to his vision by making it appear to be written upon the threshold of Asia, nearly opposite Ephesus, and by addressing it with counsels which remind one of those of a director of the conscience to the churches of Asia, it is because Peter has been at Rome and John has been in Asia. Dionysius of Alexandria at the end of the third century feels perfectly the great embarassment which the question thus placed presents. Shewing that antipathy against the Apocalypse which all the Greek fathers possessed in a true Hellenic spirit, Dionysius accumulates the objections against attributing such a writing to the Apostle John, but he recognises that the work cannot have been composed except by a personage who had lived in Asia, and he puts aside the homonyms of the apostle; so much does this proposition agree with the evidence that the true or supposed author of the Apocalypse has really been connected with Asia.

M. Scholten's discussion relative to the text of Papias is very important. It has been the lot of this ἀρχαῖος ἀνήρ to be badly understood since Irenæus, who has certainly wrongly made him an auditor of the Apostle John, until Eusebius, who also wrongly supposes that he knew directly Presbyteros Johannes. M. Keim had already shewn that the text of Papias, well understood, proves rather to be against than for the residence of the Apostle John in Asia. M. Scholten goes much further; he concludes from the passage in question, that even Presbyteros Johannes had not resided in Asia. He believes that this personage, distinct in his view from the Apostle John, resided in Palestine, and was a contemporary of Papias. We agree with M. Scholten, that if the passage in Papias is correct, it is an objection against the residence of the apostle in Asia. But is it correct? Are the words ἤ τί Ἰωάννης not an interpolation? To those who find this idea arbitrary, I would reply that, if they maintain ἤ τί Ἰωάννης, the words οἱ τοῦ κυρίου μαθηταί, placed after Aristion kaí ὁ πρεσβύτερος Ioannes made a bizarre and incoherent collection. What, nevertheless, confirms M. Scholten's doubts is a passage in Papias, quoted by George Hamartolus, and according to which John was killed by the Jews. This tradition appears to have been created to show the realization of words of Christ (Matt. xx. 23); Mark x. 39; it is not reconcilable with residence of John at Ephesus, and if Papias had really adopted it, it is because he had not the least idea of the coming of John into the province of Asia. Now it would be very surprising that a man zealous in research in apostolic traditions should have ignored such an important fact, which would take place in the same country as that in which he lived. The omission of all reference relative to the residence in Asia in the epistles attributed to St. Ignatius and Hegesippus gives certainly cause for reflection. At the beginning of the year 180 A.D., tradition is definitely fixed. Appollonius, the Anti-Montanist, Polycrates, Irenæus, Clement of Alexandria, and Origen, have no doubt as to the remarkable honour which the city of Ephesus enjoyed. Among the texts which might be alleged, two are especially remarkable, that of Polycrates, Bishop of Ephesus, about 196, and Irenæus (at the same time) in his letter to Florinus. M. Scholten puts aside too lightly the text of Polycrates. It is important to find at Ephesus at the end of one century all the traditions so distinctly affirmed. "The small critical mind of Polycrates," says M. Scholten, "draws from this circumstance that he represents John to us as decorated with the πέταλον, thus making recede by an anachronism to the apostolic age the usage existing then of giving to the Christian Bishop the dignity of high priest." Formerly, M. Scholten did not judge thus; he saw in the πέταλον and in the title of "high priest" given to the Apostle John by Polycrates, a proof that the apostle was in Asia, the head of the Judeo-Christian party. He was right. The πέταλον, far from being an episcopal mark of the second century, is only attributed to two personages, and to two personages of the first century, to James and John, both belonging to the Judeo-Christian party, and this party believed to exalt them by attributing to them the prerogatives of the Jewish high priests. M. Keim and M. Scholten likewise reproach Polycrates with believing that the Philip who came to settle at Hierapolis with his prophetess daughters, is the apostle. I believe that Polycrates is right, and that if we compare attentively Acts xxi., v. 8, with the passages in Papias, Proclus, Polycrates, and Clement of Alexandria, as to Philip and his daughters, residing at Hierapolis, I think we shall be convinced that it is the apostle that is spoken of. The verse in Acts has all the appearance of an interpolation. M. Boltzmann seems to adopt upon this point the hypothesis which I have proposed in my Apostles. I hold to it more than ever.

The most curious passage in the Fathers of the Church on the question which occupies as is the fragment of the epistle of Irenæus to Florinus, which Eusebius has preserved for us. It is one of the finest pages of Christian literature in the second century. "These opinions of Florinus are not of a sound teaching; . . . . . these opinions are not those which the elders who have preceded us, and who knew the Apostles, transmitted to thee. I remembered that when I was a child in Asia Minor where thou didst shine first by thy office at court, I saw thee near Polycarp seeking to acquire his esteem. I remember things which happened first rather than things which come later, for that which we have known in infancy grows with the mind, identifies itself with it; so much so that I could tell the place in which the blessed Polycarp sat to speak, his walk, his habit, his method of life, the features of his body, his manner of rendering assistance, how he related the familiarity he had had with John and with the others who had seen the Lord, and what he had heard them say as to the Lord and his miracles, and as to his doctrine. Polycarp reported it as having received it from eye witnesses of the Word of Life conforming all to the scriptures. Those things, thanks to the goodness of God, I listened to from the first with appreciation, not consigning them to paper, but in my heart, and I always, thanks to God, recorded them with authenticity. And I can attest in the presence of God, that if this blessed and apostolic elder had heard something like thy doctrines, he would have closed his ears and would have cried according to his custom: Oh good God! to what times hast thou reserved me, that I should hear such words!' and he would have fled from the place where he had heard them."

We see that Irenæus did not make an appeal as in the greater part of the other passages in which he speaks of the residence of the apostle in Asia, to a vague tradition; he recites to Florinus some remembrances of childhood, under their common master Polycarp. One of these souvenirs is that Polycarp spoke often of his personal relations with the Apostle John. M. Scholten has seen thoroughly that it is necessary to admit the reality of these relations, or to declare apocryphal the Epistle to Florinus. He decides for this second view. His reasons seem to me to be very weak. And first in the book Against Heresies Irenæus expresses himself nearly in the same manner as in the letter to Florinus. The principal objection of M. Scholten is drawn from this, that to explain such relations between John and Polycarp, there must be supposed for the apostle, for Polycarp, and for Irenæus, an extraordinary longevity. I am not much moved by that; John could not be dead, until about the year 80 or 90, and Irenæus wrote about 180. Irenæus was therefore at the same distance from the last years of John, as we are from the last years of Voltaire. Now without any miracle of longevity whatever our fellow worker and friend M. Remusat knew with great intimacy the Abbé Morellet, who conversed at length with Voltaire. The difficulty which it is believed we find in the fact recorded by Irenæus, is that the martyrdom of Polycarp is placed in 166, 167, 168, 169 under Marcus Aurelius. Polycarp was at that time eighty-six years of age; he would therefore be born in the year 80, 81, 82, or 83, which would make him too young at the death of John. But the date of the martyrdom of Polycarp should be modified. This martyrdom took place under the Pro-Consulate of Quadratus. Now M. Waddington has demonstrated in a manlier which leaves no room for doubt, that the Pro-Consulate of Quadratus, in Asia, ought to be placed in 154-155, under the reign of Antoninus the Pious. Polycarp was therefore born in 68-69. If the Apostle had lived until the year 90, which nothing contradicts (he might be twelve years younger than Jesus), it is not unlikely that Polycarp had in his youth some conversations with him. It is not the Acts of the martyrdom of Polycarp which assigns as the date of that martyrdom the reign of Marcus Aurelius, it is Eusebius who by an erroneous calculation, of which M. Waddington gives a clear exposure believed that the Pro-Consulate of Quadratus fell under that reign.

A difficulty in the chronological system, which we would explain is the journey which Polycarp made to Rome, under the pontificate of Anicet. Anicet, according to the received chronology, became Bishop of Rome in the year 154, or rather sooner. There is, therefore, some little difficulty to find a place for the journey of Polycarp. M. Waddington's results appeal decisive; if it be necessary to be in sequence with these results, to ante-date a little the elevation of Anicet to the pontificate, we ought not to hesitate, seeing that the pontifical lists offer some trouble in that direction, and that many lists place Anicet before Pius. It is to be regretted that M. Lipsius, who has published recently a very good work upon the Chronology of the Bishop of Rome up to the Fourth Century, had not known M. Waddington's treatise; he would have found there matter for an important discussion.

Is it likely, says M. Scholten, that an old man, already nearly a centenarian, would have taken such a voyage and that at a time when it was much more difficult to travel than in our days? The voyages from Ephesus or from Smyrna to Rome would have been more easy. A merchant of Hierapolis tells us in his epitaph that he had made seventy-two times the distance from Hierapolis to Italy by doubling the Malean Cape. This merchant continued therefore his journeys up to an age advanced as that when Polycarp made his voyage to Rome. Such navigations (they travelled very little during the winter) did not entail any fatigue. It is possible that Polycarp carried out his voyage to Rome during the summer of 154 and yet suffered martyrdom at Smyrna on the 23rd February, 155. M. Keim's hypothesis, according to which the John whom Polycarp would know would not be John the Apostle, but Presbyteros Johannes, is full of improbabilities. If this Presbyteros was as we believe a secondary personage, the disciple of John the Apostle flourishing in the year 100 to nearly the year 120, the confusion of Polycarp or Irenæus would be inconceivable. As to the Presbyteros being really a man of the great apostolic generation, an equal of the apostles, who might be confounded with them, we have already presented our objections to this theory. Let us add that even then the error of Polycarp would not be much more easy to explain.

One of the most curious parts of M. Scholten's treatise is that in which he recurs to the question of the fourth gospel, which he had already treated with no much fulness some years before. M. Scholten does not only admit that this gospel may be the work of John, but he still refuses it all connection with John. He denies that John is the disciple named many times in this gospel with mystery and designated as "the disciple whom Jesus loved." According to M. Scholten that disciple is not a real person. The immortal disciple who, as distinguished from the other disciples of the Master, should live until the end of the ages by the force of his mind, this disciple, whose evidence, reposing upon spiritual contemplation, is of an absolute authenticity, ought not to be identified with any of the Galillean apostles. He is an ideal personage. It is quite impossible for me to admit that opinion. But let us not complicate difficult questions by another more difficult still. M. Scholten has removed many supports upon which formerly rested the opinion of the residence of the Apostle John in Asia. He has proved that this fact does not arise from the penumbra through which we see nearly all the facts of Apostolic history. In what concerns Papias he has raised an objection to which it is easy to reply; nevertheless he has not set forth all the arguments which can be alleged in favour of the tradition. The first chapters of the Apocalypse, the letter of Irenæus to Florinus, the passage in Polycrates remain three solid bases upon which we cannot build up a certainty, but which M. Scholten, in spite of his trenchant dialectic, has not overturned.

www.ingramcontent.com/pod-product-compliance
Lightning Source LLC
Chambersburg PA
CBHW021239090426
42740CB00006B/611